Schooling for the Dole?

YOUTH QUESTIONS

Series Editors: PHILIP COHEN and ANGELA McROBBIE

This series sets out to question the ways in which youth has traditionally been defined by social scientists and policy-makers, by the caring professions and the mass media, as well as in 'common-sense' ideology. It explores some of the new directions in research and practice which are beginning to challenge existing patterns of knowledge and provision. Each book examines a particular aspect of the youth question in depth. All of them seek to connect their concerns to the major political and intellectual debates that are now taking place about the present crisis and future shape of our society. The series will be of interest to those who deal professionally with young people, especially those concerned with the development of socialist, feminist and anti-racist perspectives. But it is also aimed at students and general readers who want a lively and accessible introduction to some of the most awkward but important issues of our time.

Published

Inge Bates, John Clarke, Philip Cohen, Dan Finn, Robert Moore and Paul Willis
SCHOOLING FOR THE DOLE?
The New Vocationalism

Angela McRobbie and Mica Nava (eds)
GENDER AND GENERATION

Forthcoming

Philip Cohen and Harwant Bains (eds)
MULTI-RACIST BRITAIN

Philip Cohen and Graham Murdock (eds)
THE MAKING OF THE YOUTH QUESTION

Andrew Dewdney and Martin Lister
YOUTH PHOTOGRAPHY

Dan Finn
TRAINING WITHOUT JOBS:
From the Raising of the School-Leaving Age to the New Training Initiative

Schooling for the Dole?

The New Vocationalism

Inge Bates, John Clarke, Philip Cohen,
Dan Finn, Robert Moore and Paul Willis

MACMILLAN

First published 1984
Reprinted 1985

Published by
Higher and Further Education Division
MACMILLAN PUBLISHERS LTD
Houndmills, Basingstoke, Hampshire RG21 2XS
and London
Companies and representatives
throughout the world

Printed in Hong Kong

British Library Cataloguing in Publication Data
Schooling for the dole
1. Curriculum planning—Great Britain
2. Unemployment—Great Britain
I. Bates, Inge
375'.00941   LB1564.G7
ISBN 0–333–36728–6
ISBN 0–333–36729–4 Pbk

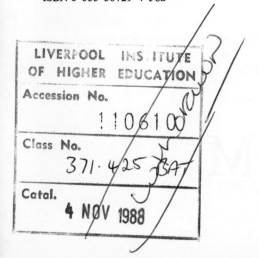

Contents

List of Tables

Preface

This book arises out of discussions and collective work in a group of sociologists, researchers and educationalists with an interest in the relationships between school and work. The group was convened by Paul Willis, changed its composition somewhat over time and met in a number of contexts – first under the auspices of a conference organised by the Socialist Teachers Alliance, and subsequently in the framework of a series of workshops financed by the Social Science Research Council on the Transition From School to Work.

The introduction and conclusion are the product of discussion in the group as a whole. In other chapters, although subject in most cases to lengthy collective discussion and analysis, individual contributors have drawn on their own work and express their own views and opinions. Editorial work and decisions were undertaken by the whole group collectively.

I.B.

J.C.

P.C.

D.F.

R.M.

P.W.

1

Introduction

John Clarke and Paul Willis

This book has been prepared in the midst of the most profound economic crisis that has been experienced in post-war Britain. Many of the features of that crisis are now self-evident. Each month brings its tally of closures, the steady growth of unemployment figures, and a rapidly rising concern about the young unemployed.

Almost everyone, of whatever political persuasion, has identified the position of the young unemployed as one of the most significant features of the crisis. This significance is shown in the endless stream of commentary, analysis, explanations and initiatives about youth unemployment. The riots of the summer of 1981 and the prospects of future instability have had the effect of focusing the spotlight of public and political attention on the young even more closely.

We have decided to add to this mass of comment on youth unemployment because we believe that the predominant focus of commentary and explanation has been on young people and implicitly, young working-class people, as the problem. Equally, government initiatives aimed at 'solving' this problem have also focused on youth and their failings.

The work collected in this book has a different starting point. We have tried to look at youth in the context of those social institutions and processes which shape the transition from school to work – or, more accurately, the transition from school to non-work. We have focused on the relation between schooling and work: on the ways in which 'work' appears within schools and the contradictions between the official and informal knowledges of work which surface in the classroom.

We know we are not alone in our opposition to the current solutions being prescribed for youth unemployment. The **young** unemployed themselves have expressed their lack of faith in these schemes, their hostility at being used as cheap labour. And, in both mundane and dramatic forms, we can see their growing alienation from the main social institutions that rule their lives. Some trade unions have become increasingly critical of the uses to which the young unemployed are put in training schemes, as well as of the sorts of pressures that are put on youth to take advantage of these dubious 'benefits'. Finally, those working in schools, colleges and under the MSC have also expressed an increasing disenchantment with the sort of offerings they are supposed to provide for the young.

This book is addressed to this movement of disaffection and opposition in two senses. First, we have tried to provide a critique of the state's responses to youth unemployment, particularly as they affect the content and processes of schooling. Second, we have tried to identify the material cultural experiences of the young themselves as a powerful element in the process of transition. It is a force which is absent from 'official' accounts, but which we believe demands to be taken seriously.

These are the purposes of the book. In the rest of this introduction we set out some of the general context within which these arguments take place.

Blaming the victim

Official accounts of youth unemployment have developed two main strands of explanation. The first focuses on young people themselves or, more precisely, on the things which young people lack. Government reports, investigations and commentaries have centred on the assumption that the young school leaver is *disadvantaged* in a highly competitive labour market because he or she lacks *both* the necessary work skills *and* the appropriate work experience and the habits of mind that go with it. Employers, they have argued, are understandably reluctant to take on young people who have no developed skills to offer, and who do not have a properly mature and sensible attitude to work itself.

When, as now, the labour market is 'highly competitive' (that is, there are lots of people unemployed), these 'failings' of skill and character place the young at a disadvantage compared to skilled, mature, experienced and sensible older workers. This is an explanation which leaves several important processes out of account. But, however implausible as a rational explanation, it has not only achieved massive credibility but has also produced very real consequences. Not the least of these is that this explanation has shaped the state's initiatives to 'solve' this problem. The schemes and programmes developed by the state have been founded on the assumption that since what the young unemployed lack are skills and work experience (and the habits and maturity that come from such experience) the state should take a hand in filling these gaps. This explanation also has an important *ideological* consequence. It accomplishes the apparently difficult task of blaming the young for the position they are in. At the same time it excludes other possible explanations. This form of explanation was called 'blaming the victim' by William Ryan, who identified it as a central theme in American poverty programmes which explained the economic position of black Americans as being the consequence of black Americans' cultural failings. They, too, didn't have the right 'habits of mind'.

There is, however, a second theme in these official accounts. Another guilty party had contributed to this situation.

Blaming the schools

The 'Great Debate' about education, inaugurated by James Callaghan, began an attack on the education system based on one central assumption that fits elegantly into the previous explanation for youth unemployment. Schools were accused of failing to equip their pupils with the necessary basic skills *and* attitudes to enter work. Employers, it transpired, had been appalled at the quality of school-leavers applying to them for jobs. They lacked not only technical skills, but even the basic standards of literacy and numeracy required for employment. Worse still, school-leavers seemed not to have the right attitudes to work, nor the right sort of 'social skills' to cope with the process of finding work. They dressed badly, wrote letters badly and spoke badly.

Schools, then, perhaps because they had become too caught up with 'fashionable' educational theories and practices, had begun to fail in their responsibility to the nation's economy. They were not preparing young people adequately for the world of work. Once again, however implausible these explanations might be rationally, the weight of evidence appeared to be on their side: there was, after all, a growing number of unemployed school-leavers whose presence clearly testified to these failings. By mid-1982 the unemployment rate for under-18s was 33 per cent compared with the national rate of 13 per cent. How else could such a difference be explained?

The collapse of the transition

These explanations focus on one specific part of the transition from school to work – the entry of young people to the labour market. The initiatives which followed from them, in schools, colleges and the MSC, have likewise concentrated on the moment of entry. But, obviously, the *process* of transition involves more than this. To put it crudely, the idea of transition also involves the notion of having somewhere to go *to*. To understand the breakdown of the transition from school to work, it is more important to understand the changes in employment, and in particular youth employment, than to examine the conditions of entry to this process. For the transition has become a transition to nowhere.

The recession, and the strategies adopted by British capital to escape from the recession, are the 'prime movers' in the growth of youth unemployment. It is these processes which have profoundly reorganised the market of labour – which have made it 'highly competitive' – and which have changed the position of youth labour.

The economic crisis is a crisis of profitability, and it has had the consequences of sharpening the process of capitalist competition. Competition for markets, and thus for profitability, means that the *least* competitive lose out. The first result of recession is the flood of closures and shut-downs of the 'inefficient' factories, plants and enterprises that we have seen over the past few years. This purging of the economic body has two main consequences: to free sources of capital from inefficient and unprofitable enterprises and allow them to seek out more profitable ventures (typically, *outside* Britain) and secondly, to throw workers back into the market for labour.

These are the first, most dramatic and most visible consequence of the crisis – and are reflected in those which follow. For enterprises that aim to remain in business and become more profitable, the goal is to increase their efficiency. In Britain, the crisis of profitability has been defined as a problem of 'productivity' and 'over-manning'. Various euphemisms have been coined to describe the solutions developed for this crisis: 'streamlining', 'rationalisation' and 'shaking out' excess labour. Their central object is the same. Profitability can be restored through making labour more productive: essentially by producing the same levels of output with fewer workers. Again, more workers are thrown back into the market for labour. Even where new investment does take place, this is in the form of 'new technology', forms of mechanisation and automation of production which will reduce the numbers of workers needed.

Why the young?

The 'transition from school to work', then, is taking place in the context of an economic strategy (endorsed by both private capital and the state) which stresses getting rid of 'excess labour'. The character of the labour market has been dramatically transformed before the young worker even enters it. But within this context, these economic strategies have come to bear particularly on the young in a number of ways.

First, the 'shake-out' of labour involves not merely the attempt to get rid of 'excess' numbers, but also to break down barriers to 'rational' management controls such as traditional skill demarcations among workforces (usually known as 'restrictive practices'). The same emphasis upon reorganising and rationalising the labour force also accompanies the introduction of new technology. This means that long-standing methods of recruitment of young workers, such as apprenticeships, need to be reduced since they reproduce the existing, and unwanted, division of labour.

Second, in a context where employers are concerned to reduce their labour force, they are unwilling to substitute young workers for existing workers. Economically, this means they can minimise the cost of redundancy by not 'shaking out' more than their immediate needs. To substitute young workers would involve the costs of making redundant more existing workers. This calculation of the costs of different sorts of labour is especially powerful for the group of workers whom employers see as the most interchangeable with young workers: women, and married women in particular.

Since many women work in the lowest-paid jobs, little immediate economic advantage in wage costs would be gained from this substitution. More importantly, since many women work under part-time employment conditions (with less employment protection, and less union organisation) they are a more attractive employment prospect, because employers can bring them into and out of production more 'flexibly'.

Finally (and here is the hidden truth of claims about the young's 'attitude') employers do prefer a workforce of 'mature' workers. Mature in the sense that they are more tied by financial and social responsibilities, and therefore more securely bound by the discipline of wage. In this sense, the young worker is indeed less 'disciplined', less habituated to the 'dull compulsion' of waged labour.

The consequence of these strategic considerations is that the young are unemployed not because of failings of their own, but because of the way that the labour market is being reorganised in the midst of the recession.

Youth and the transitions

We have, like everyone else, talked of youth, 'young people' and the 'transition'. But this generality of 'youth' disguises a more profound set of differences. Youth is not a homogeneous social category.

This conception of youth as a homogeneous group is one which rests on deeply rooted biological and psychological assumptions. They are assumptions about universal patterns of human development and growth to maturity, in which youth appears as the transitional stage between childhood and adulthood. According to this, youth is distinguished by all sorts of biological changes, and a variety of psychological changes and adjustments – the 'Acne and Valderma syndrome'. Youth then, is natural, universal (a 'phase' that we all go through), and inherently unstable (a period of difficult adjustments).

But this disguises two ways in which youth is profoundly social, rather than natural. Youth, as we know it, is the consequence of social arrangements designed to regulate the transition not of child to adult in a universal sense, but of the child to worker and citizen in *our* society, with all the appropriate habits and attitudes that are supposed to belong to such an individual. Youth, in this sense, is a social product which accompanied the rise of mass schooling as a way of regulating and controlling this *social* transition. It is the process by which potential labour-power (the child) is recruited and transformed into actual labour-power (the adult). The 'development' of youth in our society has very specific goals in mind.

Once we understand this social character of the transition, we can follow it to the second sense in which youth is social. Because the transition is not a 'common' process, it is differentiated by the social divisions of British society: by class, gender and race. The transition is differentiated in its starting points, the experience of the transition itself, and in its destinations.

Class affects how young people enter it and where they are expected to go when they leave it. Class also shapes the process of transition itself – its length (at what age do people leave it?) and the sorts of institutions in which it is experienced (school; school plus college; school plus university). Gender, too, differentiates the transition. The different destinations assumed for boys and girls structure how they enter it, the sorts of experiences and direction they encounter within it, and the manner in which they leave it. Finally race impinges on the transition, again partly on the different experiences with which groups enter it and partly on the different destinations presumed for them.

These social divisions, then, produce not a transition from school to work, but a whole variety of transitions. They bear on the process of transition in two ways. First by locating individuals in different starting points and secondly, through the social division of labour, they determine the different destinations to be arrived at: skilled worker, white collar worker, manager, wife and mother, or unemployed.

These points about the social differentiation of youth are not merely part of an abstract academic argument – they bear on everyday reality encountered by teachers and the young themselves in the institutions of the state. We have emphasised their importance not because we have somehow 'discovered' them but because they are systematically *not* recognised in official accounts of the confused and contradictory everyday life of institutions. Workers in these state institutions – teachers, lecturers, youth workers and so on – have to face the task of negotiating the gap between the *reality* of the structural and cultural differentiation of the young and the *official accounts* of youth which structure the institutions and programmes within which they work. This book is addressed to those contradictory demands and pressures which those working in education have to confront. In it we have attempted to examine and assess these pressures from 'above and below' which shape the boundaries of educational practice.

Bridging the gap: the role of the state

In spite of the recent revival of 'classical' free market economics, with its avowal of the importance of supply and demand and with its contempt for government interference, the social reality of youth unemployment is not simply a matter of the market in labour. The state has, throughout the history of British capitalism, always taken an interest in 'surplus labour' – an interest expressed in a diversity of institutions ranging from skill centres to the workhouse. Since the mid-nineteenth century the state has also taken a hand in 'managing' the transition from child to worker – first in schooling, and then in further and higher education. These two concerns have come together in the current crisis – . . . a crisis involving not just 'surplus labour', but surplus *youth* labour.

Even under the direction of a government committed to a 'rolling back the state' and 'freeing the individual', the state's commitment to managing this broken transition has not only continued but been expanded. 'Thatcherism' (for all its hostility to 'quangos') has maintained and increased the role of the Manpower Services Commission. The MSC's role in youth employment was initially that of 'filling the gap' between the end of school and the arrival of work. To this end, it has provided or financed its own training and education schemes and invested heavily in the Further Education sector, providing finance for suitable courses. At the end of 1982, however, the Minister of Education (Sir Keith Joseph) and the Minister of Employment (Norman Tebbit) announced a scheme to extend the financing of approved courses to secondary education.

This proposal is a logical consequence of two earlier developments. First, it is a development in the career of the MSC as the 'master institution' responsible for both defining and responding to youth unemployment. Secondly, it is a consequence of the attack on the schools' 'failure' to equip young people adequately for their entry to work. Once the 'Great Debate' had identified the failings of the schools, what could be more reasonable than that an organisation which 'knows better' should step in with advice (and funds) to improve the situation.

'Work' in the schools

Nevertheless, what the 'Debate' and subsequent responses have played down is just how far 'work' has already penetrated the school curriculum. What is startling is not the 'failure' of school to prepare for work, but the extent to which such 'preparation' has been embodied in secondary schooling. The pressure for 'relevance' (particularly for the 'non-academic' strata) has meant that the world of work increasingly has come to be represented in the school curriculum, in the guises of social education, vocational guidance and preparation, social and life skills and so on. The Debate and its subsequent echoes were not the point at which 'work' was suddenly discovered by schools – at best, they accelerated an already well established trend.

Such innovations indicate that the 'pressures from above' on teachers do not remain fixed and permanent. These institutional demands are responsive to the external spheres of economics and politics – although these changing external conditions are always translated into the language of education before they arrive at the teacher. 'Work' – the demands of the economy for particular sorts of labour – may undergo a variety of transformations before its appearance in the classroom. It is translated through the languages of knowledge, values, skills, relevance and pedagogy on its way from the commanding heights. In this book we have tried to examine some of the ways in which these 'translations' have been accomplished; the processes by which work appears in the curriculum. But we have also tried to examine the processes by which 'work' has been negotiated in the classroom itself: how teachers attempt to manage the gulf between the official formula of youth and employment and the diverse structural and cultural realities of young people in the classroom.

Where to begin?

We have sketched in some of the main changes in the world outside of the school. Most important is the fundamental and trenchant economic crisis, the various attempts to understand it, allocate blame, and to take steps towards its resolution. These external changes are affecting the school in a number of ways. Indeed, schools are an important battleground between contending interests as these interests try to define the general crisis in a certain way, and therefore offer certain kinds of solution. What are teachers to make of the situation? What are they to do? What are those teachers to do who are involved in the most contested terrain of all – careers?

In this book we offer, not particular answers, but some general principles and ways of thinking to clear the undergrowth for a progressive position in the school – a position which supports the interests and future of working class and oppressed groups. It might help here to lay out our general approach. All of the following chapters bear upon a particular aspect of this basic position – enlarging and emphasising what we mean.

Most basically we try always to bear in mind the perspectives, experiences, and position of pupils in school. Of course, all writing on education purports to take young people as the main stake – it is they who are to be 'helped'. But in most approaches and accounts – never more than now in the age of 'the new realism' – the pupil is taken as an essentially malleable bit of human clay. The child is not anything yet in his or her own right. He or she is only an undeveloped adult. The business of schooling is to mould this adult – hence the argument over the shape of the mould. The argument is over the 'ideal' model of the future adult – honest citizen, good worker, caring family person, critical and informed voter and so on – which the school is then organised and empowered to produce. Currently we can see a clear battle over whether school should produce an 'ideal worker' to help resolve the economic crisis or a 'critical and independent person' who can develop their own capacities to the full. As we shall see, this is often apparently resolved by the former pretending to be the latter.

But this is not the way in which we want to be 'interested in' the pupils. We do not want these ideal constructions. Actually we do not believe that, for the most part, the actual products of our schools ever bore much resemblance to these ideal models. We have tried to keep at the forefront of our minds the *real cultural diversity* of young people and to emphasise that this diversity brings experiences, expectations and evaluations of work to the school. The youth of this book are not the abstract generalisations of sociology, psychology or pedagogy, but *specific* social groups who are actively 'knowledgeable' about the world.

We would argue, for example, that most working class children have never been concerned with what the ideal models are supposed to be. Their concern is not with the ideal future worker to solve the problems of capitalism, nor is it with the ideal citizen to solve the problems of democracy, nor is it with the self-developed individual to solve the problems of civilisation. Their problems concern survival in scarcity and the need to make material adjustments and plans to cope with their real – and future – situations. Gaining a wage to survive; hoping to enjoy some power as a buyer and consumer through the wage; going through the adolescent sexual dance and setting up the working class home in straitened circumstances; adapting to the strengths and enablements as well as the oppressions of quite strictly policed gender identities – these are the real themes of working class apprenticeship to adulthood in our society. In relationship to this apprenticeship there is often a general and uneasy sense of the *irrelevance* of the school. School is often rejected, rebelled against or treated as a comic interlude before 'real' life begins.

Schools and their ideal models have never really taken into account this *material culturalism* of growing up in the working class. Indeed many of the educational prescriptions do not even recognise how far *their own practices*, and teaching regimes, have less to do with theory than with responding to the *material cultures* of pupils in schools – that is in supervising, controlling and often negotiating with them. This gap between the official and the real – and the problems of managing it – are, of course, the stuff of which the everyday life of teachers is constructed. The tasks of making these two versions of the world match, of managing the antagonisms between them, of controlling unfulfilled expectations, are those around which many of the problems of classroom centre.

These problems are contradictory ones: a commitment to either the official or unofficial versions of reality encounters the antagonism of its opposite. It is in this sense that one can speak of teachers 'negotiating' these pressures: of trying to hold these tensions and conflicting interests in some sort of balance within the classroom. Containing and handling this situation is often as much as teachers can do – and this is what dictates teaching styles and methods, even though they may be dignified at another level by philosophies of teaching.

Meanwhile, as the 'ideal' models for future citizens miss their mark, we would argue that it is, importantly, from pupils' *own* cultures and experiences, from their *own* struggles actually to make a life, that a connection with the future is made at all. It is here that the transition into work, adult and family life is accomplished, that jobs and functions are filled irrespective of the quality or attitudes deemed ideally to be necessary for these things. Crudely we are saying this: life goes on and 'transitions' are accomplished in all the complexity of normal everyday life, and although this is continuously 'moulded' and 'developed' in part by direct official policy, it is also achieved through experiences, knowledges and cultures of the people involved. The current crisis is also experienced at that everyday level. This is where it is dealt with and suffered. So long as we try to understand this experience only through the school, its constructions, mystifications and specifically 'educational models', we will be lost and confused. The fundamental aim of this book, in various ways, is to keep in mind the material experiences and cultures of the pupils and to see how far teachers can respond to *these* problems – rather than to the problems of something called 'the school'.

Whether it was ever accomplished through the intentions of teachers, or actually as an escape from school, the transition into work is a thing of the past. A guillotine has fallen on the traditional couplet school/work – and chopped out an empty chunk of time for most youngsters: five years before their first job, or perhaps before permanent unemployment, or before motherhood, domestic labour and family life intervene anyway. The changed situation can be stated very simply – 'there ain't no jobs'. That is at the heart of the educational crisis and it is not surprising that careers education, and 'work in the curriculum' should be caught up in the storm.

But this central material fact is constructed, understood and acted upon in different ways. Most accounts of why this has come about, and what action must be taken, come from the state or from industrial interests. As we have just said, our approach is to try to see how the crisis is understood and *survived* by the young people involved, and to start from here in trying to work out a relevant curriculum. But the 'problem' of youth and education has actually been massively dealt with by grown-ups, and certain kinds of grown-ups at that. Perhaps the dominant definition of the 'educational crisis' has come from those who represent the power of industry and the power of capital. Of course this has filtered into the 'debate' in a variety of ways and has also now become an educational argument, and even a liberal argument, *apparently* in support of young people. In the new age of international commercial competition and of 'high tech', industry needs better workers – more skilled and especially more loyal and hard working. Just like the Japanese are held to be. If they are not like this, then it is no surprise that the economy is declining – and incidentally that there are no jobs for the young. Industrial interests and those speaking for them interpret changes in 'the transition' in the light of their own problems and therefore propose certain kinds of solutions. The 'mould' for the model pupil here becomes the mould for the model worker – trained, skilled, flexible and above all disciplined. There is no room for reluctant heroes in the sinking ship of HMS UK Plc. In a word, this view wishes to subjugate young people more completely than ever before to the needs of industry and, therefore, to the needs of capital. Youth can only be helped by their *own* contribution towards making a more successful economy and along with it, more jobs. The implications for careers teaching and for work in the curriculum are obvious. The needs of industry, their 'sympathetic' presentation, and production of 'model workers' threaten to carry all before them.

An almost equally powerful 'definition of the problem' comes ultimately from the state and from its problems in maintaining law and order and a peaceful society. In one way more realistic than the industrial view, this perspective accepts that, at least for the moment, youth unemployment will not be spirited away by up-skilling and higher qualifications. The empty chunk of time chopped out of most young people's lives by the guillotine of the recession is also a *social* problem – it might be used collectively to roam the streets, conspicuously colonise shopping centres, to frighten the citizenry or even to riot and directly challenge the social order. It is safe to assume that the riots of summer 1981 helped wonderfully to concentrate the Tory government mind on youth unemployment, and it can be no coincidence that state expenditure on special measures for the young unemployed is one of the things to have escaped the cuts and actually to have been increased dramatically. However the transition into work had been accomplished before, the situation had one over-riding merit – young adults were in work and causing trouble nowhere else. It is therefore hardly surprising that the most immediate – and still dominant – fundamental response has been to keep as many youngsters as possible in something as close as possible to work for as long a period as possible – via YOPs and later YTS. Perhaps no-one will notice the difference! At least they're off the streets!

Of course, many of the YOP and YTS schemes display a combination of the two perspectives. Discipline, compulsory attendance and work experience attempt to duplicate the social discipline of work and also pre-empt alternative and perhaps 'anti-social' styles of consumption, leisure habits, modes of thought and action. The double and partly contradictory aim is to produce people who want and are able to work, but who are also willing to maintain these qualities in suspended animation for a period without letting them deteriorate or allowing the human capacities behind them be turned to other, perhaps dangerous, activities.

In confusing and multi-form ways, the 'industrial' and the 'state' views can combine together in schools to produce a liberal, humane, child-centred view which stresses the individual well being and development of the child. Indeed, it is to the benefit of the individual child not to be unemployed, not to be locked up by the police. Social and life skills training, and work in the curriculum, can be important and relevant to pupils while still serving also to promote a certain view of society, to promote social control and to offer certain solutions to the problems of the economy. We hope in the course of this book to see in what ways curriculum innovation and development in these areas can be examined, to separate out some of these elements and to promote strongly those which offer most support and development to the actual position and dilemmas of working class youth – from its own perspective.

But, to repeat, our position in this book is that the variety of student 'moulds' – principally those of 'good citizen' and 'good worker' – do not actually produce very good copies! In a certain sense they are phantoms in the illusions of power that our controllers need in order to make sense of society. The reality of how life and its futures are experienced by the different sections of the pupil population, the actual processes, uncertainties and ambitions which govern how the 'transition' or the 'empty chunk of time' is lived and accomplished, are likely to be quite different. But if the powerful 'definitions' and the solutions which flow from them owe more to phantasm than a serious material analysis of the position of youth, and if they reveal more about the problems which the controllers are trying to solve rather than the problems experienced by youth, they nevertheless have very real effects. They help to give justification to certain kinds of control and to the suppression of other cultures and possibilities within the school. Despite their contradictions, they can also imprint on many student minds certain attitudes and beliefs, even if only to mystify and make less coherent their own views of what is happening to them. Certainly alternative pursuits, alternative styles and types of consumption and behaviour are prevented from emerging or castigated as dangerous or ignorant. Most of all, the weight of the (ironically disappearing) world of work is brought to bear in a certain threatening way which seeks to place the burden of the world on its children. Perhaps the most damaging general tendency is to promote self blame amongst young people – unemployment is the result of *their* lack of ability, skill, capacity and discipline. Individual or collective action or understanding suggesting anything different is anti-social and reflects badly on the moral fibre of those involved.

So 'industrial' and 'state' interests and views, and combinations of both, do have real effects. And yet we argue it is still the young people who face the material aspects of their changed situation. They are often more likely to see the real dimensions and possibilities of their situation than their mentors. The fundamental aim of this book is not to add more acres to the print on how education might respond better to 'state' and 'industrial' interests – masquerading as educational interest in youth – but to try to think through the real situation of the variety of pupils and to see how careers teaching and work in the curriculum might really begin to help them, and to help more in *their* terms.

The book

Each chapter in this book addresses a particular aspect of the issues we have identified here, examining specific ways in which 'work' makes its presence felt through both the official and informal cultures of the school. The chapter by Dan Finn considers the informal knowledges of school pupils. He draws out the implications of the depth of unacknowledged experiences of work which pupils possess and looks at the consequences for official assumptions about careers education. Robert Moore's chapter focuses on the development of 'social education' and its commitment to the construction of 'relevance'. He considers its development as a teaching strategy related to the issues of classroom management and its role in handling 'knowledge' which arises at the intersection of the school and the world of its pupils.

Philip Cohen critically examines the 'new realism' and the 'new vocationalism'. His chapter then goes on to describe a concrete example of an alternative practice for teaching about work and vocational preparation which attempts to bring out the issues ignored in 'official' versions.

Inge Bates' chapter examines the career of vocational guidance itself. She provides a critical study of its development as a professional theory and practice, and highlights the social and theoretical assumptions on which it has been based. Her assessment points to the particular models of employment choice which structure official accounts of the transition to work.

The final chapter aims to draw out the consequences of these studies for practices within the school. It considers the contradictory world constructed by the competing demands of official and informal cultures. This conclusion tries to make explicit the consequences for educational practice of 'taking youth seriously'. We do not claim to be able to prescribe detailed programmes, but believe that these studies can contribute to the developing debate about how best to work with and for the young.

2

Leaving School and Growing Up: Work Experience in the Juvenile Labour Market

Dan Finn

In the interminable arguments about the forms of educational and training provision thought to be appropriate for the current generation of young workers, it seemed to me that not only had this debate served to obscure the material causes of youth unemployment – by focusing on the capacities and qualities of young workers, as against the ability of employers to provide *any*, let alone meaningful, work – but in so doing it also misrepresented and misrecognised the actual processes whereby school leavers make the transition to work or, increasingly, unemployment.

In a context of escalating youth unemployment the noises of reform issuing from the education and training infrastructure, with the occasional sounding from the Employment Secretary, have created the illusion of dynamic change and hard-won concessions. However, with the aid of the research material below, I want to raise certain questions about the key presuppositions underlying the various training programmes currently being constructed.

Centrally, it has been a fundamental assumption that the young unemployed are both ignorant about, and lack experience of, work and working life. Sir Richard O'Brien, then chairperson of the MSC, expressed the point in Birmingham a week before the inauguration of the Youth Opportunities Programme in 1977:

> The key in helping young people lies in giving them experience of work and some knowledge of what it means to have a job. Things which you and I might take for granted [sic] . . . [the] young people who entered the scheme have been learning about work with an employer – its opportunities, desciplines and rights – and in the process finding out about themselves at work. (O'Brien, 1977)

What O'Brien, and the new army of industry/education specialists (with their numbing vocabulary of social and life skills, discipline, generic skills and so on), seem to take completely for granted is that the mass of working class youth is actually ignorant about work and the somewhat dubious pleasures of 'its opportunities, disciplines and rights'. It is precisely this assumption that I want to question.

By analysing the responses to a questionnaire of almost 150 boys and girls in their last year of compulsory schooling, I want to argue that the reality for most young people is far more complex. Indeed, not only has the debate about training and education misrecognised the nature of their involvement with work and the labour market, but in their programmatic form the new schemes have denigrated the youngsters involved by suggesting they are responsible for their own unemployment, and circumscribed (not to say eliminated) the already limited material options and freedoms they possessed to exercise some control over their future destinies.

The youngsters surveyed came from a mixture of class and ethnic backgrounds, and whilst I do not want to suggest that they faced a similar class destiny (some of them, for example, would be going to university), I want to demonstrate that, irrespective of their ultimate position in the complex roles of domestic and wage labour, their first contacts with the social relations of work took place in the twilight zone of unskilled labour where a variety of employers make use of their flexibility and cheapness. That their first contact with the 'dull compulsion' of capitalist economic relations is with capital at its dullest.

Equally, I want to question the suggestion, implicit in much recent literature on the transition from school to work and bound up with elements of MSC and educational practice, that the transition itself is abrupt (both socially, in terms of the transition to an adult role, and materially, in terms of longer hours, different working conditions, the discipline of the wage, and so on) and that its dislocation is therefore damaging. In fact, as will become clear in the responses, the pattern is more complex than this; the damage lies elsewhere, and very few youngsters make the abrupt transition from absolute innocence at school to the 'harsh' realities of economic life that the dominant model suggests. Many of the young people had a lengthy history of job involvement and a repertoire of experiences which both predisposed them to certain destinies in the labour market and could be drawn on to make sense of the move into full-time employment or unemployment.

Over that period I want to suggest that through their involvement in forms of domestic and wage labour, and through their involvement with the work disciplines of schooling (whether those of the academically 'able' or 'disabled'; whether experienced as a necessary evil or as a ticket for the future), they experienced a pattern of material and social constraints and freedoms which, when articulated to their wider experiences of domestic and class cultures, precipitated their choices to move towards certain locations in the labour market or further education. Experienced as a set of individual transitions and choices (which at least half of them would be denied), it is through these wider structural processes and the living meanings they are given that the youngsters take their places in the social and sexual division of labour.

Finally, I want to emphasise that I am not suggesting that when young people make the transition from school there is not an important change. Indeed, in terms of their own perceptions and in the reactions of their parents there is a qualitative shift. But it is only for a minority that this change involves the acquisition of new technical competences or skills at work. For the vast majority this change has more to do with the leisure options and commodity choices they attain with the 'freedom' of the wage, and its effects on their relation to the family economy and wider peer groups, than it has to do with their newly acquired status of wage slave. It is these freedoms and choices which are most directly threatened by unemployment and by the extended dependence on the family wage implicit in the new training schemes. As to the more narrow social relations of wage labour, there are important continuities between their pre- and post-school work experiences.

In what follows I want to outline, briefly, the form of the research and the nature of the schools and areas in which it took place. I will then outline the kinds of work the youngsters wanted to do, how they evaluated the relevance of what was offered in school, and their feelings about their likely job prospects. After that I will be examining the extent of their involvement in forms of part-time work and their experiences with different kinds of employers. I will then look at their pattern of involvement in domestic labour and the family economy. Finally, I will be considering the complex pattern of constraints and freedoms they experienced in their leisure time, and the nature and extent of their consumption of commodities. In other words, I will be examining the multitude of social and economic transitions they were going through in their last year of compulsory schooling.

The research. The questionnaire which the youngsters filled in was handed out and collected by four individual teachers in separate schools (three in Coventry and one in Rugby). There was no attempt to construct a 'technical' sample, but rather, after discussing with the teachers the broad object and structure of the questions, I asked them to distribute the forms to a group of their fifth years who were academically mixed and seemed interesting in terms of the research.

This does not accord with the technical and formal strictures of most statistics textbooks, or resemble the sanitised consumer surveys adopted by many projects in the burgeoning youth education and training industry, but I would suggest that the groups chosen were as 'representative' as many of those reported on elsewhere. The object of the research was to illuminate some central features of the lives of young people, not to display proofs or technically correct propositions on the basis of simple numbers made incomprehensible by arithmetically exact formulae.

The teachers chose the groups surveyed as interesting, though not particularly unrepresentative of their fifth year populations. The schools from Coventry formed an interesting mix:

A. Roman Catholic comprehensive, with a large sixth form, drawing its pupils substantially from a large Irish community. It had a nine form entry, and in 1981 had 1400 pupils.
B. Comprehensive, with a smaller sixth form in an older working class area, with a substantial Asian population. It had a ten form entry, and in 1981 had 1500 pupils.
C. Comprehensive, again with a large sixth form, and located in and drawing on a middle class and skilled working class catchment area. It had an eight form entry, and in 1981 had 1250 pupils.

Finally, school D in Rugby, which provided over a third of the respondents, was chosen for two basic reasons. In the first place it drew substantially on a working class rural area and, secondly, it was in Rugby where the educational structure is still determined by the feudal squirearchy of Warwickshire who, in the interests of 'quality' and 'choice', have successfully resisted full comprehensivisation. The school's effective existence as a secondary modern, partially reflected in the examination entries shown in Table 2.1, is heavily influenced by a pattern of resources and curriculum structure which clearly demonstrates the legacy of 'parity of esteem' espoused in the 1950s. It had no sixth form, had an eight form entry and in 1981 had just under 1000 pupils.

Overall then, the schools drew on a variety of catchment areas and local labour markets, and whilst each had unique features, together they represented a rough cross section, not unusual in many areas, whose response could illuminate some of the processes on which I wanted information. Flowing from this, and reflecting my own objectives, in what follows I have compressed the responses from individual schools and, where I have emphasised differences amongst the pupils, have focused on gender and the number of qualifications the youngsters were entered for. This has certain consequences for the accuracy of the material: for example, the respondents in School B were less involved in part-time work and this may have reflected the nature of the local labour market, the population of the catchment area or the choice of the sample. However, for a number of reasons, I have been unable to avoid collapsing these differences.

Given the object of the research, the variables of gender and educational level were obviously the most salient, particularly in relation to future destinies in the social and sexual divisions of labour.[1] Because of the diversity of the catchment areas and, consequently, local class cultures, it seemed to make little sense to follow the conventional model and relate responses to parents' occupations, important though they may be. Instead, I wanted to look at them in relation to the pupils' occupational destinies, and that could only be done with reference to their potential level of qualification – imperfect a measure as it is. Also, for want of better terminology and despite its lack of accuracy, I will be referring to those with four or more 'O' level entries as the 'academics' and those with less as the 'non-academics'.[2]

In using categories derived from levels of educational attainment, and adopting terms such as academic or non-academic, I want to emphasise that I am not operating with implicit notions concerning levels of innate ability or competence. Despite their occupational importance, what these formal examination entries measure are degrees of performance at school; they say nothing about the capacities of the young people in general. They only indicate what they are prepared to do in response to the demands of formal education.

From Table 2.1 it can be seen that overall there were 75 boys and 72 girls, a total of 147. Of the boys, 27 per cent were entered for more than four 'O' levels and 73 per cent for less than four; for the girls the respective proportions were 33 per cent and 67 per cent. In terms of destinies, 75 per cent of the boys and 48 per cent of the girls were intending to leave school by the summer of 1981; together 61 per cent of the total. 20 per cent of the boys and 26 per cent of the girls were intending to go into the sixth form; 23 per cent of the total. Finally, 5 per cent of the boys and 26 per cent of the girls were intending to go to college; 16 per cent of the total.

Table 2.1   *Young people surveyed by sex, school and qualifications*

School:	Academic			Non-Academic			All		
	M	F	Total	M	F	Total	M	F	Total
A	11	13	24	10	7	17	21	20	41
B	1	3	4	19	5	24	20	8	28
C	6	5	11	4	9	13	10	14	24
D	2	3	5	22	27	49	24	30	54
TOTALS	20	24	44	55	48	103	75	72	147

Although it was clear that just under 75 per cent of the non-academics were intending to cease full-time education at near enough the earliest possible moment, and that a substantial minority of the academics (32 per cent) were of a like mind, it is worthwhile, before moving substantially into what they intended to do, to say something about the structure of job opportunities that was to confront them in the summer of 1981.

In Coventry, the post-war boom town of the motor trade, the prospects were bleak and getting worse. An area which provided massive profits for the multi-nationals who dominated the city in the

1950s and 1960s, particularly in engineering, had been devastated by a catalogue of closures which had seen the general unemployment rate escalate from a few percentage points in 1975 to over 14 per cent in 1981, and had seen the collapse of apprenticeships which in the same period had fallen by over 80 per cent (Hencke, 1981). In terms of the young unemployed, before 1981's summer leavers came onto the market in July, there were 2100 youngsters already on MSC schemes and another 1700 registered unemployed. Of the 5500 pupils who were expected to leave school that summer, it was estimated that only 2500 would get jobs or places in further education; the other 3000 would be joining the dole queue.[3]

In Rugby, as with the rest of the West Midlands, unprecedented post-war levels of unemployment have been experienced. In common with the rest of Warwickshire it was expected that only one in five of 1981's school leavers would obtain permanent work; half of them would be accommodated on MSC schemes of one kind or another, and the remaining 30 per cent would be signing on and, if lucky, drawing benefit.

With this backdrop, it may have seemed perverse to ask some of the youngsters affected what they would 'choose' to do, when clearly *any* job would be at a premium. However, it seems to me to be symptomatic of the bureaucratised and insensitive youth industry that the voice largely absent from its deliberations – except in the form of a 'client' to be processed, 'skilled' and packaged for a potential employer – is that of the young people trying to make the entry into work. As I want to show, the choices they wanted to make and the aspirations they had were not unrealistic, atavistic or peculiarly idiosyncratic; and the attempt to substitute for them with a seemingly bewildering array of job taster, preparation or experience courses cannot disguise the moral and social bankruptcy of an economic system which was condemning a generation of young workers to arbitrary and increasingly lengthy periods of unemployment.

Leaving school: the impact of unemployment

Following the stark prospects just outlined, and recognising that these statistics directly affected the whole texture of economic and social life shared by the youngsters, I wanted to get some indication of how difficult they thought it would be to get work when they left school or further education.

Overwhelmingly, they thought it would be difficult, if not impossible: just under 90 per cent of them were worried about the prospect, and it was a concern common to both sexes and all ability ranges. While some pointed to issues related to racism, or levels of qualification, the vast majority just pointed to the scale of unemployment, the seemingly never ending sequences of closures and redundancies, and the consequent ability of employers to pick and choose from a queue of applicants.

However, there were 19 of them who felt they would not have difficulties, largely because they had guarantees of work. Eight per cent of the youngsters had already been offered full-time work either by their part-time employer (7) or by relatives or friends (3). Although the latter group did not particularly want that work, only one of the former (a male academic) felt that way. The rest actually wanted the work they had been offered; three female and one male non-academic, and one female academic, were going into full-time shop work; and two male non-academics were either going into farm work or full time in a small engineering workshop.

Another five of the youngsters had already been offered full-time work, though two of them had been offered places by the RAF and the Army on condition they attained the necessary formal qualifications. Three other youngsters felt that because of their particular job choices – chef or hotel receptionist – the nature of the work or the unsociable hours and conditions of the job would either maintain a high level of labour demand or an absence of other applicants. Finally, there was one academic boy who felt – true to the principles of market economics – that there were always jobs around if one was not too choosey.

Nevertheless, despite this group, who in the main had good reasons for being optimistic about their job chances, there was also a substantial group who, despite recognising the paucity of job opportunities, still wanted to leave school as soon as possible.

Assessing the experience of school

Given that urge to get out of school and into what was seen as a tight labour market, it seemed important to find out how the youngsters assessed their educational experiences. Were they in fact looking forward to leaving school? Did they have mixed feelings? Or, were they apprehensive about the prospect?

The latter category, which only involved nine youngsters, predominantly mentioned a fear of unemployment coupled with the fact that they would miss their friends and the atmosphere of school. Two made it clear that they did not really want to go out to work. As one academic male expressed it: 'I would rather be at school than working all day for my keep'.

The majority of the youngsters, just over half, clearly had mixed feelings about the prospect. Many were obviously reluctant to leave behind friends and experiences that they might have enjoyed, or else were clearly apprehensive about the prospect of unemployment. Alternatively, they emphasised a desire to get jobs and all that implied, or else, particularly in the case of those going to college, emphasised their desire for a change and to be doing something they saw as more relevant to their future.

Undoubtedly it is from these groupings that the increasing recruitment for the sixth forms was likely to come, but it was also clear that in the latter group the majority actually wanted to work, despite ambiguities about leaving school and old friends, or fears of unemployment.

Among the group who were positively looking forward to leaving there was a basic split between those who emphasised their dislike of the institution, the petty rules they thought were imposed – 'they treat us like children' – or their personal antagonism towards some of the teachers; there were 18 non-academic males and females in this group and one male academic. However, the vast majority of youngsters in this category stressed the maturity and independence they would get from either going to college, or going to work. Importantly, it was here particularly that youngsters started to stress the connection between maturity and independence and starting to earn money. Again a high number of this group stressed the ability, through going to work, of being able to buy things and start bringing money into the home.

It seemed important then to begin to explore how the youngsters assessed the value of what they were told in school in helping them to get a job. However, before outlining their responses, it is important to grasp that the dominant influence on the way young people make choices or decisions about their futures comes from their class and cultural backgrounds. This does not occur mechanically, either through the iron laws of genetics or through the equally rigid laws of a vulgar Marxism. Rather it is through the assimilation over time of a set of preconceptions about what kind of work is meaningful and relevant to them, and makes sense to them in terms of how they understand their own destinies and how they perceive opportunities in the labour market.

Obviously, the process of schooling has an important impact in translating those cultural experiences into scholastic attainment – thus, in some cases, opening avenues for forms of social mobility. But also this process clearly reinforces middle and upper class privilege which, through qualifications, can be retranslated into a new generation of economic privilege. However, for many working class youngsters who choose not to follow the academic route the critical influence lies outside school.

Research over a long period, from Carter (1966) to Willis (1978), has shown how disaffected male, white, working class youth clearly develop their understanding of wage labour, of 'good' and 'bad' jobs, in relation to the informal knowledges and cultures of working class life. Indeed, it can be the case that what appears as 'failure' at school can in fact be part of a very successful cultural preparation for work, and that those most at 'risk' during the transition are not the apparent 'failures', but those who assimilate and believe aspects of the formal educational exchange (Clarke, 1980, p. 11).

Similarly, young girls are more critically affected by processes outside the school, especially by their perceived role in the family. For middle class girls, and some of the working class, the possibilities of an extended education, with its access to certain professions, are now available. But, in common with the mass of early leavers, they also make job choices in the short term, within a longer term context of their future roles as home makers and child rearers. For many young working class women, job choices made on this basis have the paradoxical effect of making marriage all the more necessary to escape from the low paid and monotonous work they have initially accepted – and to which, after child rearing, they are increasingly likely to return. Moreover recent research demonstrates that particular job choices for young women are also influenced by the necessity to get the 'right mate': 'One of the central criteria according to which waged work is seen as more or less attractive is the relative possibility it offers for meeting eligible men' (Griffen *et al*., 1980, p. 23).

So, the responses of the boys and girls to the value of what the school purveys in the context of getting jobs, have to be considered within that wider context of how particular work is chosen.

Overall, just over 70 per cent of the youngsters gave a positive response to some aspects of the schools' provision, though a substantial minority – about a quarter of the academics and a third of the non-academics – were critical of what they had been offered. In the main the criticisms focused on the perceived irrelevance of academic subjects to the jobs they wanted, with the related opinion that the curriculum should either have been more job specific or that there should have been more time spent on careers advice and work experience. More specific information was requested on signing-on procedures, social benefits, the individual's rights at work and concrete knowledge of working life.

Even those giving a positive evaluation tended to focus on the value of instrumental provision, either in the form of subjects such as wood and metal work, typing and so on, which employers specifically demanded, or in terms of more immediate advice on how to look for jobs, get and perform at interviews, write letters and applications and obtain references. Although these attitudes were predominantly expressed by the non-academics, only a small group of the academics endorsed the general value of the school curriculum and examinations as such. However, even these were clearly seen in terms of access to further education or the universities, or as a necessity for gaining access to particular kinds of work.

The vast majority of the young people emphasised those parts of the curriculum which they saw as directly relevant to their own possibilities of work – irrespective of whether they thought these had been provided adequately or not. This applied as much to the broader curriculum as to the more specific and direct forms of provision concerning the mechanics of getting jobs. Thus, it is only for a minority of the youngsters, whose job choices specifically depend on qualifications, that the formal curriculum has a direct instrumental connection. For the rest, a proportion of whom criticised the irrelevance of academic subjects, the more substantial elements of school life were largely seen as irrelevant to their future job chances and destinies.

Instrumentalism

This instrumentalism and pragmatism in relation to the value of schooling is a well documented response of young people, particularly on the part of those identified as the early leavers, and their parents (Schools Council, 1968). Indeed, it resonates closely with the responses of working class families to earlier phases of educational expansion. Critically, it creates a key contradiction for teachers who, on the one hand, have to respond to that instrumentalism and also do their best for the individual child within the constraints of the syllabus, but on the other hand are confronted with an objective situation where as many as two out of three of their pupils will now be unemployed, and at best they are reduced to helping them compete more effectively for a diminishing number of jobs. Some teachers have been able to respond to this creatively, but the majority have undoubtedly attempted to reinforce the importance of competition within the school, to reinforce the value of the educational exchange – 'work hard, get your exams, and get a good job'. For the 'less able', alternatively, we get an increasing emphasis on meeting their social and developmental needs, and an attempt to break, even ignore, the links between school and work/unemployment. Fortunately, for the schools, the comprehensive nature of the Youth Training Scheme eases the pressure of the contradiction, and recreates a modified version of the educational exchange by pointing to the diversity and the 'choices' opened for the young through the schemes.

Two more features of this instrumentalism are worth examining. In the first place, over 80 per cent of the boys and girls were aware that other young people would be getting better jobs than they would, and that was predominantly understood as a function of an extended education and better examinations. However, this recognition did not have the consequence of making them work harder on the academic route; it was a commonsense explanation of the division of labour that had no real connection with their own destinies – as one young boy expressed it: 'Most people have got better qualifications than me, but as long as I am doing a job I like I don't mind'.

In other words, although schools have been effective in convincing the youngsters about the legitimacy of exams and job position, for many of the boys and girls this was irrelevant to their own position and the jobs and destinies they saw awaiting them.

The second point worth extracting is that, increasingly, schools have developed curricula and courses which attempt to respond to that instrumentalism which rejects the formal academic curriculum. However, these programmes have clearly evolved as an attempt to make schooling more relevant to the youngsters, rather than make the schools more relevant to employers and their needs. Thus, the increasing emphasis in the curriculum on the interest of the youngsters in work and in getting jobs, will confront a material situation of mass unemployment where that curriculum will increasingly not work. The contradiction, where schooling for unemployment means more efficient education for employment, has as its consequence a curriculum which increasingly cannot deliver the goods in terms of jobs.

Leaving school: expectations of work and job choices

In considering the expectations that the youngsters had about work and the kinds of work they were after I wanted, initially, to get some idea of how much money they expected in their first jobs; while these averages conceal wide differences in expectations, they do give some impression of what the youngsters anticipated.

Nearly a fifth of them did not know what to expect, or gave no answer. On the average, academic boys expected £42 a week and non-academic boys £37 a week; academic girls expected £43 a week and non-academic girls £34. These amounts, in fact, were not dissimilar to the actual average wage rates of young people in this period; but they did stand in sharp contrast to the weekly allowance on YOP, which had been frozen at £23.50 since 1979, and was only increased to £25 a week in January 1982. In all, only ten of the non-academics had expectations as low as the YOP allowance, and for many of those who had done part-time work this allowance (for a 40-hour week) would actually represent a cut in wages.

Constructed by the MSC on the time-honoured principle of 'less-eligibility' the YOP allowance, which awaited many of these youngsters, was not to be seen as a wage, with the property rights that implied, and most assuredly should not become a disincentive to finding work. This underlines the role of the allowance (which

Table 2.2 *The jobs they wanted or expected to get*

	Academics			Non-Academics			All		
	M	F	Total	M	F	Total	M	F	Total
Nursing/nursery nurse	0	4	4	0	7	7	0	11	11
Working with children/old people	0	1	1	0	2	2	0	3	3
Teaching	0	1	1	0	2	2	0	3	3
Office, clerical, secretarial work	0	3	3	0	9	9	0	12	12
Shop work	1	0	1	5	13	18	6	13	19
Miscellaneous job after FE (e.g. receptionist, beautician, etc.)	1	3	4	0	4	4	1	7	8
Craft/technician apprenticeship (inc. hairdressing, lorry driving, etc.)	5	0	5	27	3	30	32	3	35
Professions (e.g. law, accountancy, engineering, etc.)	6	1	7	1	0	1	7	1	8
Armed forces, police merchant navy	3	1	4	7	5	12	10	6	16
Labouring, factory work	0	0	0	2	0	2	2	0	2
Farming, agricultural work	0	0	0	3	2	5	3	2	5
Artistic, design work	0	1	1	1	0	1	1	1	2
Miscellaneous	0	2	2	0	0	0	0	2	2
Don't know	4	6	10	6	0	6	10	6	16
TOTAL	20	24	44	55	48	103	75	72	147

also applied to 17 and 18 year olds), in preparing these youngsters for cheap labour and making their expectations more 'realistic'.

If their financial expectations were relatively modest – though unlikely to be realised – what were their expectations of work in general? Here the focus was overwhelmingly on work that was interesting (though across the categories that meant different things), accounting for the responses of 59 per cent of the boys and 64 per cent of the girls. Only 15 per cent of the boys and 6 per cent of the girls emphasised good pay; and 13 per cent of the boys and 3 per cent of the girls prioritised possibilities for promotion. The other main criterion, particularly emphasised by non-academic girls, was for their fellow workers to be sociable and friendly; this wish was expressed by 7 per cent of the boys and 24 per cent of the girls.

In other words, their demand was not particularly for high wages, though it was important that these were adequate. Rather, the predominant emphasis was on having jobs that were interesting, whether that was defined in terms of the social or the technical relations of the work. In an objective situation where these young people will be confronted in many cases by deskilled work or forms of labour which are an extension of the types of part-time work they have already rejected, or increasingly no work at all, we are presented with a vivid illustration of the bankruptcy of the labour market for meeting their needs.

So what, then, were the actual jobs they wanted? In Table 2.2 we can see that in any 'equitable' system they were not making particularly unrealistic demands. However, as has been demonstrated in survey after survey, and in the chilling reality of the monthly unemployment statistics, even these modest demands had little or no chance of being met. On top of the virtual collapse of apprenticeships and other 'youth' work in the manufacturing sector, even previously expanding areas in the service sector–such as local authorities or banking – had decimated their recruitment. Similarly, whole sectors in further and higher education have been forced to contract at a time when the age group is increasing, and even young professionals have experienced unprecedented levels of unemployment.

Without exploring the hierarchical and sexual divisions implicit in these job choices, it was clear in the summer of 1981 that many of these expectations would be blocked. In their place, the youngsters were to be confronted with the training schemes of the MSC and its related institutions, or the dubious 'freedoms' of the dole, all designed to accommodate the youngsters to cheap labour and the acceptance of *any* job which was on offer.

A further consequence of these restricted opportunities is brought out when we examine Table 2.3 and see that it is precisely around job and educational options that many of the youngsters saw their transition out of the family of origin. Clearly, delay in achieving the financial autonomy necessary for marriage or leaving home, or the denial of places on courses of higher education, will have a critical impact in extending the period for which the youngsters are dependent on the parental wage and remain in the parental home.

Table 2.3   *When they expected to leave home (as a percentage, n = 147)*

	Academic			Non-Academic			All		
	M	F	Total	M	F	Total	M	F	Total
When they go to:									
College/university	5	7	12	1	1	2	6	8	14
Armed forces/ police/ merchant navy	1	0	1	5	3	8	6	3	9
As soon as they can afford to	3	1	4	12	7	19	15	8	23
When their parents throw them out	0	0	0	5	2	7	5	2	7
When they get married	5	7	12	11	20	31	16	27	43
No answer	0	0	0	2	0	2	2	0	2
Don't know	0	1	1	1	0	1	1	1	2
TOTAL	14	16	30	37	33	70	51	49	100

What I have tried to demonstrate is that most of these youngsters, particularly those intending to leave in the summer of 1981, were prepared in the social and cultural sense for making the transition to work, though they may not have been particularly attractive to employers who, to be frank, had a choice of thousands. They made realistic choices for largely reasonable jobs which, minimally, should at least offer interesting work. Despite mass unemployment they wanted to make the transition. They were motivated, had already started to look for work, and would undoubtedly put a lot of energy and activity into the search for work (Markall and Finn, 1982, part I).

However, in reality, most were to be confronted with the debilitating experience of unemployment or a set of schemes and options which were designed to restructure and deflect their expectations and their potential frustration. Dressed up in a rhetoric of not simply meeting employers' requirements but responding to the 'needs' of the youngsters, the move in unemployed skills training was away from any notion of providing power on the labour market, through control of particular technical or labour processes, towards the forms of 'skill' training needed to provide the adaptable and flexible young workers who could float from job to job at the bottom end of the labour market, to be recruited as and when employers wanted them.

By extending the dependence of many of these youngsters on their families, and by taking them out of the formal wage economy, the intended consequence seemed to be to socialise and prepare them to act as 'pliable' and cheap workers, who would subsequently take any work that was on offer and forget even the minimal expectations that they had when leaving school.

But where did these expectations about working life come from? Out of what concrete experiences were the young people able to evaluate the various options and possibilities they saw on the labour market? How ignorant were they about the realities of working life?

Child labour: the involvement of school children in paid labour

> We can forget how long abuses can continue 'unknown' until they are articulated: how people can look at misery and not notice it, until misery itself rebels. In the eyes of the rich between 1790 and 1830 factory children were 'busy', 'industrious', 'useful'; they were kept out of their parks and orchards and they were cheap. If qualms arose, they could generally be silenced by religious scruples. (Thompson, 1968, p. 377)

Although the gross abuse and exploitation of child labour associated with the rise of industrial capitalism has largely, though not entirely, been eliminated, it is often forgotten that this form of labour did not simply disappear with the wave of the legislators' wand. The last 150 years has been marked by a *continuous* struggle over the conditions and regulations governing the work of children. A complex relationship between wage labour, the working class family and state education has created a situation where the direct involvement of young people in work and domestic labour has been submerged beneath the rhetoric of compulsory school attendance and the assumed 'innocence' of childhood.

Today, apart from the occasional 'splash' over a particular case in the newspapers, things are assumed to be largely equitable with the taken-for-granted newspaper delivery, milk round and stacked shelves in the supermarket. Indeed, the problem presented today is one concerning the absence of work experience from youngsters' lives, and schools are extolled to provide more of it, for longer periods to greater numbers. Indeed, the rationale for many of the MSC youth unemployment schemes assumes an 'ignorance' on the part of the young, and the necessity to expose them to more or less extended periods of work experience – a view echoed persistently in reports and pronouncements from LEAs and the DES.

I do not wish to dispute the argument that school children's work experience smooths the transition to work. However, rather than underline its purported beneficial effects (for whom?), I would emphasise that it points to the existence of a complex and largely hidden labour market where many young people first confront and experience the social relations of wage labour and which also, in its complex relation to forms of domestic work, prefigures for many youngsters their future destinies in the social and sexual division of labour.

It has to be recognised that this extensive labour market – estimated at any one time to involve from a quarter to a third of all 13–16-year-olds (MacLennan, 1980, p. 13) – does not exist for the benefit of the children, whose 'smiling faces' are rarely seen as the newspaper drops through the letterbox early on a February morning. Rather, child labour, whilst complicated by features of the domestic economy, represents for employers a particularly flexible and cheap labour force which, because of its location in and dependence on the family wage, can be paid far below the costs of its reproduction.

Alongside part-time women workers (though in the main even cheaper) they are particularly attractive to many kinds of employers because they can be paid far below the adult rate; their labour power has a specific flexibility in terms of tasks, hours and days and, finally, the employer can evade the obligations to comply with normal employment requirements, such as, collective bargaining and National Insurance contributions. Indeed, for many young women their work 'career' will be dominated by the experience of part-time work.[4] The 1975 UK 'Labour Force Survey' showed that whereas only 0.8 per cent of young male workers were part-timers, 8.2 per cent of young women workers were part-timers, and as a proportion the number of part-time female workers increases in each age category (OECD, 1978, p. 108).

Furthermore, as reported by the Low Pay Unit in 1980 (Mac-Lennan, 1980), child workers are peculiarly vulnerable to exploitation because there are few enforcement agencies and personnel, who in any case have difficulty in gaining evidence or access, and are also charged with implementing and enforcing an excessively complex set of regulations with only minimal sanctions for offences. Dr Emryn Davies, in a piece of research commissioned by the DHSS in 1972, covering 2500 youngsters, found that not only were nearly half of them involved in some form of paid work, but also that a large majority of the employers involved were guilty of some kind of statutory infringement – covering areas such as hours of work, rest periods, age of employment and so on (MacLennan, 1980, p. 16).

At this point, it is worth emphasising the salience of age relations, particularly as they are defined in employment legislation, as they very actively influence access to and exclusion from portions of the labour market. Just as the pensioner (and married women) are discarded by the bureaucratic and rigid structures of the primary labour market simply through age or domestic commitments, so too is juvenile labour. Necessarily connected to their future class and occupational position, it is also their age and gender which is critical in placing them predominantly within a secondary labour market – characterised by insecurity, low wages and bad conditions – whilst at school. Of course there are massive differences even within age-related class positions, but a powerful element in their consciousness of giving their labour power, particularly whilst at school, is its clear association with culturally defined life stages.

In turning to the experiences of the youngsters surveyed in Coventry and Rugby, I want initially to look at the nature of their involvement in part-time labour; how they gained access to such work; their experience of changing jobs; their hours of work and rates of pay; the kinds of jobs they held and employers they worked for; and whether they wanted to do this work after leaving school. Finally, I want to assess the implications this material and analysis has in a context of mass unemployment, where youth is being redefined institutionally.

The extent of part-time work

When questioned, it became clear that the vast majority of the young people were either currently involved, or had been involved, in some form of paid employment. 65 per cent of the academic boys, and 62 per cent of the academic girls had had some paid work experience; and 80 per cent of the non-academic boys and 86 per cent of the non-academic girls had also had part-time jobs. Overall, 75 per cent of the youngsters had had some involvement in this juvenile labour market.

No particular pattern emerged between the sexes or academic groupings in terms of the age at which they first got involved in part-time work. 27 per cent had started by the time they were 12 years old – indeed two of them had started working either for the family or relatives by the time they were nine years old. A further 28 per cent commenced work at the age of 13, and a similar proportion when they were 14 years old. 17 per cent started when they were in the last year of school. From the age of 12 or younger then, an increasing proportion of the school pupils were progressively involved in forms of paid employment. By their last year at school, nearly four out of five of them had had experience of part-time work.

It was also evident in the survey material that there was a considerable degree of fluidity in relation both to the number of jobs held and their duration. In Table 2.4 it can be seen that while a considerable proportion of the young people – 38 per cent – had held only one job, an equivalent proportion of 36 per cent had held two jobs. 13 per cent had held three jobs and 13 per cent had held four or more jobs. Quite clearly this latter group, though small, was

dominated by non-academic males. In fact this pattern of movement around the child labour market is one which resonates with
the experience of a proportion of working class youth in their first
full-time years on the labour market. However, the stability of some
of the youngsters holding two jobs is emphasised when we take
account of the fact that 23 per cent of the academics and 32 per cent
of the non-academics *currently* working actually held two jobs; one
male non-academic held three part-time jobs at the time of the
survey.

Table 2.4 *Number of part-time jobs held (as a percentage, n = 113)*

	Academic			Non-Academic			All		
	M	F	Total	M	F	Total	M	F	Total
One	4	7	11	12	16	28	16	23	39
Two	5	4	9	15	12	27	20	16	36
Three	0	3	3	4	6	10	4	9	13
Four or more	2	0	2	8	2	10	10	2	12
TOTAL	11	14	25	39	36	75	50	50	100

Where multiple job holding did occur there were a number of
patterns, though predominantly for the young women concerned it
would consist of their doing paid baby sitting whilst also holding a
Saturday job – doing shop work or, less frequently, a paper round.
For the young men concerned many of them, while doing a weekly
paper round, would also commonly hold a Saturday job in some
form of shop work.

Already emerging here, and to be largely confirmed when we
turn to look at the kinds of work held by all the youngsters, is a
pattern similar to that identified by Spittles in 1973 (Frith, 1978,
p. 31), where the paid employment done by school children reflects
their different destinies in the sexual division of labour. Girls were
predominantly involved in casual, home-based tasks like baby
sitting or light shop work; the boys went into the more systematic
work of milk and paper rounds, stacking and warehousing in shops,
or on market stalls. Although this obviously reflects employers'

preferences and definitions of appropriate workers, it also points to the sexual characteristics ascribed to particular kinds of work, even within the informal structures of the child labour market.

Obtaining work and job turnover in the informal labour market

It is important to emphasise that this child labour market is highly localised and informal, and that the youngsters' experience and knowledge of it become particularly important when they leave school and start looking for full-time work. In a research project in Salford in 1980, for example, I found that over 70 per cent of the jobs held by young workers had been obtained through informal job finding networks (Markall and Finn, 1982).

Table 2.5 *Methods of obtaining current and last part-time jobs (as a percentage, n = 170)*

	Academic			Non-Academic			All		
	M	F	Total	M	F	Total	M	F	Total
Told by a friend	2	2	4	10	8	18	12	10	22
Told by a relative	3	2	5	6	14	20	9	16	25
Just went in and asked	3	6	9	16	8	24	19	14	33
Advertised in window	1	0	1	4	2	6	5	2	7
Advertised in a newspaper	0	1	1	1	1	2	1	2	3
Worked for relatives or parents	2	2	4	1	5	6	3	7	10
TOTAL	11	13	24	38	38	76	49	51	100

It is rare to find children's work advertised in the press or by public agencies – as is the case with some important sectors of subsequent full-time youth work. As we can see in Table 2.5, only four of the 170 jobs I got information on had been found through such routes. The vast majority had been found through friends or relatives, or just by asking around. The point I want to make is not so much that the full- and part-time job markets are coterminous; obviously they are not. Rather, I want to emphasise that the social and job hunting skills (as MSC terminology would put it) evidently displayed by the youngsters whilst at school are also those required for an important sector of the job market which confronts them after leaving. Although the bureaucratised practices of application forms, telephone calls, interview procedures, and so on (which seem to form the core of 'social and life' skills training), are obviously important after school leaving, they are not exclusively so. Further, the implicit suggestion that the youngsters are ignorant of the operations and practices of the labour market, denigrates the real skills and competences they obviously display whilst looking for and finding work while still at school.

Having earlier pointed to the degree of movement in the part-time job market, in terms of job turnover and multiple job holding, I now want to consider the reasons the youngsters gave for leaving their last part-time job. Overwhelmingly, the majority of those leaving a job had done so of their own accord. It can be seen in Table 2.6, that this accounted for 78 per cent of those leaving their last job, though 22 per cent had been given the sack. This latter group was dominated by non-academic males.

Table 2.6 *Reasons for leaving last part-time job (as a percentage, n = 147)*

	Academics			Non-Academics			All		
	M	F	Total	M	F	Total	M	F	Total
Never had a part-time job	5	6	11	7	5	12	12	11	23
Only had one job which they still held	3	3	6	3	7	10	6	10	16
Left of own accord	4	6	10	18	19	37	22	25	47
Dismissed	2	1	3	9	2	11	11	3	14
TOTAL	14	16	30	37	33	70	51	49	100

As to why they had been given the sack, over half of them (10) had an early experience of what is afflicting the adult population currently – they were 'surplus' to requirements, had been laid off, or the employer had closed down. Another six had been dismissed for disciplinary reasons, particularly in relation to absenteeism and punctuality, though one had been sacked for fighting. Finally, three of them had been shown the door because their employer felt that they were not up to the work or were not working hard enough, though the youngsters themselves did not necessarily agree.

As to those who had left of their own accord, the vast majority, 38, or 55 per cent, had done so either because they found the work boring and had disliked it, or they felt the pay was too low and the work was too hard. As one young woman graphically expressed it: 'Because it was not very well paid – 10p an hour – and I had to carry heavy weights'. Similarly, within this group were half a dozen youngsters who had found the pay, weather conditions, and hours of work associated with paper rounds too much to put up with. A further four had left either because they did not get on with the employer or, as some of them put it, felt he was a 'slave driver'. Again these patterns and reasons are not dissimilar to those identifed with many early school leavers in the first few years at work, and if nothing else it demonstrates their material ability to forego the wage rather than accept what they experience as intolerable working conditions.

As for the rest in this category, 13 or 19 per cent had got another job, and a small number (three) had either moved from the area or felt it was too far to travel. There were some fairly specific individual cases where, for example, youngsters had left work because of medical reasons or, alternatively, their parents had sold the shop where they had worked. The final category, accounting for seven or 10 per cent, referred to seasonal work ending or short term jobs in the summer being given up when going on holiday.

The connection between part-time work and subsequent full-time jobs

Overall, then, we can see that a substantial group of the young people had had some experience of the vagaries of wage labour, and had either voluntarily or involuntarily rejected what they considered to be bad working conditions. Whilst not making a direct equation between this experience and that awaiting them on the full-time labour market, it seems reasonable to suggest that these learning experiences, and those implicit in the experience of the ostensibly more stable, are important factors predisposing them towards certain positions in the full-time labour market. Indeed, evidence suggests that employers themselves value this labour market experience, in preference to time-tabled work experience, as demonstrating a youngster's 'initiative' and 'discipline', and it becomes an important selection criterion in their recruitment practices (Richards, 1982).

As we pointed out earlier, over half of those youngsters not worried about future employment prospects had been offered jobs by their part-time employers, though as can be seen from Table 2.7, there were a few more youngsters who would move into that work full-time (including three female non-academics) if nothing else turned up. Altogether then 21 per cent of the youngsters with experience of part-time work were prepared to go into that work full time, particularly amongst the non-academic girls where the proportion was 32 per cent.

Table 2.7 *Would they want to do the work full-time (as a percentage, n = 82)*

	Academics			Non-Academics			All		
	M	*F*	*Total*	*M*	*F*	*Total*	*M*	*F*	*Total*
Yes	1	1	2	5	10	15	6	11	17
No	11	14	25	27	28	55	38	42	80
Maybe, if nothing else	0	0	0	0	3	3	0	3	3
TOTAL	12	15	27	32	41	73	44	56	100

Those youngsters who said 'no' pointed predominantly to the low pay and monotonous nature of the work; as one young girl put it: 'Because it has no atmosphere to it and it's as if you are closed in a cardboard box'. In addition there were many specific objections to particular working conditions, such as unsocial hours, bad working practices and lack of security. There was also a small but significant group, predominantly male, who saw no trade or skill at the end of it. Obviously these reactions need to be seen in a context where many of the youngsters had other jobs in mind to which they were more positively committed.

Having discussed the reactions of the youngsters to their experience of part-time work, and finding a considerable degree of dissatisfaction both with the pay and the nature of the work on offer, it is now important to go on to consider the kinds of work, hours and conditions on offer in the twilight economy of child labour.

The nature of the employers: hours and conditions of work

We can see, from Table 2.8, that the kinds of employers involved clearly represent the peculiar combination of domestic relationships, small employers and large retail/distribution companies who control and structure the child labour market. It is also important to recognise that the kinds of work the youngsters are involved in are not simply those we commonly define as 'child's' work, such as newspaper rounds, but include many jobs which are done by adult workers. Nor is it simply a tiny minority of employers who are involved. From this and wider evidence, it is clear that a large number of employers are involved, ranging from the smallest to the largest business corporations which dominate the retail outlets in most high streets and shopping centres.

Further, while there are manifest sexual divisions between various categories of work (noticeably between domestic and mechanical), even within the categories, as was indicated earlier, there were important divisions prefiguring the structure of opportunities in full-time work, such that boys and girls would do different types of 'shop work'.

In terms of their conditions of work, the majority of youngsters were working less than ten hours a week. However, a large number, over 30 per cent, were doing more, and over 10 per cent were doing more than 16 hours per week. The youngsters in this latter group were primarily employed in supermarkets and shops (six), or in the case of two youngsters doing more than 25 hours a week, working for their parents (one in a market garden; the other in a pub). These amounts may seem trival, but as the Low Pay Unit has pointed out

Table 2.8 *Nature of jobs held (includes multiple job-holder) (as a percentage, n = 108)*

	Academics			Non-Academics			All		
	M	F	Total	M	F	Total	M	F	Total
Babysitting/ child-minding	0	3	3	0	21	21	0	24	24
Paper, milk, egg rounds (inc. leaflets)	2	2	4	10	5	15	12	7	19
Shop assistant/ market work	4	5	9	8	9	17	12	14	26
Cleaning (inc. cars)/ domestic work	0	0	0	3	1	4	3	1	4
Waitress work/ catering	2	1	3	0	2	2	2	3	5
Garage, mechanical, electrical work (inc. forecourt attendants)	1	0	1	5	1	6	6	1	7
Farm work (inc. poultry picking)	0	1	1	5	2	7	5	3	8
Office work	2	1	3	0	0	0	2	1	3
Miscellaneous (e.g. Punk band, and other self-employed)	0	1	1	1	2	3	1	3	4
TOTAL	11	14	25	32	43	75	43	57	100

(MacLennan, 1980), if these hours were added to the normal school week of 30 to 35 hours, then many of the youngsters were already working over 40 hours per week.

When considering the hours worked during the holidays I am only able to consider those youngsters who were actually working during term time as well. Due to an ambiguity in the questionnaire, those who solely worked in the holidays were excluded, and while this has, if anything, led to an understatement of the numbers involved in part-time work before leaving school, it is still possible to say something about the hours the rest worked. For 37 (45 per cent) of them there was no change in hours worked. Seven of them reported an increase to between 11 and 20 hours per week; five increased to between 20 and 30 hours; 10 were up to between 30 and 40 hours; and 14 non-academics (nine boys and five girls) were working over 40 hours a week, primarily in shop and market work.

The final responses to be considered in this section concern rates of pay. Although five of the youngsters gave no answer, or received nothing as they worked for their parents, it is possible to give some rough averages. For academic boys the average hourly rate was £1.03, and for girls 77p. For non-academic boys the average was just over 70p and for the girls 68p per hour.

Obviously, these averages conceal fairly large disparities: for example, seven boy and 13 girl non-academics were receiving less than 50p per hour, as against six academic boys who were getting in excess of £1 an hour. Further, rates of pay were directly related to the nature of the employer and clearly – apart from those working for their families – the aristocracy of paid jobs were in the large supermarket chains, such as VG, Sainsbury's or Marks and Spencers.

The importance of part-time work and the impact of unemployment

From this examination of the pre-school-leaving labour market we can see that the experience of young people within it is important for two major reasons. In the first place, it is important both because it can give a proportion of them direct access to forms of full-time work, and also because the nature of the work on offer, and their experience of it, prefigures in some important ways their future destinies in domestic and wage labour.

Secondly, it represents a learning experience which, whilst the particular kind of work might be rejected, makes for a continuity between pre- and post-school economic life, and ensures an early exposure and subjection to the rigours of the labour market. That is, a subjection to the discipline of the wage, where the individual experiences the material constraints and limitations imposed by work discipline in exchange for the powers of consumption given by the wage.

Finally, the extent of part-time work points to the contradictory legacy left by compulsory schooling and the regulation of child labour at work. The history of such legislative interventions and their enforcement has had unintended and sometimes radical consequences both for the organisation of the family economy, and also in the creation of a hidden labour market which revolves around child labour both outside and within the formal statutory regulations.

In a context of rising unemployment and declining real wages, it has to be recognised that this hidden and informal labour market and its use of labour reserves is dynamic and complex. However, my own material was essentially static; yet it is possible, by looking at the situation in Birmingham (one of the few areas on which it is possible to get *some* data), to evaluate some of the implications of changes in this labour market in the 1970s (Forester, 1979, p. 259).

In 1979 evidence was given of a massive increase in child labour in the Birmingham area. Registered child employment rose from 4683 in 1963 to 7821 in 1971. But as unemployment rose in the mid-1970s, the total climbed steeply to 13 336 child employees registered in 1978. This could only be partially explained by improved registration methods, and also did not include another extimated 3000 children illegally employed in the city on building sites, industrial cleaning, street trading, coal delivery, fairgrounds and rag trade sweatshops.

Research evidence suggested that the pressure on living standards and unemployment in the home was forcing many youngsters to look for work in order to get some independence from their parents and obtain the commodities which their parents would not, or could no longer afford to, supply. Equally, it was clear that employers were absorbing this willing source of cheap labour.

The significance of these latter two points has since been emphasised dramatically by the return to mass unemployment. In the first place, mass youth unemployment, in further delaying the transition to an adult wage, has had important implications for the structure of the working class family economy. One study, undertaken in January 1977, found that one in seven of the young unemployed had fathers out of work; one in five had a brother or sister unemployed, and the same proportion lived in households where no one was in full-time work. In all, nearly 80 per cent of the young unemployed had friends out of work (*Department of Employment Gazette*, December 1977, p. 1346).

Although an elaborate scheme of training programmes has been introduced, they have hardly ameliorated the scale of the impact of unemployment on the financial resources of families implied by the above statistics – which reflect a period where registered unemployment was much lower than it was to become. Not only has this deprived working class youngsters of access to a wage, and forced them on the mercies of what has been romantically described as the 'hidden economy', but the material costs of their reproduction have been forced back on the family. Moreover, the training schemes, which have helped create a new and even more inadequately protected reserve army of youth labour, have also implicitly opened up the young unemployed to new forms of exploitation which employers could easily extend from the twilight economy of child labour.

The involvement of children in the economy of the family

Although it is evident that the physical maintenance of children remains one of the primary objects of women's labour in the family economy, financed by the male wage and part-time earnings, it is also clear – particularly within working class families – that with increasing age children are expected to make an ever more positive contribution to the tasks and chores of day to day social reproduction. It is within this context that young people largely learn about appropriate gender behaviour in the home, and clearly for many young women this experience constitutes a more powerful education than the purported 'equal opportunities' on offer in the school.

In this and following sections, I will be assessing the extent to which children are differentially involved in domestic labour, the tasks they perform, and the extent to which their leisure activities and forms of consumption are supported by the family wage.

Quite clearly, the costs of children – in terms of clothing, food, school meals, transport, and so on – are considerable and, along with the physical necessity to look after them, constitute the major constraints on the time and money budgets of the family. However, the initial questions I asked were to assess the actual money given to the youngsters for their own disposal. I found here that the vast majority did receive 'pocket' money, though a significant minority, particularly of the young men, did not. Altogether 20 per cent of the boys and 13 per cent of the girls, noticeably those in paid part-time employment, provided their own disposable income *without* aid from their parents. Indeed, on further examination of those with experience of part-time work it was found that 10 per cent of the non-academics (six boys and two girls), and 7 per cent of the academics (one boy and one girl) actually contributed some of their part-time earnings to the family wage – though I got no indication of the frequency or amounts involved.

I also tried to get some indication of the amounts of money given to the youngsters by their parents, but while the following averages give some part of the pattern of the income at the disposal of the youngsters, the variety of things included (ranging from some who included school meal money to those who included travelling expenses) makes it hard to generalise. Nevertheless, the vast majority got less than £3 per week; indeed 22 per cent of the non-academics were getting less than £1 a week, and only five of them, all male, were receiving more than £5 a week pocket money.

Patterns of consumption

In addition to obtaining information on their disposable income, I also wanted to get some indication of how young people obtained their own clothing; in a sense the material basis of style and cultural self expression. Although there was a considerable variety of methods – whether they bought them with their own money (17 per cent of boys and 15 per cent of girls), or with money their parents gave them, or with their parents, or a combination – it was massively the case that, irrespective of the method of purchase, all but three boys and one girl were given autonomy as consumers; that is, they chose their own styles.

What seems to be clear in the last year at school is that while the young men and women are still largely economically dependent on their parents for their maintenance and material goods, they are given considerable autonomy in relation to the style of commodities they buy. Further, the cash contribution of parents to the young is

Table 2.9   *The principal items of expenditure*

	Academics (n = 132)			Non-Academics (n = 309)			All (n = 441)		
				percentage					
	M	F	Total	M	F	Total	M	F	Total
Savings	5	9	14	6	6	12	6	7	13
Clothes	5	16	21	5	12	17	5	13	18
Make-up	0	1	1	0	4	4	0	3	3
Sweets	2	3	5	4	3	7	3	3	6
Hobby (e.g. karate, fishing, pets, etc.)	2	1	3	1	0	1	2	1	3
Magazines	1	4	5	2	2	4	2	2	4
Concerts, gigs, dances, discos	5	6	11	3	8	11	4	7	11
Football matches	3	1	4	2	1	3	2	1	3
Films	1	2	3	1	1	2	1	1	2
Beer, alcoholic drinks	3	0	3	7	1	8	5	1	6
Records	7	4	11	5	3	8	6	3	9
Cigarettes	2	1	3	6	4	10	5	3	8
Bus/train fares	2	5	7	2	1	3	2	2	4
Motorbike/bicycle	1	0	1	5	0	5	4	0	4
Snacks	1	1	2	1	1	2	1	1	2
Space invaders, pool, etc.	5	1	6	3	0	3	3	1	4
TOTAL	45	55	100	53	47	100	51	49	100

clearly inadequate, except in a small number of cases, to give them access to more than bare leisure provision. Thus, to finance those activities – to get access to the more expensive forms of youth leisure – the youngsters need the extra income from part-time work; indeed many of them were obviously financing most if not all of their own leisure activities.

To reinforce the point, the youngsters did not work simply for its intrinsic merits or to fill in empty hours (as we saw earlier most of them disliked its nature or conditions), but for the access to forms of leisure and consumption it facilitates. Given the identification of economic independence and forms of consumption with adulthood and maturity, it is clear that the instrumentalism of many young workers has some of its roots in their early exposure to the disciplines and freedoms of the wage.

The information in Table 2.9, based on the three major items of each youngster's expenditure, already indicates the developing transition to more adult forms of consumption. It also demonstrates clear sexual cleavages, with the boys spending more money on beer, pub and arcade machines, motorbikes, cigarettes, and so on, and the young women spending more on clothes and make-up. Again, even within general categories such as records, concerts, magazines and so on, the commodities in question are constructed in relation to masculine or feminine 'tastes' and characteristics. However, we should in no way see these young people simply as the 'happy' and passive consumers so beloved by the advertising companies. There is a complex relationship between the images created and exploited by the advertising industry and the producers of 'youthful' commodities, the nature of their use by young people, and the meanings and constructions they may give to particular styles (see, for example, Hebdige, 1981; Frith, 1978).

In returning our focus to 'pocket' money, it should be recognised that this form of income for the young is not a simple gratuitous gift, but in many cases this power to consume is given in return for work in and around the home. Particularly in the case of young working class women, as Angela McRobbie (1978) points out, they will be expected to earn their pocket money in return for domestic labour – a form of domestic sub-contracting to the mother.

Involvement in domestic labour

Although the information in Table 2.10 has to be seen within a context of size of family, number of parents, age of siblings etc, it was clear that the girls were more frequently involved in domestic chores than their male counterparts. In all, 38 per cent of the academic and 46 per cent of the non-academic girls were involved every day in domestic labour, compared with 10 per cent of the academic and 25 per cent of the non-academic boys. Indeed, 75 per cent of the girls were doing tasks in the home either regularly or daily, compared with half of the boys.

Table 2.10   *Frequency of jobs done around the house (as a percentage, n = 147)*

	Academics			Non-Academics			All		
	M	F	Total	M	F	Total	M	F	Total
All the time, at least once a day	1	6	7	10	15	25	11	21	32
Regularly, several times a week	5	6	11	10	10	20	15	16	31
Occasionally, once a week	6	3	9	10	5	15	16	8	24
Hardly ever, not every week	1	1	2	5	2	7	6	3	9
Never	1	0	1	2	1	3	3	1	4
TOTAL	14	16	30	37	33	70	51	49	100

In terms of the tasks actually and most frequently performed, it can be seen in Table 2.11, that clear sexual patterns emerged. Although some tasks were nominally shared, the young women were almost exclusively involved in the task of washing and laundry work, cooking meals, cleaning the house, looking after other children, and sewing or mending clothes. The young men were predominantly involved in gardening, painting, fixing things and washing the car. Even within tasks which were nominally shared, however, specific sexual divisions existed. For example, while boys will commonly look after young children in terms of keeping an eye on them, particularly when they are past the toddler stage, girls will more commonly be expected to feed them, change their nappies, clean them, and so on.

This differential involvement of girls in domestic labour is a crucial part of their preparation for their future domestic role – from which men derive direct material benefits and comforts. For women, the

Table 2.11 *Tasks most frequently done* (as a percentage, n = 550)*

	Academic			Non-Academic			All		
	M	F	Total	M	F	Total	M	F	Total
Looking after smaller siblings	1	2	3	2	4	6	3	6	9
Looking after children of relatives and neighbours	0	1	1	0	3	3	0	4	4
Washing/laundry/ ironing	0	1	1	1	5	6	1	6	7
Sewing or mending clothes	0	1	1	0	3	3	0	4	4
Cleaning the house	2	3	5	3	7	10	5	10	15
Cooking meals	1	2	3	2	5	7	3	7	10
Washing up the dishes	3	3	6	5	7	12	8	10	18
Shopping	2	2	4	5	6	11	7	8	15
Painting, decorating, fixing things in the house	1	0	1	4	1	5	5	1	6
Gardening	1	0	1	4	1	5	5	1	6
Washing the car	1	0	1	4	1	5	5	1	6
TOTAL	12	15	27	30	43	73	42	58	100

* Different number of tasks mentioned by each respondent, and one non-academic boy gave no answer.

amount of time taken up by their domestic duties is one of the most significant constraints on their daily lives, both structuring the form of relationship they have to the labour process, and their pattern of subordination within the family. Even though men are becoming increasingly involved in domestic tasks, these tend not to be a direct substitute for women's routine domestic work (Land, 1981, p. 251). Equally, despite mechanisation in the home and increased involvement in part-time work, time budget studies have shown that the total time women spend on their domestic tasks has declined very little in the last half century (ibid. p. 250).

Children themselves, initially the cause of much of the labour, as they come into adolescence increasingly share some of the chores and burdens of domestic labour. But the apprenticeship in the home of boys and girls, and the material tasks done, are not shared evenly and prefigure their unequal futures.

The impact of domestic labour and part-time work on school attendance

It is also important to grasp that the primacy of the domestic economy, and the demands of part-time labour, can in themselves make more or less frequent incursions into the formally regulated time of schooling. Although working class families may, over the last century, have been 'educated' to the formal requirements of rational schooling, this has not eradicated forms of absenteeism; rather it has made them a pathology – 'truancy'. The incursions into school attendance of domestic and part-time work may, to some extent, help us understand some of the reasons for the 90 000 or so secondary school children who, according to Mark Carlyle, Education Secretary in 1981, were absent without 'reasonable explanation' on any one school day (*Youth in Society*, July 1981, p. 51). Anecdotal evidence itself suggests that some of the 'reasonable' explanations themselves concern girls having time off to help in the home, or recalcitrant fifth year boys being allowed to leave early to work for their prospective employers.

The answers in Table 2.12 were affected by the question's structural position in the questionnaire; but if anything this helped to understate the incidence of time off. Nevertheless, it is clear that a much higher proportion of the non-academics took time off because of domestic responsibilities or to do part-time work. Of those answering the question, it was also more likely for the non-academic boys to take time off for reasons of work than it was for the girls. Altogether 18 per cent of the non-academic boys had had time off for work-related reasons, as against 6 per cent of the non-academic girls. In relation to domestic responsibilities and tasks, it was evident that the non-academic girls were more heavily involved,

Table 2.12 *Number having time off school between Xmas and Easter and their reasons*

	Academics			Non-Academics			All		
	M	F	Total	M	F	Total	M	F	Total
None	12	18	30	22	19	41	34	37	71
No answer	3	2	5	17	4	21	20	6	26
To work for an employer	0	0	0	5	2	7	5	2	7
To work for relatives or friends	1	0	1	5	1	6	6	1	7
To look after relative or someone in family	1	1	2	2	17	19	3	18	21
To do some shopping	2	2	4	2	7	9	4	9	13
To help in the home	1	1	2	8	6	14	9	7	16
TOTALS	20	24	44	61	56	117	81	80	161
NB Those giving more than one reason	0	0	0	3	6	9	3	6	9

particularly in looking after relatives or someone in the home. Overall, 52 per cent of those girls had had time off for domestic reasons, as against 22 per cent of the non-academic boys.

As regards the incidence of time off, for most of the youngsters involved it had only amounted to one or two absences. However, a significant minority of non-academic boys and girls had taken time off on more than three occasions in the previous term. Obviously, this gives no indication of the scale or pattern of general school absenteeism. It simply reinforces the point that the domestic and economic lives of the youngsters' structures their relationship with schooling not only indirectly, but also directly in terms of attendance.

So far we have been able to establish that the young persons' time outside school is never simply free time – that their substantial and differential involvement in forms of domestic labour and part-time work are powerful material and educative experiences which, in their continuous exercise, provide many of the skills and disposi-tions which propel the youngsters to their positions in the sexual and social division of labour. This is not to underestimate the powerful impact that schooling and certification have on their life chances, or the cultural and social importance of the transition to full time labour. Rather, what needs to be emphasised is that these processes do not operate on a previous experience of innocence or ignorance; that the young people have established particular skills and dispositions before leaving – both inside and outside – the site of the schooling, which point them to and prepare them for the giving of their labour power. Essentially, they are not really in need of many of the social and life skills on offer from the MSC and its training programmes – of 'coping', 'resisting provocation', 'taking orders', 'getting on with fellow workers', and so on – because they have already had many of these experiences and learned how to deal with them competently and realistically. What they actually need, and explicitly want, are opportunities for real jobs, with a reasonable wage and decent conditions of employment.

Leisure and 'free' time

In this final section I wanted to obtain some information on how the young people spent their 'free' time. However, the kind of self-reporting involved has massive problems associated with it, so rather than outline any definitive pattern that might have emerged, I simply want to make some observations on the material collected.

In the first place, it was clear that the youngsters identified themselves predominantly as members of small peer groups, though a substantial minority (20 boys and 24 girls) claimed that they spent most of their spare time – though not necessarily all – with a particular friend of the same or the opposite sex. The groups largely consisted of less than six youngsters – though 12 of the boys and six of the girls reported hanging around in groups of ten or more.

When considering the sexual composition of the groups, it was found that of those who reported themselves as being in groups for most of their spare time, 39 per cent of the girls and 36 per cent of the boys were in single sex groups. Although 61 per cent of the girls and 64 per cent of the boys were in mixed groups this did not necessarily imply that all leisure activities were shared, particularly as this question was commonly interpreted as relating to who one went with when 'going out'. The youngsters were clearly in the process of making the transition from simple friendship groups to activities and peer groups that were sexually oriented.

Predominantly, the boys and girls claimed that the groups were more or less stable, varying only a little in composition. The only crude quantitative difference to emerge, in Table 2.13, was the tendency for more of the academics to draw their friendship groups from their schools, and the non-academics to draw them from where they lived. This could have reflected internal school processes and their relation to the neighbourhood or, more probably, differential material access to transport and leisure facilities.

Table 2.13 *Where their peer groups come from (as a percentage, n = 107)*

	Academics			Non-Academics			All		
	M	F	Total	M	F	Total	M	F	Total
From school	10	10	20	8	12	20	18	22	40
From where they lived	8	5	13	25	18	43	33	23	56
Relatives	0	0	0	2	0	2	2	0	2
Outside school, but not where they lived	0	1	1	1	0	1	1	1	2
TOTAL	18	16	34	36	30	66	54	46	100

Despite the crudeness of these measures, what needs to be stressed is the importance of the group as a form of social organisation. It is through this affiliation that the transition from dependence on the family of origin to the responsibilities and constraints of the family of the future is articulated. Notwithstanding specific differences and inequalities of gender and race, it is within a group of people of roughly the same age and status that adolescents experience for the first time social relationships involving some notional semblance of equality and choice.

Having established the generality of the social form, however, it is important to recognise that these groups operate in a context of real material and social disparities in access to different forms of leisure and leisure choices. While parental resources are important, so too are the youngsters' own. To obtain disposable income the youngsters had an involvement in part-time work and domestic labour and, alongside their differential commitment to academic work, this imposed a set of material constraints on their 'leisure' activities.

Moreover, particularly for young women, it has to be grasped that 'leisure' in itself can be hard work. As pointed out in an article by Chris Griffen and other women from the Cultural Studies Centre, constructing femininity to attract men is hard work, and takes time and money:

> The construction of femininity takes a considerable amount of women's 'leisure' time, both inside and outside work. It is of crucial importance in attracting a 'steady bloke who won't bash you around', and who has a secure job. It must be seen as work for women, since – quite literally – their lives will depend on it. The time, effort and money spent on the construction of femininity is an integral part of women's final appearance at the disco or club. (Griffen *et al*., 1980, p. 24)

In terms of how they spent their free time, and what they did when they were in groups, it was quite clear that a different pattern of leisure emerged around their gender; with activities for the girls having a focus around the home and consumption, involving visiting each other's houses, babysitting, window shopping, and so on. Some examples of how they responded were as follows:

> Go dancing and up town shopping.
> Go up town and do window shopping or buy the occasional thing.
> Go around to one another's houses, go to discos, listen to records.
> Go to clubs, listen to records, go to each other's houses.
> Go to shops in town, listen to records, go to discos.

This was in contrast to many of the boys, particularly the non-academics, whose reported activities tended to focus on the streets and open places or, when they could afford it, the up-market provision of pubs and clubs. Clearly, the absence of money for transport or spending, and the freedom from domestic chores, meant that for many boys their leisure was more 'free' than that of the girls and would tend to occur in public places, with the consequence of putting them in potential confrontation with the controllers of those spaces – police, shop and cafe owners, residents and so on. As Simon Frith (1978, p. 45) pointed out, home for some similar boys in the North was not much freer, 'and so the boys went out most nights, doing nothing, having a laugh, aware that this was their youth and that their future would be much like the past of their working class parents'. Examples of their activities included the following statements:

Doss about.
Just walk about.
Hang around the village causing trouble.
Concerts, discos, go to Birmingham for clothes, fight mods, hang around in village and have a laugh.
Drinking in pubs.
Go to the park, pictures or just down the town dossing about.
Go down cafe, play on space invaders, hang around streets, go to pubs.
Go round picking up birds, making trouble, going round the city.

One qualification for the boys, particularly those on the academic route, was a related tendency to spend time in each other's houses – presumably reflecting parental circumstances. Similarly, those on the academic route shared the material constraints imposed by homework to a much greater extent than the non-academic. Otherwise, there was a great deal of shared activities – dominated in the home by watching television and listening to records, and outside the home predominantly involving discos and dances, going to the pub and to a lesser extent using cafes. While it was clear that a lot of the young people used the facilities available from youth services, particularly when they provided discos, there was actually very little recorded membership of formal youth organisations, such as the Scouts, Girl Guides, and other such bodies.

It is important to emphasise at this point that the constraints on how these young people spend their time are not simply material ones. Clearly the exercise of parental authority, and the real and potential threats of sexual, racial and territorial violence, are equally important. As an indication of the former, it was predominantly the case that the youngsters would be punished or told off if they came home late without forewarning their parents. Although 21 of the boys and 11 of the girls claimed that their parents would not mind at all; parental anxieties and constraints exercised an important influence for the rest on the length of time which they could stay out, and no doubt, though with less direct enforcement, on the places they could go to and the activities they could indulge in. However, it should be emphasised again that the exercise of parental authority was increasingly tempered by the developing maturity of the young people themselves.

Nevertheless, fear of getting into 'trouble' – both for parents and the young – is also a powerful constraint on leisure, though with specific and differential connotations. For male youth, particularly black youth, the fear of police harassment and violence, racial or otherwise, can act to keep them off the streets, especially when there is no money for access to clubs and pubs. Female youth also have the additional and pervasive fear of sexual violence to deal with:

> The threat of violence, and particularly of rape, is something against which girls have no protection. They are restricted geographically – cannot go out without the means of getting home safely – and parents will impose restrictions on the time they can come home because of this constant threat. Girls will concur, because the threat of violence induces a fear which is just as powerful in forcing girls and women to 'voluntarily' limit their own freedom. Needless to say, there is no equivalent threat or limitation for boys because boys and men *are* the threat to girls. (Griffen *et al.*, 1980, p. 22)

What the argument in this, and preceding sections, has been establishing is the extent to which young people's access to leisure is both dependent on the money they have, and constrained by the activities participated in to get that money – whether in the home or part-time work, or from parental support. Clearly, an important aspect of the transition to full-time work is the power of the wage to give access to forms of consumption and leisure choices which have previously been blocked or only partially secured.

Within a context of mass youth unemployment, however, this partial access is extended and the attainment of economic independence increasingly blocked. The ever increasing presence of unemployed male youth on the streets should not blind us to those increasingly confined in the home. Equally, there should be no surprise when sections of male youth respond to police violence with rioting and by forced access to the material commodities that their unemployment denies them.

Redefining youth

There are two main implications of this research for the criticisms levelled at young people in the wake of the Great Debate.[5] In the first place, on a number of important levels, the youngsters on leaving school were ready culturally and socially to make the transition to work. Secondly, it is quite clear in related research that for most young workers the transition has never been particularly difficult, and indeed has usually been marked by as many continuities as ruptures in experience (see, for example, Carter, 1966; Willis, 1978; Clarke, 1980).

As a consequence, when examining the discourse constructed by the training and educational infrastructure, which suggests that young people have a problem in making the transition to work, it is very important to grasp that the problem is not one about their adjustment to working life. Instead, the problem is about how that transition has been arbitrarily extended by employers' refusal to employ the young. The key issue for the MSC and other similar agencies, in the context of mass unemployment, has been how to structure that longer, perhaps indefinite, transition in a way that improves employability (primarily, I would argue, by making youth labour cheap) *and* that also defuses and deflects potential opposition from young people and from the wider labour movement.

However, it can also be seen that the new programmes for school leavers and the young unemployed also misinterpret the relation of young people to waged work, and generalise programmes for all from the practices of the primary labour market, which can only apply to a minority. For example, if we look at the informal labour market – populated predominantly by what the statisticians label as the 'unskilled' – we can see that it contains within it a complex range of social practices. These range from the casual quiet 'word in the ear' or knock on the door, to the complex social forms of being 'spoken for' or the 'lump pub', where labour contractors will appear on a Monday morning. So when I stress the experience of young workers in these areas I am not simply referring to arbitrary and disconnected events, but to forms of social and economic activity which require particular forms of knowledge and experience to negotiate: a cultural knowledge which has to be learned and assimilated. Nevertheless, the courses and educational programmes being provided presuppose an involvement with the bureaucratic procedures and processes of the primary labour market. Given to all, this type of advice and information can only benefit the few. With the extent of unemployment, and the choice and screening devices available to employers, it is clear that the majority of young people are being set up for a competition they cannot win. The programmes pretend to offer to *all* youngsters what can only inevitably be enjoyed by a minority – those who 'fail' have only themselves to blame!

This new political and economic redefinition of youth is fundamental. The attempted absorption of large segments of this pauperised generation within the institutional constraints of education and training, and the implicit attempts to force young women firmly back into the economy of the family, are of enormous significance. Not only does the extension of the period of dependence between school and work have important material implications for the family economy, as I hope I have shown, but it also has more general social and cultural implications for the family and working class culture. It will undoubtedly restructure the age relations which shape both the internal social relationships of the family and the family economy itself. Most directly, these changes will defer, for different lengths of time, the entry of children to full-time waged labour and extend their involvement in the 'shadow' economy of part-time work, thus necessitating new economic adjustments within family patterns of social reproduction. The material conditions of full employment, and the rising disposable income of youth it brought in its wake, which created the conditions for new forms of youth's *cultural* autonomy, are now threatened with permanent disruption.

In many ways these courses and training programmes are the institutional vehicle through which a transformation in patterns of working class social reproduction is being achieved. But this involves no simple transmission of new competences and skills to a generation of working class youth which is allegedly bereft of them. Instead it involves an ambitious attempt to restructure the forms of knowledge and cultural expectations that young people have hitherto displayed in making the transition to wage labour. As the White Paper on the New Training Initiative made clear in December 1981, the Government:

> is applying these extra resources to help secure longer term reforms in the quality of training and bring about a change in the attitudes of young people to the value of training and acceptance of relatively lower wages for trainees. (HMSO, 1981, p. 13)

Young school leavers, then, are not just accidental victims of the recession and economic decline; they are not simply the luckless few marooned by a maelstrom of natural forces. Rather, having been excluded from the labour market, they are now being actively redefined as a key element in the state's solution to the crisis of mass unemployment.

Notes

1. It is important to emphasise that in combination with the social and sexual divisions of labour an individual's job opportunities and life chances are also massively affected by ethnicity. The persistence of overt and covert racial divisions at work and in most other areas of our culture is a well documented one. However, while the relationship between black and white youth of both sexes is of fundamental importance, particularly in a context of increasingly belligerent forms of white racism, within this chapter I focus on the sexual and class experience of youth.
2. The choice of *entry* to four 'O' levels or equivalent was not itself arbitrary, but reflected a number of important considerations. In the first place, despite a proliferation of forms of certification from CSE to GCE, it is quite clear that four 'O' levels represents to a large extent the bottom end of a significant cut-off point in relation to access to certain

sectors of the youth labour market and to forms of higher education (Markall and Finn, 1982; Ashton and Maguire, 1982). Secondly, although CSEs are of considerable importance in internal hierarchies in the school, they are largely discounted by employers, save for the elusive Grade I.

Numerous empirical surveys confirm this assertion. From research in Scotland which concluded: 'below apprentice level, the large majority of employers did not ask for qualifications' (Hunt and Small, 1981, p. 24); to a survey of employers in Coventry and Nottingham which summarised their response to CSEs:

> Apart from one respondent, all the employers agreed that they took little or no notice of the CSE examination or its results in selection procedures . . . The vast majority of employers knew nothing about 'Modes' as such, and indeed seemed unaware of the structure of Grades below Grade I. (Freedman, 1981, pp. 48–9)

3. To emphasise the extent to which 'monetarism' has achieved its object of de-industrialising vast tracts of hitherto productive areas, Coventry's unemployment position was to deteriorate even further between 1981 and 1982, when registered unemployment reached 18 per cent. By November 1982 only 11.3 per cent of that year's school-leavers had actually obtained jobs. 31.7 per cent were unemployed and on youth opportunities schemes; 12.7 per cent were unemployed and not on schemes; 12.5 per cent were in further education and 27.3 per cent had gone back to school. Finally, 4.5 per cent had left the area (*Coventry Citizen*, 4 November 1982).

4. It is important to emphasise that the growth of part-time work has been a marked feature of developments in the UK Labour Force. The MSC Manpower Review (1982) showed that the numbers working part-time doubled between 1961 and 1980, a period when people employed full-time dropped by 2.1 million. By June 1980, 4.4 million were part-timers, of whom 3.8 million were women – or 40 per cent of the female workforce. Two-thirds of male part-timers were over 60. Overall, they mainly worked in unskilled jobs in catering, cleaning, hairdressing, other personal services, clerical and related occupations and selling.

5. The Great Debate on education, initiated by James Callaghan (then Prime Minister) at Ruskin College in October 1976, represented a crucial transition in the debate about educational means and ends. It marked at the highest political level the end of the phase of educational expansion which had been largely promoted by his own party, and signalled a public redefinition of educational objectives (for a more extended discussion of the politics of schooling in this period see chapters 8–10 in Education Group, 1981).

References

Ashton, D. N. and Maguire, M. J., *Youth in the Labour Market* (London: Department of Employment, 1982).

Carter, M., *Into Work* (Pelican, 1966).

Clarke, L., *The Transition from School to Work: A Critical Review of Research in the UK* (London: HMSO, 1980).

Education Group, *Unpopular Education: Schooling and Social Democracy in England since 1944* (CCCS/Hutchinson, 1981).

Forester, T., 'Children at Work', *New Society*, 1 November 1979.

Freedman, S., 'The Certificate of Secondary Education and the Employer', in Ashton, D. N. and Bourn, C. J. (eds), *Education, Employment and Young People*, Vaughan Papers in Adult Education (University of Leicester, 1981).

Frith, S., *The Sociology of Rock* (Constable, 1978).

Griffen, C., Hobson, D., MacIntosh, S., McCabe, T., *Women and Leisure*, paper presented at BSA/LSA Conference on 'Leisure and Social Control' at CCCS, Birmingham University, January 1980.

HMSO, *A New Training Initiative: A Programme for Action* (London: HMSO, Cmnd 8455, 1981).

Hebdige, D., *Subculture: The Meaning of Style* (London: Methuen, 1979).

Hencke, D., 'How a City Prepares its Children for the Outside World', *Guardian*, 23 June 1981.

Hunt, J., Small, P., *Employing Young People: A Study of Employers' Attitudes, Policies and Practice* (Scottish Council for Research in Education, 1981).

Land, H., 'Who Cares for the Family?', in Dale, R., *et al.*, *Education and the State: vol 2: Politics, Patriarchy and Practice* (Falmer Press and Open University Press, 1981).

MacLennan, E., *Working Children*, Low Pay Unit, Pamphlet No 15, December 1980.

McRobbie, A., 'Working Class Girls and the Culture of Femininity', in Women's Studies Group, CCCS, *Women Take Issue* (London: Hutchinson, 1978).

Manpower Services Commission, *Manpower Review*, MSC, 1982.

Markall, G., Finn, D., *Young People and the Labour Market: A Case Study* (London: Department of the Environment, HMSO, 1982).

O'Brien, R., *Industry, Education and People*, The Josiah Mason Memorial Lecture, Birmingham University, 29 November, 1977.

OECD, *Youth Unemployment: A Report on the High Level Conference 15–16 December, 1977*, vol I, OECD, 1978.

Richards, G., *Work Experience Schemes for School Children – The Case of Coventry: The Shape of Things to Come?*, unpublished paper, 1982.

Schools Council, *Schools Council Enquiry 1: Young School Leavers*, Report of an Enquiry carried out for the Schools Council by the Government Social Survey (London: HMSO, 1968).

Thompson, E. P., *The Making of the English Working Class* (Harmondsworth: Penguin, 1968).

Willis, P., *Learning to Labour: How Working Class Kids Get Working Class Jobs* (Farnborough: Saxon House, 1978).

3

Schooling and the World of Work

Robert Moore

This chapter will examine the role of 'the world of work' in the school curriculum. I will argue that programmes incorporating this concept have, in reality, little to do with work at all. They are best understood as responses to *control problems* within the schools. These problems arise as a result of critical changes in the social compositions of key areas in the school system, for example, in the fourth and fifth forms in the early 1970s and in the sixth form (and also in CFEs) today. This argument implies that there is a fundamental discontinuity between the level of policy construction and the level of implementation. Objectives developed at the former level take on a very different meaning at the latter, in the everyday pragmatics of classroom teaching.

Around the time of the raising of the school leaving age (ROSLA) in 1972/73, the problem that teachers had to face was that of coping with the 'reluctant attenders' – pupils who, had it not been for the raising of the school leaving age, would have been out at work. Today the problem is that of coping with the situation arising from the *lack* of jobs and the pressure created by the ways in which the government is responding to that problem – YOPs, the YTS, and so on. The rise of the Manpower Services Commission has drastic implications for the school system. Increasingly the MSC is taking on the appearance of an alternative DES. The MSC-commissioned report from the Institute of Manpower Studies (Report No. 39, *Foundation Training Issues*) recommended the establishment of an MSC 'inspectorate' to oversee training pro-grammes. The Commission has also initiated the first moves in the creation of a training 'education' route starting at age 14 and running parallel to the schools. Seen against the background of the

1944 Education Act, this is a departure of the most radical kind. Equally significant is the fact that the training programmes are predominantly staffed by people who are not qualified as teachers.

Essentially this reflects a shift of power of a fundamental kind – from a decentralised education system whose agents had an *indirect* relationship to production and, consequently, enjoyed a high degree of 'relative autonomy', to a centralised system whose agents bear a *direct* relationship to production and who define their objectives specifically in terms of the needs of production. This is a shift from a liberal-humanist educational paradigm to a technicist training paradigm. Its most fundamental consequence is to sever the connection between practical knowledge and elaborated, theoretical knowledge. An index of this rupture is the movement from social education and its critical possibilities, to social and life skills training with its restricted, normative control objectives.[1] The processes and issues involved here are obviously complex and cannot be developed in detail. The focus of this paper will be on the world of work in the school curriculum in the ROSLA period, that is, within an *educational* paradigm, and in particular in the context of social education. I believe that the analysis has, though, more general implications. The underlying theoretical perspective is derived mainly from the work of Basil Bernstein.[2]

Education and production

A number of basic issues need to be discussed in order to establish a framework within which to set the analysis. First it is necessary to look at the basic assumption that lies behind the idea that 'the world of work' should have a place in the school curriculum – the assumption that schools can develop occupationally relevant characteristics. Secondly there is the associated view that a particular category of pupils, non-academic low achievers, *needs* to have such characteristics developed. This assumes a *deficit model* of the pupil and that alternative sources for these characteristics are not available to them, in the home and community. Thirdly it is important to grasp the significance of educational trends, such as changes in class differentials in attainment, and their implications for theories of the relationship between education and production.

1. At the most general level it is difficult to find any strong evidence to show that education makes a decisive contribution to economic growth beyond that provided by the achieving of mass literacy. Comparisons between industries of the same type in different countries, and between firms in the same industry in the same country, indicate that a wide variety of educational 'mixes' is compatible with economic efficiency. Nor is there evidence to show that more educated workers, or even those with the 'appropriate' educational qualifications, are better than less educated ones or ones with 'inappropriate' qualifications. There is, in fact, little systematic relationship between educational background and the distribution of workers in the occupational structure, and labour elasticities of substitution, movement between strata and sectors of the occupational structure, and potentials for retraining on-the-job are invariably shown to be of a high order. Both orthodox human capital and technical-functionalist type theories and certain Marxist ideological control theories, which see education as an agency of occupational socialisation and allocation, have little substantive support. The reason for all this is that the relationship between educational career paths – supposedly conditioning pupil identity – and occupational categories is not given but, rather, is dependent upon a complex set of contingent factors which mediate the relationships between the educational system, the labour market and the occupational structure. As Marx himself said: 'large-scale industry, by its very nature, necessitates variation of labour, fluidity of functions and mobility of labour in all directions' (Marx, 1976, p. 617).[3]

2. An explicit principle behind work experience, social education and vocational preparation schemes is that large numbers of young people are lacking in basic 'social and life skills'. They are portrayed as socially incompetent and unable to 'cope' with life in general and the transition to work in particular. This view is often invoked as the reason why young people are suffering high unemployment. Once again there is little substantive evidence to support this view, and the chapter by Finn in the present volume provides counter evidence. As I have shown elsewhere, even official versions of employers' dissatisfaction with young workers need careful interpretation.[4] In fact, research indicates that most young people adjust fairly easily to

working life and that those who are 'alienated' from school tend to do so even more successfully than many others.[5] Part of the argument in this paper is that their very disaffection from school results precisely from their desire and competence to enter 'the world of work'. The lack of continuity between performance at school and performance at work reflects the fact implicit in the previous chapter – that the social skills required in work are primarily developed in the home and community and not at school. Consequently there is little relationship between variations and changes in educational institutions and practices and propensities to adjust to or perform adequately at work. Changes in educational practices relate to the needs of schools to 'cope' with pupils and have little to do with the needs of pupils to 'cope' with life.

3. There are a number of factors to be considered here and it has to be kept in mind that they are not simply an ad hoc collection of empirical trends, but the inter–related phenomena of a complex structural totality. Studies of trends in education have shown the following:

    (*a*) a general increase in the levels of educational attainment:

    (*b*) this trend has been most pronounced for lower class groups;

    (*c*) consequently there has been a progressive reduction in educational inequality in attainment;

    (*d*) but this has not been associated with a corresponding reduction in *social* inequalities, for example, in increased social mobility, narrowing of income differentials;

    (*e*) this is because this trend is internally associated with credential inflation in the labour market. People in general, and lower class groups in particular, require successively higher levels of attainment simply in order to maintain existing status. Hence, as Bourdieu and Passeron argue,[6] this process is not so much one of *redistribution* of educational opportunities as of *translation*, that is, the *structure* of differentials being expressed in changing forms (for example, the difference between staying on or leaving is now expressed in the difference between 'O' level and CSE courses);

    (*f*) through time, given levels of educational attainment and their associated educational career paths are corresponding to successively lower occupational categories. For this reason, educational career paths cannot be treated as agencies of identity formation, socialising pupils into predestined occupational positions, because there is no enduring relationship between particular career paths and particular occupational positions.[7]

The structural dynamics of educational change

Within educational institutions, the statistical trends discussed above are represented as critical changes in the social compositions of pupil populations at different levels. 'Social composition' involves gender and ethnic as well as class factors. At the lower branching points – those immediately following the earliest legal leaving date – the rate of increase in numbers will be greatest for lower status groups. This is because higher status groups will already be at saturation point at those levels. Given the larger numbers of lower class potential members, a rapid rate of increase can radically change the social composition of a site in a relatively short space of time, especially if the underlying trend is suddenly 'bumped up' by external factors such as ROSLA or YOP. The kind of quantum change that hit the schools in the early 1970s is affecting the FE sector today (a similar effect occurred in higher education in the late 1960s).[8] The significance of this process is that different groups have different attitudes towards school, extended educational careers and educational knowledge and authority. Bourdieu and Passeron argue that:

> The analysis of the differential reception of the pedagogic message presented here makes it possible to explain the effects which the transformation of its public exert on pedagogic communication, and to define by extrapolation the social characteristics of the publics corresponding to the two limiting states of the traditional system – what might be called the *organic* state, in which the system deals with a public perfectly matching its implicit demands, and what might be called the *critical* state, in which, with the changing social make-up of the system's clientele, misunderstanding would eventually become intolerable (Bourdieu and Passeron, 1977, p. 90).

The key issue is how the school responds to these 'transformations of its public'.

The changing social composition of educational sites gives rise, at the critical point, to a crisis of control. Despite the structural sophistication of their model, Bourdieu and Passeron's argument can be seen as too simplistic in one crucial respect – it operates with a *cultural distance principle*. This means that different categories of pupils are seen as located at different points removed from the culture of the school and correspondingly more or less able to cope with its implicit demands – its implicit values, assumptions, conventions, and so on. The critical state is reached when a sufficiently large proportion of 'new members' are in this 'disabled' category. In this respect Bourdieu and Passeron's theory can be located within the mainstream of theories in the sociology of education which have tended, to put it in very general terms, to see pupils as either being disabled by their social background (cultural deprivation theories) or by ideological control mechanisms in the school itself (teachers' middle class expectations, conservative pedagogic practices etc). These theories share a major defect – they treat pupils as being essentially *incompetent*. Even phenomenologically inspired approaches which treat 'members' knowledge' with respect tend to see pupils as the losers in a contest in which those in authority are able to impose their meanings and models of reality. What is crucially lacking here is a view of pupils as *active and determining*; of outcomes as the positive accomplishments of pupils themselves. Perhaps this reflects to some extent an inability on the part of sociologists (reflecting their middle class assumptions!) to believe that anyone would actually want to be an educational 'failure' and actively set out to evade 'success'.

An alternative approach is available, however, in Raymond Boudon's concept of 'the educational decision field' and in the work of Basil Bernstein. D. Davies has given a succinct summary of Boudon's argument, relating it to the work of Paul Willis and to an article by the present writer:

Boudon maintains that working-class failure in school cannot be satisfactorily explained in terms of different types of material or cultural deprivation. Although working-class people do suffer from primary deprivation, e.g. frequently having lower incomes, worse housing and social conditions and hence less material wealth to spend on books or educational games and activities, Boudon argues that educational reform can progressively eliminate these effects. He shows that where pupils from the middleclass and working-class are matched for intelligence and ability, the differences in attainment in school are to be explained by the influence of 'secondary' effects. These secondary factors include the values, beliefs and attitudes that pupils hold as members of wider social groups. It is not that middle-class pupils are better motivated to succeed than working-class pupils, but rather that both groups aspire to the level of their respective parents. (Davies, 1981, p. 91)

Empirical support for Boudon's view can be found in Roberts *et al.* (1977). The important point is that pupils' aspirations are related not to an assumed common base-line (unskilled manual labour?) but to their respective starting points. Roberts *et al.* say that:

> In absolute terms, manual parental aspirations were modest compared with white collar respondents. However, in relative terms, when levels of parental aspiration were measured against respondents' own starting points, the relationship between occupational status and ambition disappeared. Whether thinking of themselves or their children, according to our evidence, there is no clear qualitative contrast between working and middle class mobility orientations. (Roberts *et al.*, 1977, p. 77)

The significance of mobility aspirations for educational careers has to be related to wider cultural fields in which identity and membership are entwined with cognitive maps of the occupational structure and their corresponding symbolic value forms. As Davies says, 'Class relations become transposed into symbolic relations at the level of culture, and school cultural experience becomes a struggle to win symbolic space and to re-assert freedom'. (Davies, 1981, p. 92).

The system of relationships is not fixed in a given cultural form. As the discussion of educational trend data above implies, it is in a continual process of transformation. The relationships between social backgrounds, educational career paths, levels of attainment and occupational categories are constantly changing. These changes are repositioning individuals from different class backgrounds and with different gender and ethnic characteristics in relation to the school. Lower levels of attainment are being devalued for middle class pupils, for example, as they become the typical requirements for working class jobs. These complex changes in the structure of relationships and the constant repositioning of groups within those relationships call forth responses at the cultural level – resignation, resentment, rejection and resistance according to and in a form appropriate to the symbolic logic of the group. For working class groups in particular, extended educational careers are not culturally embedded within the normal social career path. It is, precisely, *leaving* school that is important. The necessity to extend the educational career (even into 'training') interrupts the development of the social career at a particularly significant point. Rather than an inability to cope with the demands of extra schooling, it is the simple fact of having to be there at all that creates the critical state and the crisis of control. Given the dynamic nature of the situation, it is clear that what is important is not the *content* of relationships – *particular* pedagogies, *specific* symbolic forms or cultural values – but the principles governing the relationships *between* positions and categories in the system of relationships. The social value and the meaning of a given level of educational attainment changes through time as the social composition of the group typically attaining that level changes. These changes in their place demand changes in the pedagogy of the site as the move from an organic to a critical state occurs. We see this in the schools in the development of CSE Modes 1, 2 and 3 alongside GCE 'O' levels, for instance.

At the level of *content* of educational sites, curriculum and pedagogy, it is possible to see contradictions developing between the social relations of education and those of production. As Bernstein has pointed out:

there is a contradiction, at least in England, between the regulation of the 'less able' student ($-C-F$) in education, and the regulation of the unit of production ($++C++F$). This indicates an independence of education from production in the area of regulation. Further, the school, rather than equipping the worker with appropriate attitudes and discipline, may indirectly and unwittingly provide a range of countervailing strategies. A $+C+F$ educational code is likely to create countervailing strategies in the pupil; e.g. fixing pupil-based production norms,

resistance to discipline, avoidance techniques, implicit and possibly explicit sabotage of the means of education, operating just on
the margin of acceptable conduct. (Bernstein, 1977, p. 187)

What Bernstein says about countervailing strategies has implications for the notion of pupil competence. Countervailing strategies,
as Willis' concept of 'partial penetrations'[9] suggests, entail a
sophisticated understanding of the underlying rule system of the
school. Non-conforming behaviour can indicate not a lack of
competence on the part of pupils but a deliberate policy of
performances which undermine and reject official expectations and
which are grounded in a deep but sceptical awareness of the implicit
requirements and assumptions of the school culture. There is an
important point to grasp here; it is *precisely* these countervailing
strategies and the insights they index which end up locating working
class pupils in working class jobs. The pupils themselves do the work
of cultural reproduction. It is not that their resistance takes its stand
against the repressive character of school authority and culture and
in the end is defeated. Rather it is precisely the forms of resistance
engendered by the liberal-progressive blandishments of the school –
individual escape from your class through upward mobility – that
regulate and reproduce the position of the pupil. Educational
practices do not *in themselves* produce the ideological effects that
regulate the social allocation of pupils. The specific character of
educational practices reflects a more pragmatic concern – to
regulate the performances of pupils through transformations of the
modalities of control.

In formal terms the argument in this chapter is that schools
transform their modalities of control (the framing of pedagogic
relations) in order to preserve an underlying system of power
relationships (the system of classification). Crucially this occurs
when changes in the social compositions of educational sites reach a
critical point in terms of the positioning of the changing membership of the site. I will attempt to show how 'the world of work'
fulfilled a particular ideological function in the school curriculum by
'explaining' how and why changes should be made in the fourth and
fifth year curriculum as its social composition changed in the late
1960s and early 1970s. Beneath the official rhetoric of 'relevance'
and the needs of industry, schools at that time were primarily
concerned with pragmatic adjustments in their practices in response
to control problems in the classroom.

The Green Paper and 'The Great Debate'

The Great Debate on education initiated by James Callaghan's Ruskin College speech (1976) had two major, related, areas of concern: standards and behaviour in the schools, and the supply of skilled manpower, especially scientists, engineers and technologists. The Green Paper of 1977[10] summarised the complaints that were being made against the schools:

> Children's standards of performance in their school work were said to have declined. The curriculum, it was argued, paid too little attention to the basic skills of reading, writing and arithmetic, and was overloaded with fringe subjects. Teachers lacked adequate professional skills, and did not know how to discipline children or to instil in them concern for hard work or good manners. Underlying all this was the feeling that the educational system was out of touch with the fundamental need for Britain to survive economically in a highly competitive world through the efficiency of its industry and commerce. (DES, *Education in Schools*, 1977, p. 2)

Whilst the Secretaries of State rejected the view that educational standards had declined, they did agree that schools were failing to meet the requirements of industry.

The Green Paper sets the crisis in the educational system in the 1970s against a background of complex changes in British society to which education has had to adapt:

> Britain has ceased to be the centre of an Empire, and has become instead a medium-sized European power, albeit one with wide international connections and responsibilities. The country's economic well being depends upon its own efforts, and its standard of living is directly related to its ability to sell goods and services overseas. At home, our society has changed substantially; because of the large-scale movement of people within Britain, for instance to New Towns and expanded towns; and also of people into Britain, many from the New Commonwealth. Ours is now a multi-racial and multicultural country, and one in which traditional social patterns are breaking down. (*Education in Schools*, p. 4)

The educational system, it is argued, has coped well with the *social* changes but has failed to respond to the new needs of the economy: '. . . only a minority of schools convey adequately to their pupils the fact that ours is an industrial society – a mixed economy; that we depend upon industry to create the wealth without which our social services, our education and arts cannot flourish; and that industry offers scope for the imagination and even the idealism of young people'. The pre-monetarist tone of this social-democratic tract is striking.

Although it is tempting to see the Green Paper in terms of manpower planning, its fundamental concerns are socio-political rather than economic. It has little to say about the provision of specific skills. Its real theme is teaching *about* the world of work, and this is something much broader than simply teaching *for* it. It is a way of teaching about (and for) the social order, of promoting a particular vision of 'our society'. This vision is the social-democratic model of the new, modern Britain – a vision more clearly displayed today with the SDP than when Shirley Williams was preparing her Green Paper.

The Paper includes amongst its list of aims for schools: 'to help children to appreciate how the nation earns and maintains its standard of living and *properly to esteem* the essential role of industry and commerce in this process' (p. 7, my emphasis). The issue of 'esteem' can be related to the hostility towards industry that employers report coming from teachers. But there is a difference between the employers' view and that of the Green Paper. The type of society signified by 'the world of work' when teaching *about* industry is not the same. In the Green Paper industry should be esteemed for its part in creating the wealth which makes possible the range of provisions quoted above – 'our social services, our education and arts'. The Paper's vision is of a society dedicated to social welfare and collective, cultural enrichment rather than to privatised consumption and leisure. It is a society based on welfarism, not consumerism. Within this vision, teaching about the world of work, making education more relevant to industry, involves a particular view of the role of industry in a particular type of society and of the claims which that society can make upon the wealth that industry creates. These claims are not (and certainly were not) ones that industry itself would welcome.

The Green Paper is concerned not so much with the technical

aspects of manpower planning as with defining the role of industry within its particular vision of the good society. 'The world of work' signifies this vision of 'our society' – the new, modern Britain. It attempts to construct a common view of 'our nation'. The world of work in its interrelationships with the wider social order provides the infra-structure of that ideal. The role of industry and the reason why industry should be esteemed must be understood in terms of that wider vision. Teaching about the world of work is not a technicist exercise, it is not directed towards the technical requirements of the division of labour but towards promoting a common vision which integrates the citizen within a shared purpose and community. The reason for labour in the new, modern Britain is to participate in and contribute to the good society of social democracy.

> Young people need to reach maturity with a basic understanding of the economy and the activities, especially manufacturing industry, which are necessary for the creation of Britain's national wealth. It is an important task of secondary schools to develop this understanding, and opportunities for its development should be offered to pupils of *all abilities*. These opportunities are needed not only by young people who may have careers in industry later, but perhaps *even more by those who may work elsewhere*, so that the role of industry becomes *soundly appreciated by society in general*. (p. 35, my emphases)

The sense of communality is invoked not only directly by the phrase 'society in general', but indirectly by 'Britain's national wealth' with its implication that the wealth is a common possession. Similarly with the reference elsewhere to the economy: 'ours is an industrial society – a mixed economy'. 'Mixed economy' in conjunction with 'ours' suggesting partnership in industry, etc.

The essence of the Paper's vision is a society without inner conflicts and divisions. The aspects of social change denoted by the phrases 'technological change', 'multiracial', 'multicultural', 'the disappearance of the old stereotypes of the sexes' are associated with 'challenge', 'idealism' and 'imagination' rather than with the frustrations, tensions and conflicts they actually entail. The role of the schools is to forge that communality by promulgating the ideal community of the Green Paper's inner vision. If at the level of its *programme*, as set out in its recommendations, the Paper seems to be in line with the views of employers and manpower planners, at this deeper level it fundamentally parts company with them. The Paper's concept of making education more relevant to industry must be explicated in terms of its view of the relevance of industry to society. It must be seen in terms of its ideal of the good society and of the social good. It is this rather than the technicism of manpower planning that organises its discourse.

At its deepest level the Green Paper resonates with the values of the major traditionalist and progressive educational paradigms. The role of education is related not simply to the development of *skills*, but to the cultivation of an *idealised subject*. The world of work is not merely to do with labour and its fruits are not merely consumer goods. It signifies 'challenge', 'idealism' and 'imagination' and it creates 'social services', 'arts' and, indeed, 'education'. The Paper's rhetoric generates a sympathetic framework within which teaching *about* the world of work can be assimilated into the ideals of the educational ideologies. Within that rhetoric education can be found reconstituted as an expressive rather than an instrumental process – something very different from the utilitarianism of manpower planning. If at the level of its *programme* the Green Paper appears to be acceding to technicist instrumentalism, within its rhetoric it preserves a space for education as traditionally conceived within the *educationalist's* view.

Work experience

The Green Paper's main strategy for making schooling more relevant to the needs of industry – teaching *about* the world of work – involves teaching about what industry *does*. The world of work is a concept which gains its particular significance from the wider vision of society in which it is contextualised. In educational terms the Paper provides a rhetoric and a framework within which schools can formulate programmes for teaching about the world of work. The need for such a framework in the school situation arises from the fact that teachers themselves tend to have little direct knowledge or experience of 'the world of work'. One of the employers' main complaints about schools is the distance between education and ordinary working life. Teachers are seen as being not only ignorant about industry but hostile to it. A number of projects have attempted to close this gap by providing teachers with opportunities to gain 'work experience'. The Newsom Report provided the impetus for a joint CBI/Schools Council project in the middle 1960s. The CBI chairman at the time said:

> When we were assembling our evidence to the Newsom Committee, it became clear that there was a general feeling amongst employers that children in their final year at school would benefit from teaching more closely related to the kind of life they would lead after leaving school. (CBI Schools Council, 1966)

The Report on the project describes the problem that this idea encountered in the schools:

> many secondary school teachers felt they neither knew nor understood the industrial and commercial environments in which most of their pupils would eventually have to work. (p. 2)

The Report goes on to outline the position of employers – it is essentially the same as that expressed over ten years later in the Great Debate and, indeed, as that encountered today:

> There is indeed too great a gap between schools and industry . . . teachers have no conception of the working of commercial and industrial life; even in their private lives, teachers tend to associate with other teachers and this further lessens their chance of contact with the 'outside world'. There is even, perhaps, an inbuilt antipathy towards industry and commerce in our educational life. (p. 13)

Reading the other criticisms and the demands that employers put forward in the Report shows that contemporary complaints echo familiar propositions.[11]

Work experience schemes are one of the most obvious ways in which the world of work can be introduced into the school curriculum, and they were enthusiastically backed by the employers and the Green Paper. But clearly the teachers' lack of experience is a problem. The major impetus behind such schemes was provided by the Newsom Report and the raising of the school leaving age to sixteen. Newsom contains the features which have remained until recently the major characteristics of work experience schemes in schools. The Report says that:

> in the examples brought to our notice the experience has been designed as part of a wider educational programme of general preparation for school leavers rather than as an introduction to any specific field of future employment. (Newsom, 1963, p. 75)

And:

> Most projects of this sort could only be carried out by a few pupils at a time, but related to a larger programme they might encourage the pupils to see some relevance in their school work to the interests and work of the adult world. (p. 76)

The distinction between 'a wider educational programme' and 'an introduction to any specific field of future employment' is important. It is crucial for retaining a specifically educational definition of work experience, and remains to the fore in all the pre-MSC accounts of the activity.

The Newsom view incorporates from the very beginning the idea that work experience might help schooling seem more relevant to pupils. This is a significantly different emphasis from the view that it is a means of making education more relevant to industry. These two things are not necessarily incompatible, but given that teachers are largely unqualified to prepare pupils *for* work and the insistence that such schemes form part of a *wider educational programme*, then teaching *about* the world of work can come to mean something very different. There is a significant difference between teaching *for* the world of work and in so doing making education more relevant to the needs of industry and making it more relevant to the needs of pupils by teaching *about* the world of work. Whereas the former can be located within a manpower planning approach, the latter can be assimilated to the anti-utilitarianism of the educational paradigms, and this can be accommodated within the *rhetoric* of the Green Paper.

The important question is: to *which* pupils will work experience make schooling seem more relevant? DES Circular 7/74 on work experience states that it 'should have value for pupils of varying ability and aptitude and should neither be designed as vocational training nor aimed at a limited range of pupils only'. It was this Circular which spelt out the principles for organising work experience in the schools:

> The principle which should underlie any work experience scheme is that pupils should be given an insight into the world of work, its disciplines and relationships. This principle and the requirements of the Act that schemes for pupils of compulsory school age must form part of an educational programme would not be satisfied by arrangements made whether in school or elsewhere whose purpose was specifically or mainly to assess individuals for particular forms of employment, or to occupy pupils in producing articles for sale. Schemes should provide provision within the school curriculum for preparation before the pupils take part in work experience and for following up and discussing the experience gained. (DES, Circular 7/74, 1977)

These principles were adopted wholesale by the Inner London Education Authority in its guideline for teachers on work experience schemes. The idea that work experience should be available to *all* pupils departs from the Newsom position and that of the Schools Council/CBI project discussed above. The latter's Report, for instance, relates the introduction to industry scheme for teachers to Newsom in the following way: 'The Newsom Report emphasises the value of increasing the obvious relevance to adult life of the school studies of pupils of *average and below average ability*' (p. 2, my emphasis). It is this position rather than the DES view that worked out in practice. Work experience schemes, and the wider educational programme in which they were located, tended to be directed towards a particular category of pupils. These pupils were (and in the new YOP and Super YOP successors still are) in the main those destined for a particular sector of the labour market, and it is that sector that tends to provide the work experience opportunities.

The ILEA Guideline says:

> Obviously school pupils cannot be given experience of work calling for a high level of skills or anything more than a very short period of training. For pupils of less than average ability this usually means that they have opportunities to work in shops, on

simple assembly work in factories where they can be given tasks requiring limited skills. (ILEA, 1977, p. 3)

The limitations of the types of 'opportunities' which can be made available are reinforced by others working in the schools. The amount of time that has to be spent on work experience is relatively large. Circular 7/74 stresses that a variety of experiences should be offered to pupils and that 'it would be undesirable if the time spent in any place of work were so short as to give only a superficial impression'. The ILEA recommended one full day per week or two weeks per term. In addition there is the time spent in the classroom in preparation and follow-up work. As ILEA's careers inspector, Catherine Avent, pointed out, this amount of time excludes pupils following examination courses. She says, 'it is unlikely that enough employers could be found to provide work experience for all fifth years even if those sitting public examinations were excluded on the grounds that they had not time to spend on these extra-mural activities'.

The Guideline makes an interesting distinction between 'large-scale work experience for fifth form pupils, mainly those not sitting for public examinations', and 'work appreciation' for sixth formers. Work appreciation is described in this way:

work appreciation ... has been successfully undertaken by science sixth-formers, for example, who have already acquired certain techniques which they can immediately use in a laboratory, or girls from commercial courses whose typing skills can be utilised in an office; just as some girls spend part of the end of the summer term in junior schools before embarking upon a course in a college of education. In the case of these older pupils, the scheme is primarily designed to help them see the occupational applications of skills and interests acquired in school. It is also helpful in motivating some of them to continue their education and in helping them to distinguish between a variety of milieux in which to seek employment when they have completed their education and training. (ILEA, 1977, p. 3)

Apart from its quite remarkable gender stereotyping, this account gives an interesting insight into perceived differences between categories of pupils. Work appreciation is seen in terms of occupational choice and decision-making. These pupils are seen as having a range of options open to them, including continuing their education. Pupils on work experience, on the other hand, are in an essentially closed situation. Whereas work appreciation might be 'helpful in motivating some of them to continue their education', work experience can 'induce a welcome realism in the minds of youngsters with fantasy ideas about the level of career they can aspire to' (p. 4). There is a suggestion that the two groups are distinguished only by *age* ('in the case of these older pupils'). In reality they are quite different sets of pupils – those on work experience will never become 'these older pupils'.

It is interesting to note that a similar distinction exists in relation to community education. In the case of academically able pupils community work is usually approached through a 'service to' philosophy. The pupils 'serve' the community by using their social and academic accomplishments to aid the elderly, the handicapped, and so on. Non-academic pupils on the other hand are usually seen as being involved in a therapeutic exercise which does them good (developing 'character', 'self-confidence', 'social and life skills'), as well as those they help. This also tends to be incorporated within a 'wider educational programme' in which teachers and supervisors observe and evaluate pupils' performance. We see here another example of the widespread tendency to associate social competence with academic attainment.

These wider educational programmes are essentially interpretative frameworks within which teachers can provide accounts for pupils of their work experience. Lacking detailed personal experience of production, teachers can only draw upon their background assumptions about the world of work. These will reflect their own social backgrounds and the views and values they have internalised during their professional careers. Their accounts will, therefore, be some distance removed from the experiences, expectations and interpretations of the pupils. Neither, the evidence suggests, will they correspond too closely with those of the employers. The idea that education must be made relevant to the needs of industry implies expertise on the part of teachers. The type of vision of the world of work contained in the Green Paper will make more sense to teachers than the pragmatisms of either pupils or employers. Teachers should be in a position to determine what the needs of pupils and industry are, but it is precisely this knowledge which they lack. The dismal history of manpower forecasting suggests that no-one really knows what industry needs, and the relative isolation of teachers from the world of work as well as from the worlds of their pupils suggests that they are in no position to know what their needs are.

Pupils' knowledge and schools' authority

The factor that is continually left out of account is that pupils *do* have knowledge of the world of work. They are members of working communities and they are brought up to work. They gain indirect knowledge through parents, relations and friends and direct knowledge from out-of-school jobs. But more than this – the world of work is the experiential core of class culture. It is the everyday world of the pupil. Its introduction into the school curriculum can have the effect of reversing the normal relationship between teacher and pupil. Work experience introduces a field of knowledge in which the pupils' authority may be superior to that of the teachers. Teachers can be doubly disadvantaged through knowing neither the specificities of the skills required by industry nor the ethnography of the working worlds of their pupils.

The CBI Schools Council Report contains a significant passage which reflects this situation:

> Some teachers, who met former pupils of their own in the firms to which they were seconded, were surprised to see how purposefully young people who had been difficult at school went about their work. Among the possible reasons for the change was the difference in atmosphere. Although by no means all the school leavers seen at work were contented, many of them had responded positively to a situation they found easier to understand than that which confounded them at school, where they had been at odds with their teachers. (CBI/Schools Council, 1966, p. 11)

This difference between the pupils' difficult behaviour at school and their apparently successful adjustment to work is reflected in research in this area. Roberts has drawn attention to the fact that:

In Britain enquiry after enquiry over the last twenty-five years has reported school-leavers ill-prepared for their entry into employment, drifting into the labour market armed with little job knowledge and uncertain as to their objectives ... However, successive studies of young people in employment have concurrently been reporting a state of scarcely relieved satisfaction and vocational adjustment. Although typically vague, British school leavers' ambitions have been notably realistic, and no matter what their level of employment, the majority of young workers have been found content with their attainments, satisfied with their jobs and little inclined to seek new opportunities. (Roberts, 1975, p. 145)

This view is confirmed by the review of research in the area which has been undertaken by Linda Clarke. Interestingly, Clarke reports that it seems to be those pupils most alienated from school who adjust best to being at work.

I would argue that both orthodox and radical approaches have grossly overestimated the extent to which schools act as agencies of occupational socialisation. The thing that comes across most strongly from the material discussed here is the *discontinuity* between schooling and work. It is this very discontinuity which actually produces the problems that early leavers pose for the schools. The reason why these pupils are difficult at school, and why they see schooling as irrelevant to their needs is because it *is* irrelevant given *their* needs. These are pupils who feel themselves ready for labour and who need to take up work in order to affirm and fulfil their wider social aspirations and roles. The role of pupils is incompatible with their developing sense of self and status. Children develop their occupational aspirations and, by extension, their sense of self identity and group membership, within a network of relationships that exist outside the school. It is within these networks that they acquire the knowledge and social skills required to function as competent-members of occupational groups.

Paul Willis has shown how, for working class boys who want to take up manual labour and who reject schooling, the continuity between school and work is at the level of their *informal* culture:

Although the teacher's notion of the continuity between school and work is rejected by the 'lads', another kind of continuity is profoundly important to them. In terms of actual job choice it is 'the lads' culture and not the official careers material which provides the most influential guide for the future. For the individual's affiliation with the non-conformist group carries with it a whole range of changes in his attitudes and perspectives, and these changes also supply over time a more or less consistent view of the sort of people he wants to end up working with, and what sort of situation is going to allow the fullest expression of his developing cultural skills. We have seen that shop-floor culture is importantly borne back to 'the lads' in many ways – not least in the working class home via parents. (Willis, 1977, p. 95)

The key to understanding the rejection of schooling by pupils such as 'the lads' is in their evaluation of the significance and relevance of school knowledge in terms of their own view of things. Within that view school not only contributes little or nothing to the acquisition of the skills they need; it is also *wrong* in its account of how things are. These pupils *know* that the world of work is not as the teachers describe it. Given this position and its inherent dissonance, the behaviour of such people is powerfully affected by the demands that schooling makes upon them, and especially by the compulsion to remain within the system by forces acting in the labour market.

The pupils' view of things carries with it its own criteria of relevance. They evaluate formal accounts of the world of work in terms of these criteria. Willis' 'Lads', for example, have this to say about the career teacher's account of the world of work and job finding:

Fuzz: He's always on about if you go for a job, you've got to do this, you've got to do that. I've done it. You don't have to do none of that. Just go to a place, ask for the man in charge, nothing like what he says.

Joey: It's ridiculous.

Schools demand the allegiance and compliance of pupils on the grounds of the validity and efficacy of their formal accounts of the way things are. It is on these grounds that they can claim that pupils *need* them. Where pupils can discount these formal accounts on the basis of their own knowledge and experience, they effectively abolish the grounds of compliance with school authority. The behaviour of such pupils is intelligible in terms of their evaluation of school knowledge and its relationship to their world of work. They act from the basis of their confidence in their ability to assume membership of working groups, and of the superiority of their knowledge of the way things are. On the basis of that confidence they reject what the school has to say and resent the compulsion to remain within a role which frustrates their wider social aspirations.

On the basis of their own experience and of the received culture of their class, pupils discount the knowledge of the world of work presented by the school. They see its claim to authority as spurious. But in a similar fashion, the school discounts pupils' knowledge. Because of the way it is held and expressed, their knowledge does not appear as *knowledge* to teachers. It does not conform to their formal and informal criteria for defining 'knowledge'. Consequently pupils *appear* to be ignorant. Furthermore, the pupils' behaviour at school is interpreted as symptomatic of a basic social inadequacy, of a general lack of competence, if not actual maladjustment. The familiar cry of the teacher is: 'If you are like this at school, how do you expect to get on at work?'. The apparent inability of pupils to cope with the demands of school is interpreted as an inability to cope with *any* social situation. It is this discontinuity between pupils' reasons for rejecting school and teachers' interpretations of the behaviour in which that rejection is expressed which lies behind the kinds of discrepancies noted by the Schools Council and Roberts above. In terms of their behaviour at school, pupils *appear* to be ill-equipped to enter the world of work. But that behaviour, in fact, reflects their very ability successfully to do so.

Willis provides a case which illustrates this point:

Altogether, in relation to the basic cultural groundshift which is occurring in relation to the school and the development of a comprehensive alternative view of what is expected from life, *particular* job choice does not matter too much for 'the lads'. Indeed we may see that, with respect to the criteria this located culture throws up and the form of continuity it implies, most manual and semi-skilled jobs *are* the same and it would be a waste of time to use the provided grids across them to find material differences. Considered therefore in just on quantum of time – the last months of school – individual job choice does indeed seem random and unenlightened by any rational techniques or means/ends schemes. In fact, however, it is confusing and mystifying to pose the entry of disaffected working class boys into work as a matter of *particular* job *choice*; that is, in essence, a very middle class construct. The criteria we have looked at, the opposition to other, more conformist views of work and the solidarity of the group process, all transpose the question of job choice on to another plane: 'the lads' are not choosing careers or particular jobs, they are committing themselves to a future of generalised labour. (Willis, 1977, pp. 99–100)

In a similar vein, Roberts writes that:

Rates of occupational mobility are often taken to indicate a state of vocational maladjustment. The young worker who flits between numerous short-lived unskilled jobs is thought to be in need of vocational advice and guidance, if not psychologically disturbed in general. But really the young worker who enters and leaves a succession of routine jobs in a constant attempt to obtain the highest possible earnings and to ward off boredom is not displaying symptoms of maladjustment. In fact he is making a realistic adjustment to the job opportunity structure that his particular career situation opens up. (Roberts, 1974, p. 151)

Work experience schemes are aimed mainly at a group of pupils for whom schooling seems least relevant and which the school finds difficult to accommodate. I have argued that these pupils are 'difficult' because in terms of their own aspirations and values they *are* ready for work. They resent the compulsion to remain within the pupil role. They discount the school's formal account of the world of work on the basis of their own knowledge and experience. Occupational aspirations and the appropriate social skills are developed outside the schools. Pupils judge their own competence and the validity of school knowledge by outside criteria. Inflationary forces in the labour market compel pupils to acquire increasing amounts of education. The widening gap between pupils' own estimations of their needs and the necessity to remain at school beyond the point they feel to be justified creates the tensions which give rise to a crisis of control in the schools. I now want to examine how work experience is a response to control problems by considering social education as an example of the type of wider educational programme within which work experience schemes have been located.

Social education

The rise of social education, like work experience itself, is associated with Newsom and the raising of the school leaving age. The Schools Council ran a social education project in four Nottingham secondary schools between 1968 and 1971 (Schools Council Working Paper No. 51: Schools Council, 1974). The experiment was part of the Schools' Council's concern 'to develop programmes suitable for implementation following the raising of the school leaving age' and with 'the educational problem of the irrelevance of schooling as seen by at least a third of its recipients . . . Its aim was to explore how far it was possible to achieve a less one-sided education, a more active pupil participation and a greater awareness and involvement in relation to community affairs' (Schools Council, 1974, p. 11). Also, like work experience, social education *claims* a wider constituency than it in fact serves:

> The fact that this project was concerned with the less able children in non-selective schools does not mean that social education is only for the 'Newsom child'. The basic principle of social education – that everyone needs to develop the skills to challenge and control his immediate situation in school and community – is a principle that ought to be applied in every school in the country, and for children of all (so-called) levels of ability. (Schools Council, 1974, p. 119)

Once again here we see a striking contrast with the YOP-inspired sentiments and objectives of today (see, for instance, the MSC's *Instructional Guide to Social and Life Skills*, 1977).

A more distinctive statement of the principle of social education defines it as:

> . . . an enabling process, through which children will receive a sense of identification with their community, become sensitive to its shortcomings, and develop methods of participation in those

activities needed for the solution of social problems. (Schools Council, 1971, p. 54)

The social education philosophy is developed by the authors of the project against the background of a particular vision of community and an urgent sense of crisis in community relationships. The general situation is described as follows:

> . . . in modern urban society, government is remote and often seems incomprehensible. Even the interests and occupations of our neighbours can be a mystery. The individual is all too liable to feel isolated, trapped, manipulated by agencies which he cannot understand, even though they are benevolent. (Schools Council, 1974, p. 7)

The situation described here is contrasted with that which is assumed to exist in other contemporary or historical societies:

> In a tribal community every member knows how the groups is organised and how it achieves its ends, and every member plays a part. Much the same was true of the Greek city state – at least for its freemen. (Ibid, p. 7)

The characteristic which these societies are held to share is 'a generalised active involvement in the community' (p. 11). The same thing can be found, it is claimed, in modern Cuba, China and the Israeli kibbutzim. It is this common condition, a radical organic community, that social education seeks to restore:

> The ideal which animates social education harks back to an older concept of democracy: the democracy (real or legendary) of the Greek city state in which the chief pursuit of citizens was deemed to be their participation in running their collective affairs. (Ibid, p. 10)

The specific focus of the approach is described in this way:

> We exclude any rigorous examination of the organisation of social structures. Both institutions and persons participate in several structures. Hence they have many roles. Social education is not

concerned to formalise the relationships between roles. It is concerned with the understanding of social roles – in particular, awareness of different roles and of the sources of social conflict. This points to the need for understanding people, and the effect this has on role behaviour. (p. 130)

The significance of the concept of community, in association with the focus upon 'roles', lies in the way in which it enables the construction of a particular model of the pupil.

The project organisers report that they were unsure as to how far their wider, radical aims could be achieved within the context of a modern, urban society, but they felt that the crisis of community relations was so acute that they should nevertheless go ahead with their experiment:

Would the introduction of social education be likely to help in alleviating the problems of the community as a whole, to mitigate the alienation of some of its members, or even to bridge gaps between youth and the older generation, between home and school, between school and the surrounding community? (p. 9)

The difference between the pragmatic concerns of the Schools Council and the ideals of the practitioners is striking. Within the ideology being formulated by the committed advocates of social education, the starting point for the reduction of anomy in the community is the classroom. The pedagogy of social education is seen as leading to an increasing degree of control by the pupils themselves. By learning control in the classroom, it is argued, they will come to practice control in their communities. The transformation of classroom relationships will lead to a transformation of community relationships. This process will be encouraged by the involvement of social education in the community itself. Its activity is directed outside the classroom to the world at large. This activity may come to alleviate the anomic state described above. This model of community-based participatory democracy stands as a radical counterpoint to the patronage of the benevolent social democratic state implicit in the Green Paper, but its essentially utopian vision and psychologistic orientation precludes any critical examination of basic power relations within a capitalist social formation.

Like the Green Paper, the social education project was conceived within a particular vision of *community*. The community from which the pupils are drawn is seen as 'socially handicapped' and is contrasted with an idealised model composed of eclectic fragments of Ancient Greece, tribalism, and modern Cuba, China and Israel. Social education's wider vision provides a framework and rhetoric within which a particular type of programme can be implemented, together with a source of commitment for its practitioners. Like the Green Paper, its theme is adaptation to new conditions:

> If our students are to fulfil roles in society which will bring satisfaction to themselves and be beneficial to others, education must not only help them in the development of personality and academic ability, but also provide them with skills which are necessary to cope with a sophisticated and expanding technology. This is true even of those who will not be directly involved in development and design or in large scale organisation and planning. Equally, a good education should enable the student to cope with the increasingly bewildering pressure of life in a modern society. (p. 7)

There is a striking resonance here with the Green Paper. The social education vision and rhetoric organise an interpretative schema in which to account for and accomodate a category of pupils who were becoming increasingly problematical for the schools.

Given the model of their communities as 'socially handicapped', the pupils themselves, as the products of these communities, can be defined in the same way. The vision of community generates a particular model of the pupil, and this in turn makes possible a particular type of accomodation of the pupil within the educational paradigm and institution. It assimilates the problem they pose for the school to a wider account of their place in the social order. By defining the pupil as the socially handicapped product of a socially handicapped community, it displaces the explanation of his or her problematical behaviour in the school. That behaviour comes to be seen not as a *specific response* to the conditions of schooling in relation to the pupils' own values and aspirations, but as a *general condition* of the pupil, as a state of basic maladjustment. This move preserves the integrity of the educational paradigm whilst allowing pragmatic adjustments of the pedagogy which attempt to reduce the tension and conflict in the everyday, classroom situation. The gap between the philosophy of social education and the pragmatics of its implementation is reflected in the difference between the wider aims of the movement – the regeneration of community, etc. – and the mundane concerns of the Schools Council with the 'educational problem of the irrelevance of schooling as seen by at least a third of its recipients'. The social education philosophy (articulated by its committed advocates and practitioners) functions as an ideological device which positions both pupils and *teachers* in a particular way towards the social relations of school and the wider formation in which they are inscribed. It is important to note that in this ideological positioning of teachers it is precisely their radical commitment, and precisely the genuinely radical character of much of the social education philosophy, that enables it to function as a reproducer of the dominant system of relationships. In just the same way that the Lads' resistance leads them into working class jobs, so teachers' radicalism leads them into this. The true subtlety of the process of cultural reproduction is that it is the contending position that ends up doing the real work.

This complex mechanism can be illustrated in the technique of 'socio-drama'. This is a form of role playing which begins with elementary mimes such as 'come here (I am angry with you)', 'wonderful news', 'surprise', and progresses to more complex situations involving moral issues: 'returning a pair of shoes, which are found to be unsuitable, to a shop', 'interview with council official – need for play street'. This progression from simple to complex is seen as promoting the personal development of the pupils. The social education philosophy relates personal growth to identification with the community. As the individual's awareness of the community and of the role relationships (the basic concern of socio-drama) within it deepens, so does the sense of personal identity. Identity is a function of identification.

This approach is underpinned by a theory of observation and communication:

> If we do not 'observe', if we are not 'aware', then our capacity to participate in a situation is severely reduced. Communication skills are essential if what has been observed is to be fully understood. Observation and communication are the principal techniques that the child must acquire to enable him to advance in the process of social education. (Schools Council, 1974, p. 19)

Social education is seen as training in social sensitivity. It is interesting to note that socio-drama techniques have been carried over into present day social and life skills training, although the social education objective of the individual acquiring the ability to work collectively for social change has been abandoned in favour of pleasing the employers. The basic assumption of the approach is that the pupils are *lacking* in the social skills that socio-drama sets out to develop. This is seen as the obvious concomitant of his or her membership of a 'handicapped' community. Training in social sensitivity sets out to compensate for the pupils' supposed lack of observation and communication skills:

> He must learn to pick out things that are significant and important in the social life about him. He must learn to interpret clues: how people reveal their attitudes by their behaviour, how they express their hopes and fears. He must learn to ask questions in ways which show proper understanding. He must learn to communicate his own feelings and reactions and to share them with others. (Ibid, p. 19)

The assumption that the pupil cannot do these things indicates a view of his or her impoverishment that is quite remarkable. It is a view, however, which follows logically from the model of community and the theory in which it is located. It follows from the *radical* position of the philosophy. On the basis of this theory the aim of socio-drama is defined as:

> to activate the mind by developing and training the child's latent powers of observation and, most important, by developing functional intelligence and thus providing the child with a desire to learn, read and record; he begins to analyse his own conduct and that of others and by degrees to learn to assert himself and see himself as part of the social pattern and gain success and dignity by participating in it. (Ibid, p. 23)

Having defined the pupil in this way, it then becomes necessary to construct an educational space in which he or she can be accommodated. This space contains the content and the pedagogy of social education. The authors describe how they devised a strategy for dealing with the fact that their pupils were predominantly low achievers:

Their self-confidence had already been sapped and their willingness to display initiative in the school setting had been drained by their previous failure. They had to be made to feel that past 'failures' in academic work were not signs of uselessness or stupidity on their part. In order to do this, children were encouraged to think of intelligence as having four parts: abstract intelligence which enables us to understand abstract concepts; technical intelligence which allows us to remember processes; creative intelligence which enables us to understand new ideas and things; and social intelligence which enables us to understand people and relationships. (p. 19)

Although the schema was developed for strategic reasons, it was nevertheless felt to be 'not without psychological validity'. Social education pupils, of course, are located in the social quadrant. There is some degree of inconsistency in this in that it is precisely 'social sensitivity' which these pupils are seen to be so conspicuously lacking. On the other hand, the discovery of 'social intelligence' enables an educational programme to be developed which can be placed alongside those directed towards the other types of 'intelligence' – it legitimates the approach. The concept carves out a space in which the practitioners of the subject area can operate and claim a special expertise.

It is useful to contrast this account of a social education project with that given by Peter Dawson,[12] ex-headmaster of Eltham Green, a large, mixed comprehensive in South East London. Dawson was head of the school from 1970 to 1980. When he took over, the school had considerable difficulties and a poor reputation in the local area. When he left it was one of the most oversubscribed schools in the ILEA. An index of its relative lack of problems in the later period is given by the fact that it had an extremely low repair bill! Dawson was a highly controversial head and his style – authoritarian and egocentric – aroused as much opposition as it did support. Leaving aside the inevitable value problems raised by his example and by the very idea of a 'good' school or a successful head, at a purely pragmatic level the role of social education at Eltham Green is instructive. First, Dawson is quite clear about the *pragmatic* interest in constructing a social education department as far as the school as a whole was concerned:

The creation of a social education department at Eltham Green was without doubt the most important single factor in the school's emergence in the seventies as one of the most heavily oversubscribed in the capital. Once the needs of the most disruptive element in the school population had been met, everything else followed almost as a matter of course. (Dawson, 1981, p. 36)

However, this pragmatism was in no sense purely instrumental, let alone cynical. The social education department was seen as genuinely addressing the needs of the pupils in it, and was highly privileged in terms of resources and staffing. The department was housed in its own wing of the school and its teachers spent all their time in the department. Pupils entered it in the fourth year and spent all their time there. The department, consequently, offered a full range of subjects and, in addition to the standards such as English and Maths, organised numerous link courses with local FE colleges as well as community work and work experience. Subjects could be examined as CSE Mode 3s or as 'O' levels in some cases. The stress as far as the department's Mode 3s were concerned was on practicality and 'relevance' – traditional Newsom values. Relationships between pupils and staff in the department were far less formal than in the rest of the school but 'high standards' were insisted on in areas such as school uniform and behaviour.

As with the difference between the Schools Council's conception of their social education project and that of those implementing it, so at Eltham Green the teachers in the department had a far more radical and a much broader conception of what they were doing than did Dawson and the senior staff in the school. Obviously a programme such as social education demands a highly articulated ideology, both to motivate its practitioners and to provide them with a sense of commitment. This ideology will tend invariably to bring the teachers themselves into conflict with the senior staff or other interest groups in the school and a major problem becomes that of managing this tension. We see here the key to understanding what happened at Eltham Green. As Dawson makes clear in his book, he did not attribute any particular ideological significance to any given form of pedagogy, such as mixed ability teaching vs. streaming, integrated studies vs. subject specialism, and so on. His concerns were purely practical – does this best meet the needs of pupils. 'Needs', of course, is a problematical concept, but we can interpret it as meaning basically cognitive, emotional and social requirements of pupils and functional requirements of the school as an organisation. Essentially, Dawson's strategy can be understood as the construction and maintenance of a *structure*. This is, he determined the *mixture* of approaches which seemed to be appropriate to the school's problems, translated it into an organisational form and then worked extremely hard at maintaining the resulting structure. In particular it was extremely important to 'police' the *boundaries* between the various sectors, segments and enclaves in the school. In retrospect I feel now, from my own experience as a social education teacher in the school, that this was how Dawson worked. It is important to note that the early 1970s in particular was a time when different types of pedagogy were very closely identified with specific political and ideological *positions*. We see this in a theoretical form in the ideas of the 'new sociology of education' and the de-schoolers, and at a practical level in the events at William Tyndale School.

Dawson refers to the study carried out by Michael Rutter[13] and his team. He refers to a conference for ILEA head teachers which Rutter addressed:

> The successful secondary school, the speaker explained, was one with a tight structure, firm discipline, streaming and setting, school uniform, and a commitment to similar traditional approaches. He developed his theme further. A successful secondary school was one with a flexible structure, no great emphasis on discipline, mixed ability teaching, no school uniform, and a progressive approach to educational issues. Could one have it both ways? Indeed, one could. The truth which the Rutter Report put forward on its publication a year after the conference was blindingly obvious when one thought about it. What makes a school successful is not its organisation but its ethos. It is not what you do but the way you do it that matters most. Style and atmosphere are more important than particular methods. (Dawson, 1981, p. 168)

The term 'ethos' is particularly unsatisfactory. As Dawson himself points out, 'Michael Rutter and his colleagues have nothing new to tell us, but they remind us of some important old truths which have become somewhat neglected'. (Ibid., p. 170). He then goes on to list three factors which together can be fairly taken as defining a good professional approach to doing the job of teaching regardless of any particular commitments to approach or method. Of course there is nothing new in this and any experienced teacher would think he or she could have saved Rutter the trouble. Of course professionalism is important. But the term 'ethos' should not simply be taken as a gloss for professionalism. Although it is true that *in general* the particular method does not matter, in the sense that mixed ability teaching has no *intrinsic* virtue over streaming or vice versa, particular method *is* important within the *specific* context or set of relationships to which it might be applied. In other words, we need to approach methods in terms of the kind of structural dynamic approach I outlined earlier. This is a theoretical way of saying 'pragmatically'. In the school context teachers are able to judge the kind of approach most appropriate to particular groups of pupils at particular times. As Dawson says, 'The best teachers move from one method to another between different classes and age groups'. (Ibid., p. 168). An intuitive grasp of this may well be an important aspect of the good teacher's professional skill, but it is fairly obvious that *simply* being a conscientious professional is not enough. I am sceptical about the implication that a highly experienced, professional, country grammar school, sixth form classics master would be an effective inner city comprehensive social education teacher; neither is it at all obvious that an equally professional social education teacher would be able to fill the other's shoes. *Ethos*, I feel, should be taken as indicating that a professional group of teachers have managed to construct a system of relationships in their school, an organisational structure, in which the various groups are accommodated in a way that at least establishes a basic cohesion and stability.

In certain cases, for particular groups, the *precise character* of the 'solution' will be crucial. This might be so for pupils like 'the lads' or for West Indian children or academic working (and middle) class white girls. For others, far greater latitude is possible because their position in relation to the school is less tense. In any particular positional complex this will determine the appropriate mix of approaches and the nature of the optimum organisational structure. It is important to note that, in certain cases, what is being done for one group will preclude certain options being employed for others, because some pupils, for example, will be seen as unfairly privileged, or being allowed to 'get away with things'. It is this that leads to the variability that Rutter notes and makes it impossible to generalise or be dogmatic about particular methods or approaches. Selective schools insulate themselves from problems by being able to maintain an organic relationship between their pupil body and their structure. Non-selective schools do not enjoy this privilege. They need to be able continually to adjust to the changing character of their intake (in response to demographic changes in their catchment areas for instance) and to changes in 'climate' generated *endogenously*. Dawson's very success at Eltham Green changed the character of the school's intake. As the years went by the spread of ability widened, the level of attainment increased and the proportion of low achieving problem children declined. These changes would change the requirements for particular pedagogic responses in the school. Perhaps by the end of the ten year period Eltham Green was no longer the type of school that needed a headmaster like Peter Dawson? All the factors *within* the school have to be located and valorised within the structural complex of factors and trends operating outside the school. Hence, the structural totality in which we have to locate these processes is extremely complex.

The major error we encounter in this area of analysis is *essentialism* – the tendency to impute *intrinsic* values to particular types of pedagogy. The ability of selective schools to insulate themselves from problems creates an illusion of *ease*, *competence* and so, of *superiority*. The traditional pedagogy is held to be superior both as a means of transmission and socially. Traditional pedagogy is identified as being in some way an instrument of the ruling class. By extension, the type of pedagogy which *appears* to be the opposite of traditional pedagogy comes to be seen as radical or oppositional and identified with the interests of the working class. William Tyndale illustrates the practical consequences of essentialism. Teachers acting on the basis of their ideological commitments implement the pedagogy which 'logically' should be the pedagogy of the oppressed. It turns out not to be – it was quite simply the wrong approach for those children in that place at that time. This is in no sense whatsoever to impugn the *professionalism* or integrity of the teachers. The error is to believe that you can *deduce* the political value or significance of a form of pedagogy from its intrinsic characteristics (to be precise, you *impute* intrinsic characteristics to pedagogy on the basis of a particular commitment and ideology) rather than having to reconstitute its position within the complex structure of its field of relationships and the cultural dynamics of its recipients and agents. Pedagogies are valorised by the transformation of the structural fields in which they are located.

Conclusion

This chapter has attempted to address the complex manner in which school-pupils' material experiences are appropriated and accommodated within educational ideologies. It has focused upon the pragmatics of the implementation of programmes concerned with 'the world of work' and the everyday community lives of a certain category of pupils. The argument has *not* been posed in terms of the imposition of a 'ruling ideology' within the framework of a state apparatus; rather it has attempted to record and explicate a complex series of breaks and displacements within this process. First there are those which occur within the *vertical dimension* whereby high level policy formulations, such as demands that education be made more relevant to the needs of industry, are transmitted and translated into educational processes. I argued that we see here a set of contextualising discourses whose rhetorics enable the accommodation of positions, which actually vary considerably, within an *apparent* consensus. Secondly, in the *horizontal dimension* of classroom practices, where teachers and pupils confront each other directly in the interstice between official formulations and the bedrock of material culture, we witness the practical accomplishment of an effective hegemony. The mechanism of this process has two main components, (a) a model of the pupil which, while presenting him or her as *incompetent* and 'in need', is associated with a curriculum and a pedagogic practice which covertly trades on precisely the real skills and experiences which the young people possess (in this way 'relevance' appropriates the material culture of the pupil), and (b) a discourse which contextualises the pupil and positions the *teacher* within a *radical* educational ideology.

It is at the level of these interstitial discourses and practices that teachers may be able to intervene directly, because it is here, within the pressures and exigencies of daily life in the classroom, that we are positioned ourselves – positioned in part by *our own* constructs.

I have argued in this chapter that it is the *contending* position which does the real work of social reproduction: the oppositional practices and resistances of pupils, the progressive educational ideologies of radical teachers. It is not the *substance* of discourse and practice which counts, but its *position* within a complex of relationships. It was precisely the *radicalism* of the social education ideology which enabled both its teachers and their pupils to be positioned within the school in such a way that they effectively reproduced its essential relationships. The mechanism described above and explored in detail in the text is one which can be exploded *if* these interstitial practices cease to be the reproducers of the given and come, instead, to be the mediators between the official and the material cultural practices of the young. The condition for this is to start from what young people *already know*. On this basis 'relevance' no longer *appropriates but denies* the material experiences of the pupils – it *acknowledges and elaborates* the central cultural dimensions of lives realised through the ideologies of class, labour, gender and race.

The relationship between pupils, school knowledge and work is becoming the central ground within education and training. The transition from school to work (sic) may soon begin from fourteen as YTS moves back into the territory of the school. Although there are fundamental differences between the educationalist's social education and the trainer-technician's social and life skills, the mechanism described in this work can be seen repeated in the new concepts of vocational preparation. Yevgeny Yevtushenko ends his poem *Lies* in this way:

> Forgive no error you recognise,
> it will repeat itself, increase,
> and afterwards our pupils
> will not forgive in us what we forgave.

Notes

1. On the area of social education/social and life skills training in general see Lee (1980) and for a critical discussion of the relationship between the two approaches see Davies (1979).
2. See Bernstein (1977; 1982).

3. On the general issue of the relationship between education and production see Berg (1973), Bernstein (1977, ch. 8), Boudon (1973), Collins (1981), Hussain (1981), Mace (1977), Thurow (1977), Tyler (1977).
4. See Moore (1983).
5. For critical reviews of research in this area see Clarke (1980a, 1980b).
6. See Bourdieu and Passeron (1977).
7. See Boudon (1973), Halsey *et al.* (1980), Moore (1979), Hussain (1981).
8. For an analysis of the student revolt in France along the lines being followed here see Boudon (1980, ch. 10).
9. See Willis (1977, ch. 5).
10. See DES 1977, and for a critical analysis, Donald (1981).
11. For a discussion of complaints against schools and an extensive review of the evidence on standards of attainment see Wright (1977).
12. See Dawson (1981).
13. See Rutter (1979).

References

Berg, I., *Education and Jobs* (Harmondsworth: Penguin, 1973).

Bernstein, B., *Class, Codes and Control vol. 3* revised edn, (London: Routledge & Kegan Paul, 1977).

Bernstein, B., 'Codes, Modalities and the Process of Cultural Reproduction', in Apple, M. (ed.) *Cultural and Economic Reproduction in Education* (London: Routledge & Kegan Paul, 1982).

Boudon, R., *Education, Opportunity and Social Inequality* (New York: John Wiley & Sons, 1973).

Boudon, R., *The Crisis in Sociology* (London: Macmillan, 1980).

Bourdieu, P. & Passeron J-C, *Reproduction in Education, Society and Culture* (London: Sage, 1977).

Clarke, L., *The Transition from School to Work* (London: Dept. of Employment, HMSO, 1980a).

Clarke, L., *Occupational Choice* (London: Dept. of Employment, HMSO, 1980b).

Collins, R., *The Credential Society* (London: Academic Press, 1981).

CBI/Schools Council, *Closer Links between Teachers and Industry* (London: HMSO, 1966).

Davies, B., *In Whose Interest? from social education to social and life skills training.* (Leicester: National Youth Bureau, 1979).

Davies, D., *Popular Culture, Class and Schooling* (Milton Keynes: The Open University Press, 1981).

Dawson, P., *Making a Comprehensive Work* (Oxford: Basil Blackwell, 1981).

Department of Education and Science, *Circular 7/74* (London: HMSO, 1977).

Department of Education and Science, *Education in Schools* (London: HMSO, 1977).

Donald, J., 'Noise of Crisis' in Dale R. *et al.* (eds), *Schooling and the National Interest* (Lewes: Falmer Press, 1981).

Halsey, A. H. *et al. Origins and Destinations* (Oxford University Press, 1980).

Hussain, A., 'The Economy and the Education System in Capitalist Societies' in Dale R. *et al.* (eds), *Schooling and the National Interest*, (Lewes: Falmer Press, 1981).

Inner London Education Authority, *Guidelines for Teachers on Work Experience Schemes* (London: ILEA, 1977).

Lee, R., *Beyond Coping* (London: FEU, 1980).

Mace, J., 'The Shortage of Engineers' in *Higher Education Review* (Autumn 1977).

Marx, K., *Capital*, (London: Penguin, 76).

Moore, R., 'The Value of Reproduction' in *Screen Education 29* (Winter 1978/9).

Moore, R., 'Pedagogy, Production and Further Education', in Gleeson D. (ed.), *Youth Training and the Search for Work* (London: Routledge & Kegan Paul, 1983).

MSC/TSA, *Instructional Guide to Social and Life Skills* (London: MSC, 1977).

Newsom, J. H., *Half Our Future* (London: HMSO, 1963).

Roberts, K., 'The Entry into Employment' in Williams, W. M. (ed.), *Occupational Choice* (London: George Allen & Unwin, 1974).

Roberts, K., 'The Development Theory of Occupational Choice" in Esland, G. *et al.* (eds), *People and Work* (London: Holmes MacDonald, 1975).

Roberts, K., *et al.*, *The Fragmentary Class Structure* (London: Heinemann, 1977).

Rutter, M. *et al.*, *Fifteen Thousand Hours* (London: Open Books, 1979).

Schools Council, *Choosing a Curriculum For the Young School Leaver*, Working Paper 33 (London: Evans/Methuen Educational, 1971).

Schools Council, *Social Education: an experiment in four Nottinghamshire secondary schools*, Working Paper 51 (London: Evans Brothers-/Methuen, 1974).

Thurow, L., 'Education and Economic Inequality' in Karabel, J. and

Halsey, A. H. (eds), *Power and Ideology in Education* (Oxford University Press, 1977).

Tyler, W., *The Sociology of Educational Inequality* (London: Methuen, 1977).

Willis, P., *Learning to Labour* (Farnborough: Saxon House, 1977).

Wright, N., *Progress in Education* (London: Croom Helm, 1977).

4

Against the New Vocationalism

Philip Cohen

I Elements for a theoretical critique[1]

When I first joined Marks and Spencer, I was lucky enough to get selected for a Unified Vocational Preparation Course. We were taught canoeing, horse-riding and archery. We had lectures on home economics, personal development, hygiene and retailing. Since they I have stayed with the firm but am very unhappy there. I have twice applied for a Junior Development course, but I didn't get it. I think maybe the reason is because I went on the other course, so perhaps they feel I have done enough training, and I am too old now anyway. So I am at a dead loss, and get very bored and frustrated with the job. – *18-year-old shop girl*

Contrary to popular belief, when you leave school, you can't just go out there and get a job because you're smart, or, if you're a girl, because you look attractive. You've got to sell yourself, and you've got to deliver the goods as far as management is concerned. The main thing that trainees have to learn when they come here is discipline. I tell them, if you don't conform at home, if you put your feet on the table or come in late, then sooner or later you'll get your marching orders. It's the same at work. The employer is looking for punctuality and willingness, and if he doesn't get it, then you become a luxury he simply can't afford. – *YOPS Training Manager*

In the first part of this chapter I want to look at some of the hidden agendas of the new vocationalism, and at their relation to a wider debate about the future shape of British society. I want to suggest that the new approach and emphasis given to 'skilling' in both the secondary school curriculum and 16–19 training provision, is primarily about the inculcation of social discipline; but this is no simple harking back to 'Victorian values'; on the contrary, it represents an attempt to construct a more mobile form of self-discipline, adapted to changing technologies of production and consumption, and to link this to a modern version of self-improvement aimed at the reserve army of youth labour. In unwrapping this ideological package I will be chiefly concerned to assess its likely appeal to teachers, trade unionists, working-class parents, and not least, school leavers themselves.

Most of the criticism so far directed at MSC policies has concentrated on their immediate political and economic effects.[2] The role of the MSC in pioneering more directive forms of State intervention into education has been much stressed; so too has the way YOPS served to substitute or dilute adult labour, while simultaneously cheapening the youth wage. These effects are important. They must be resisted. But we also have to ask why opposition to MSC programmes, whether from trade unionists or teachers, has been so divided and weak. This cannot simply be put down to force of economic circumstance or lack of political strength, though both, of course, play their part. It has just as much to do with a failure to contest the *ideological* ground staked out by the not-so-great educational debate, and subsequently claimed by the new vocationalists.

For a long time, the view that youth unemployment was due to faulty supply, rather than lack of demand, and could be solved by educational rather than by economic means went virtually unchallenged. Then, as soon as it became recognised as a structural phenomenon, youth unemployment was simply accepted as an inevitable concomitant of new technology. These twin views, a voluntaristic notion of educational processes, and a fatalistic view of technology, continue to dominate the responses of the teaching profession and the labour movement. Neither has proved capable of confronting the real and changing relations between State education and the capitalist economy; it was left to Black Paperites and Tory industrialists to make the maximum capital out of these changes, to exploit popular discontent with schooling (especially its more progressive forms) and the manifest inadequacies of the apprenticeship system. In the process, many of the arguments developed in radical critiques of working class education during the 1960s have been used in support of policies and practices which have very different aims and priorities.

For example, I have listened to MSC spokesmen extolling the virtues of YTS to a group of FE teachers, on the grounds that it will increase young people's self-confidence and prepare them for 'life'; to an audience of trade unionists the scheme was represented as equipping school leavers with working skills, and, moreover, reuniting education with material production in a way that Robert Owen, even Marx himself, might have approved. But with only a slight change in emphasis, (different adjectives, same nouns!) I have heard the new vocationalism being sold to a conference of small businessmen, not as creeping socialism, or as an extension of liberal education, but as part of Thatcherite strategy to restructure the economy, sweep away archaic labour practices and instil the virtues of discipline, hard work and respect for authority, in modern youth. This does *not* need to be an exercise in calculated duplicity, because the new vocationalism does indeed incorporate elements from both liberal and polytechnic traditions; but it subordinates these practices to quite a different set of organising principles, in a way that makes them work *against* their own articles of faith.

As an example of this process, consider for a moment the two faces of training portrayed in the opening quotations. The girl from Marks and Spencer is sent on a Unified Vocational Preparation Course. This 'quality training' encouraged her to see in shop work, not an extension of the domestic apprenticeship she had already served at home, but an incremental structure of promotion and reward belonging to a career code. Yet far from enhancing her prospects, the course seems to have blocked them. Her 'personal development' is arrested by the conditions of the job itself. This is the *human face* of the new vocationalism, but in so far as it raises young people's hopes, which are then dashed either by the kinds of job they are forced to do, or by ending up still on the dole, then its effect may be to increase the sense of frustration it is expressly designed to counteract. This is a familiar dilemma for liberal education of course, but in so far as 'liberal elements' are incorporated within training regimes, it is raised in a particularly acute form here.

There is also, however, the more overtly disciplinary face of training, as represented by the quotation from the YOP manager.

Here the renewed emphasis on work-discipline, explicitly cross-referenced to family discipline, reproduces the most authoritarian and patriarchal aspects of the old apprenticeship system, with the position of master, as at once employer and instructor, now subsumed in the role of State manager. The regime is justified in purely utilitarian terms – delivering the goods; yet from my observation of this scheme (an MSC showpiece originally opened by James Callaghan) the only 'really useful knowledge' the trainees were likely to learn was how to look busy while leaning on brooms – and get away with it.

There is currently a wide variety of regimes to be found under the MSC youth training programme. But it would be misleading to think that schemes where the stress is laid on personal development are necessarily more progressive than those which emphasise work discipline. If the shop assistant is sent on a UVP course, it is to acquire 'qualities' (poise, charm, etc.) to attract more customers and sell more goods – in a word, to make patriarchy more productive. The YOP manager is no less concerned with inculcating 'qualities' (punctuality, obedience, etc.), and is even more blatantly sexist in his assumptions. The difference is not in the 'quality' of the training, but the 'qualities' being instilled – those associated in the first case with personal servicing jobs; in the second, with manual work. These are simply two different but complementary disciplinary forms, corresponding to specific divisions of labour. But what *is* significant is the way liberal ideals of 'education as self-fulfilment' are now being made to work for crudely utilitarian forms of training. In the UVP example, expressive practices are invested with a purely instrumental function; in the YOP example obedience to positional controls is transformed into a personal achievement. By such sleights of hand the old-fashioned contradiction between what employers demand and what young workers want for themselves is supposedly conjured away. Yet, of course, it remains to cast its shadow over both kinds of regime.

What then is new about the new vocationalism? Its supporters claim that it is a bold experiment which will turn a whole generation of school-leavers into a new kind of model worker. The new worker is to 'transcend' narrow trade practices or occupational loyalties, to be highly mobile and individualistic, infinitely adaptable to technological change and yet conserve all the traditional virtues of the work ethic. If it is objected that this is an industrialist's pipe-dream, and that no amount of adaptability may 'deliver the goods' in terms of a well-paid job, the new vocationalists tend to change their tack.

It is argued that self-employment in the hidden economy or small enterprises will be the only major source of job creation for young people in the foreseeable future. The priority then must be to equip them with entrepreneurial skills so that they can successfully become their own boss. If it is pointed out that this is hardly a realistic prescription for half a million school-leavers, the ground of argument is shifted yet again. It turns out that we are moving towards a leisure society, in which paid employment only occupies a minority of the population for a part of their time. The task then becomes to 'educate for leisure'; unemployed youth, far from being regarded as a reserve army of labour, are now hailed as the advance guard of a brave new world. Leisure counselling, and courses in 'life-style enhancement' are to be introduced to prevent demoralisation and teach them to make the most of the opportunities opened up by life on the dole. Finally these two 'ideas' are combined to take the argument a step further. Dance, music and other elements of do-it-yourself youth culture can be turned into means of livelihood as well as leisure; alternative life-styles can generate 'alternative work' provided young people are taught how to make capital out of these cultural resources.[3]

The slogan 'small is beautiful' thus reaches its final destination in a more hedonistic vision of free enterprise capitalism, whose formula might be 'what is practised for pleasure can be practised for profit'. This combination of romantic individualism and penny-capitalism has a potentially wide appeal to young people whose routes into wage-labour have been blocked. In reality what is offered to them in the guise of 'alternatives' to the dole is decidedly less glamorous and lucrative. Within the youth service, quite traditional forms of leisure provision – sports, hobbies, arts and crafts – are simply being topped up with various types of counselling, as the basis of 'new' programmes for unemployed youth. What lies behind them is all too often the old-fashioned notion that the 'devil makes work for idle hands' and that at least these activities keep a potentially 'dangerous class' out of trouble and off the streets. But it is where these same activities are represented as preparing young people 'vocationally' for the New Jerusalem of the 'leisure society', that the cat is really let out of the bag.

A more significant, but no less problematic development has

been the growth of small self-help enterprises run by young people, often with starter-finance from public funds. Whilst these projects certainly avoid the worst features of the hidden economy and the old juvenile market, they do not, and indeed cannot amount to 'alternative work' in any real sense. The majority involve the kind of work already performed by young people in domestic or leisure contexts – bicycle-repair workshops, 'odd job' collectives, window cleaning, gardening, decorating, baby-sitting and the like. Traditionally this type of work was included within the category of 'blind alley' occupations; now it is suddenly 'rediscovered' as a stepping stone to a better future! In so far as these set-ups survive it is often only by systematically undercutting the rates for the job charged by unionised firms in the service sector. Many of these enterprises do undoubtedly begin with a genuine desire to create socially useful jobs, and to organise themselves according to principles of democratic self-management. Yet the names they give to themselves (e.g. 'Bootstraps', 'Ladders') seem to indicate other sources of inspiration, not a million miles away from Mrs Thatcher's. The logic of their economic situation, as well as the present ideological climate means that in many cases it is the competitive rather than the co-operative aspect which prevails.

It is all too easy to see the training of young people in practices which militate against their identification with organised labour, the displacement of job creation to the unregulated margins of the economy, and the construction of leisure as a cottage industry for the unemployed, as all forming part of a grand offensive against the working class with the MSC playing the co-ordinating role as Big Brother. Such conspiracy theories should be resisted; it is both fallacious, and self-defeating to try to read off conscious intentions from structural effects; for mediating both, and reducable to neither, is the discourse of ideology itself. And here what is significant is the role of vocationalist discourses in defining the terms of public debate about youth unemployment. Through this mediation what began as a debate about education and the economy between 'modernising' elements of British capital and the labour movement has increasingly been connected to another older debate, about leisure and the quality of life, in which libertarians of the Right and Left have traditionally locked horns. As in every debate the protagonists share more common ground than they care to admit. In the education debate, for example, there was a shared optimism about the benefits of a 'high tech' consumer society, the argument being over which class should bear the brunt of the costs of transition to it. Similarly in the leisure debate most of the interested parties shared a common vision of a return to England's 'green-and-pleasant-land' based on organic communities, small-scale production, and freedom from centralised state control; here the dispute is about which class is the authentic voice of this way of life. This pre-industrial vision of the good life might seem a long way from the permanent technological revolution heralded by the champions of the 'post-industrial society', but just how easily the two problematics are connected in youth training regimes was illustrated by the UVP course quoted above. For here we have a shop girl being 'prepared' for computerised systems of cash flow and stock control by being inducted into the kind of rural pursuits (horse-riding and archery) which do indeed belong in a *tableau vivant* of 'Merrie England': lord and peasant shown in common enjoyment of 'ancient liberties' subsequently destroyed by the advent of those dark satanic tills!

The ideological matrix which has governed and linked the hidden agendas of debate on education and new technology, unemployment and leisure, originated in an historical compromise between the bourgeois work ethic and aristocratic pleasure principles in mid-Victorian Britain.[4] This compromise was cemented in a civilising mission to the working classes centred on the rational recreation movement. Mr Gradgrind was forced to admit that 'all work and no play made Jack a dull boy' (though it made Jill a good wife!), while the Marquess of Queensbury wrote 'Leisure Earned is the Devil Spurned' into his rule book. The construction of the Great Outdoors as a playground for the urban masses was designed to both spur them on to greater industry and channel their interests away from politics and crime. But more than that it symbolised a peculiar alliance between different sections of the governing class, which in turn made it easier to neutralise popular anti-industrial sentiment and even convert it to a programme for modernising both capital and state. In this unique coalition of forces, the dissenting voice of English socialism, as represented by Morris and Ruskin, was squeezed to the margins of public debate, where it was tolerated as an eccentric or merely utopian presence. The emergence of a new middle class with a decidedly merito-technocratic view of progress only briefly disturbed this picture in the 1960s; it was quickly drawn into the matrix of pre-existing positions. In this context the Thatcherite bricolage (strong state + *laissez-faire* economics/high tech + 'Victorian values') attempts to *reverse* the terms of the historical compromise in favour of a reconstructed bourgeois work ethic whose pleasure principles unite popular opposition to the aristocracies of labour, learning *and* leisure.

Youth training schemes have acted as a major conduit for this new 'civilising mission' in several ways which I shall explore later. But first it is necessary to establish the fact that the common-sense terms in which these schemes have been represented as a solution to youth unemployment owes more to the way the new vocationalism has orchestrated these ideological motifs than to actual performance in terms of job placement rates. I interviewed a sample of FE teachers, trade unionists, training instructors and employers, all of whom had a stake in the management of MSC schemes in Southwark. There was considerable disagreement among them over the value of YOPS and what criteria to apply to its evaluation. Many of these differences were clearly the expression of conflicting vested interests, but beneath them and cutting across them I also discovered a pattern of assumptions about 'the working-class', 'youth' and 'societal trends' which seemed to belong to rather more hiden set of agendas.

For example a left-wing trade unionist and a Thatcherite training manager shared the same view of the working class as 'rather sheepish' but 'responsive to firm leadership'; youth in contrast, were 'irresponsible' with 'more energy than sense' and the role of training was to 'discipline them into productive activity'. Both were equally suspicious of new technologies, placed 'intellectuals' high on their list of *bêtes noires* and were firm supporters, and practitioners of rational recreation. Both condemned the schools for failing to equip pupils with the basic skills and 'right attitudes to life'.

A high tech employer and a local FE teacher exhibited a dramatically different pattern of positions. The problem with working-class culture in their view was that it bred 'rigid and inflexible attitudes' and was 'highly resistant to change'. The very inexperience of youth was now an asset; they were 'impatient of tradition' 'not yet stuck in a rut', and the 'natural allies of progress'. Progress itself was about technology 'liberating people from unwanted toil' *and* 'getting back to a more natural way of life'. The purpose of schooling and training was to prepare young people for these developments and 'release their talent for innovation and change'. Unemployment could be a 'positive experience' giving school leavers time to consider what they wanted to do with their lives.

Two things became clear from analysing this data. First, that it was not possible to read off, or predict these patterns of common sense simply from class location or party-political ideology; still less were they derived from 'experience'. Rather they reproduced historical configurations of *inter-class discourse* as chains of association to particular fixed reference points. Second, these reference points were imaginary, projecting a subject position on to an object (the working class, youth, technology, etc.). They did not correspond to actual social conditions or practices.

For example, the majority of unemployed youth I interviewed were not engaged in any great soul-searching exercises, nor were they turning into anarchists. They wanted real jobs with living wages, because without them they felt bored and useless, trapped into domestic roles, if they were girls, and pressured into other despised ways of earning money if they were boys. Equally the majority of those who were in full-time employment, or training, saw in this neither an occasion for rejoicing, nor for demonstrating the special qualities attributed to them. They simply followed the time-honoured practice of creating little islands of free time to break up the boredom and monotony of the working day. The unemployed envied the workers their regular wage, and the workers, in turn, thought how nice it must be not to have to get up so early in the morning if you were on the dole. But both groups knew you could not have it both ways, and neither made a virtue out of a necessity.[5]

In this, they showed themselves far wiser, and more realistic than the ideologues of the new work or leisure ethics who take their name, so often, in vain. I have already indicated how far the New Deal being proposed for youth training wants to have it both ways. As for 'making a virtue out of a necessity' that might indeed sum up the home-spun philosophy preached by the new vocationalist. For here we have a framework within which the structural aspects of youth unemployment – the elimination of youth labour from bottlenecks in capitalist production, and the decline of the apprenticeship system consequent on deskilling – these developments appear *only* in a positive light, as both inevitable and desirable, opening up a new field of training opportunities.

On closer inspection, this piece of optimism appears to pivot on a hidden agenda for redeploying the notion of skill itself. And on this operation, I believe, hinges the fate of the whole ideological enterprise. It is quite a complex manoeuvre. First skill is dissociated both from specific practices of manual dexterity, and from general forms of mental co-ordination exercised by workers over the immediate labour process. It is no longer entailed in a power of social combination, or embodied in cultural forms of apprenticeship. Instead skill is defined in terms of certain abstract universals – as a set of instrumental properties common to the functional co-ordination of isolated operations of mind/body/machine. Training in these so called transferable skills is essentially training for abstract labour, i.e. labour considered in its generic commodity form as an interchangeable unit/factor of production. The main function of this reclassification, in fact, is to increase elasticities of substitution between different occupational categories, and thus indirectly, to undermine the residual forms of control exercised by skilled manual workers over conditions of entry and training in their trades. What 'transferable skilling' corresponds to in reality is the process of *de*skilling set in motion by new information technologies, a process which is here represented at its opposite, i.e. a basis for perpetual retraining and reskilling.

At the same time the form and function of discipline is being redefined. For if skill is being objectified in a way that minimises the bargaining power of the 'collective worker', discipline is being 'subjectivised' in a way that serves to maximise the symbolic power of the individual.[6]

The traditional form of work discipline involved both a system of class control exercised by management over labour, and a system of patriarchal control exercised by male elders, over youth and female workers. However, this involved more than simply a delegation of disciplinary functions from capitalist to master craftsman or family wage earner; as the history of the shop stewards and apprentices movements shows, shop floor discipline had a contradictory structure; it also created the conditions of organised resistance against despotic forms of line management, *and* against trade-union complicity in the no less brutal forms of 'domestic' discipline meted out by elders to youth.

As our YOPS example indicated, these old forms are quite capable of reproducing themselves. But in general MSC policy is concerned to sweep them away; the new strategy of skilling requires a new approach to discipline. The shift is from a system of external controls and negative sanctions, towards a more invisible process of regulation aimed at eliciting a voluntary reform of working-class structures of feeling and motivation around a system of personal controls. For youth labour is now to be socialised in and through the *discipline of impression management*. Under this rubric, trainees are taught how to sell their labour power successfully by carefully editing their public image in conformity with dominant representations-of-self. Training in so called 'social and life skills' is essentially training in behavioural etiquettes which concretise in a subject form the general commodity form of abstract labour. And then this new discipline is made a special site of 'transferable skilling'.

In real, meal-ticket, terms SLS relates to personal service industries, where the ability to handle clients and customers, rather than goods, is at a premium. Futurologists of both Left and Right are currently pinning most of their hopes for eventually solving youth unemployment, in terms of both the expansion of this sector, and its labour intensive capacities. Unfortunately, here as elsewhere, rates of economic growth and labour intensity seem to be inversely correlated! But that only highlights the fact that the reconstruction of skill/discipline, like much else in YTS, is of little importance as an exercise in indicative economic planning. The primary significance of the new vocationalism is ideological.

Here two features stand out. First, what is in reality a position of class subjection (the sale of labour power as a commodity) is represented as its opposite – a position of individual mastery (the marketing of a self-image). And second, what is represented as the liberation of young workers (of both sexes) from the disciplinary power of male elders is in practice a means of also subjecting them secretly, and individually, and hence all the more effectively to the 'discipline' of market forces. The fact that the indenture form *is* obsolete has provided a pretext for dismantling the whole cultural apparatus of working-class apprenticeship. As we have seen, the substitution of state training regimes does little more than create a new site in which patriarchal attitudes have to be contested. What it *does* achieve is the final destruction of those social practices which made it possible for young people to acquire, besides trade skills, a living legacy of 'really useful knowledge' under the tutelage of 'old hands' in shopfloor struggle. In its place the MSC has developed training forms in which knowledge is radically disconnected from the power of social combination. But do other payoffs from these schemes compensate for that loss, as their supporters claim? How does the new approach to skill and discipline work out in practice?

In a good, or rather bad, proportion of the schemes I visited in South London, the trainees seemed to spend a lot of their time sweeping floors, cleaning up, running errands, etc. Clearly they were being taught how to lend a hand, make themselves useful and look sharp – part of the traditional discipline of apprenticeship. Yet I was told that these trainees were actually mastering 'transferable skills' that would enable them to find work in a variety of occuaptions. Now, in the old juvenile labour market this may well have been true. The generic 'proto-domestic' features of youth labour made it very transferable indeed – between a whole series of dead-end 'fetching and carrying' jobs. Somehow, though, I do not think this is quite what the MSC had in mind! Yet when a girl who is using a pair of scissors to cut her nails can be described as learning how to 'put together two metal blades unpowered', then we are clearly living in a universe of discourse in which anything goes!

Trainees on these same schemes could also be found learning social deportment, good interview manners and dress sense, a whole variety of techniques of impression management which seemed to belong more to a finishing school for the children of some rising middle-class. These, I was informed, were social and life-skills (SLS). I was shown a list of some 250 such skills, graded in complexity from simple (how to address letters) to advanced (appropriate modes of address for different social occasions and groups). I will come back to what is involved in SLS in more detail later, but for the moment, what concerns me is the practical outcome of these schemes.

Many of the instructors I met were openly dismissive of aspects of MSC policy, especially this 'new-fangled' approach to skilling. They preferred to get on with the job of teaching bricklaying, carpentry or electronics, using the traditional pedagogy of craft apprenticeship or technical education. Perhaps not surprisingly, their approach proved very popular. But it also had some quite unintended side-effects.

In the area I studied, these 'old-fashioned' schemes were overwhelmingly dominated by white male trainees, of the kind who would hitherto have got craft apprenticeships or gone to college. Schemes which emphasised the 'new style' approach were equally over-populated with black youth and girls – and fewer found work on leaving. There is obviously a very complex relationship between type of regime, form of skilling, patterns of recruitment, local opportunity structures and processes of sexual and racial discrimination. But certainly there is little evidence so far that the re-organisation of skilling is equalising these relations in the operational contexts of youth training schemes themselves.[7]

The reformation of skill has wider ramifications however. Skill is constructed through a discursive apparatus whose networks embrace not only the specialised fields of education, counselling and occupational training, but radiate into the general forms of the dominant and popular culture, connecting a whole range of political, moral and behavioural ideologies related to class and gender, on the way. The new vocationalism derives much of its legitimating support from these wider relay systems, and, in turn, seeks to articulate them to its more specialised sites of intervention. It may then be worth looking for a moment at this wider context.[8]

The dominant construct of skill is the outcome of an historical compromise between two leading reproduction codes – the code of the aristocracy, with its paradigm of the amateur and the gentleman, and the code of the bourgeoisie predicated on the position of the professional and the self-made man. Under the former, skill is constructed as a natural aptitude, an *inheritance* of cultural capital, a birthright and a legacy of effortless mastery. The latter code, in contrast, defines skill in terms of personal initiative and drive, measured through an incremental grid of status or *career*. The rise of the 'career code' can be traced in the history of its meaning. From its eighteenth century usage as a largely derogatory term applied to the rake's progress of younger sons of the aristocracy ('careering about') the word gradually took on the sense of orderly progress up an occupational ladder associated with competitive success in examinations. By the end of the nineteenth century careerists have made their appearance, and by the 1960s we not only have a careers service for young people whose school 'careers' have disqualified them from pursuing one, but even criminals and delinquents are said to have 'careers', albeit ones closer to the original meaning of the word! The extent to which it is a male construct can be judged from the derogatory connotations of 'career woman'.

However, the code of inheritance is far from having been eclipsed. It continues to dominate commonsense constructs of skill, such as the 'natural athlete', the 'born teacher', etc. In combination, the two codes thus relay a contradictory message: skill is both an inherent property and a socially-achieved practice, both the cause and the effect of mastery.

There is, though, another major construct of skill, which increasingly mediates between the terms of this contradiction. It has its own distinctive history, and moreover has come to lend its name if not its substance to the preparation of young people for work.

From the time of the Puritan revolution, the code of vocation has offered an image of skill as a special gift or calling, acquired through a purely interior process, governed by the voice of conscience or the presence of an 'inner light'. Skill here becomes a sign of grace, which may be spiritual, aesthetic or purely physical in mode. In any case it remains the prerogative of the self-elected few.

This code was open to multiple articulations. In one such, the notion of natural aptitude is reworked; it is divorced from its rendering as a congenital mark of birth or breeding, and constructed instead as an 'inner bent', a decidedly more mystical reading of 'innate dispositions'! A quite different set of relays enabled careerists to claim that personal drive had nothing to do with a material quest for fame and fortune, but was simply the realisation of a 'God-given' gift. But in its most powerful and popular articulation the code invested the 'congenital destiny' to labour for capital, with a special sense of inner-directed purpose or mission. For according to the protestant work ethic, skill, like virtue, was to be its own reward, measured as an index of an inner, moral worth, rather than in terms of wage differentials.

Yet the vocation code also retained an independent existence albeit one confined to feminine, or bohemian pursuits, both, of course, being regarded as equally 'unproductive'. If these activities continued to be valued as skills, it was precisely in so far as they remained economically marginal or unpaid – as generations of housewives, artists, nurses and others have found to their cost! The code thus instructed middle- and upper-class girls that their true calling was caring for men, rather than the 'selfish' pursuit of career. Motherhood was constructed as an exercise in creative self-fulfilment, on the same plane as the male pursuit of the Muse. Whereas the code of inheritance reproduced the patriarchal order as a quasi-biological grid of origins and destinies, under the vocation code this was inscribed in the subject as a project of desire – a far more insidious mechanism.

Working-class ideologies of skill, though no less patriarchal, operate according to quite different principles. Here skill is constructed under the sign of an *apprenticeship*, as the progressive mastery of techniques of dexterity associated with the performance of manual labour, both in the home and for wages. However, these skills could only be legitimately mastered from a position of subordination *vis à vis* elders – who always 'know better'. Apprenticeship, in other words, has customarily been to an inheritance of sorts, a patrimony of concrete skills, transmitted through the family, the shop-floor or the wider institutions of the class-culture and community. This reproduction code was never just confined to the labour aristocracy or the workplace. In different modalities, it informed practices of rational recreation and popular pleasure, structures of sexual initiation and political socialisation too.

However, in the post-war period there has occurred a pervasive weakening and fragmentation of these grids. Cultural apprenticeships are no longer so easily or frequently connected to occupational inheritances. The practice of dexterity is no longer anchored to the sign of manual labour; it takes place increasingly in leisure contexts, in the mastery of popular dance forms or video games for example. As a result positions of 'skill' and 'unskill' are no longer tied so rigidly to divisions of labour or their relations of generational transmission, but are negotiated primarily through the peer group. The body is no longer engendered solely as a bearer of labour power, specialised according to productive (male) or reproductive (female) functions. One effect of this is to make the forms of adolescent sexuality more dependent on what Freud called 'the narcissism' of minor differences, i.e. differences of taste, clothes, and personal life-style. Whether the escape routes this opens up are more imaginary than real, and just how far they undermine working-class sexism may be open to debate. But the desire to escape a universe of fixed reference, whether of gender or class, could potentially be connected to the kind of mobile individualism currently being promoted through the new regimes of skilling.

The systematic preparation of school-leavers for their future occupational roles, by State agencies, is a relatively recent development. It is designed to gear the transition from school to the requirements of the economy in a way which, it is argued, neither individual employers, nor market forces, alone can do. It is no coincidence that these initiatives came to be defined as *vocational* guidance and preparation, or that a *careers* service should initially have been put in charge of implementing them – since the aim is precisely to establish the hegemony of these codes over working-class constructs of skill.

At first sight, State intervention in this field appeared to be progressive, in that it challenged fixed constructs of origins and destinies in favour of an ideology of occupational choice. But in practice a kind of class double standard was operated. For the middle-classes the ideal of an 'existential' calling was conserved, on condition that it was realised through the normative grid of career. The task of guidance was to help the individual realise his or her 'inner bent' in terms of an appropriate profession. The 'vocational' guidance and training of working-class school-leavers had nothing to do with their inner desires, still less with preparing them for a professional calling or career. If they talked about 'dream jobs' this was usually attributed to a passing flight of adolescent fantasy, to be cured by some stern counselling in the reality principles of earning a living and growing up. Instead they were offered guidance and training in how to make the best of a bad job.

The new vocationalism carries this a stage further. Certainly, young people are no longer being blamed solely as individuals if they cannot find work on leaving school. In addition, and in anticipation of actual outcomes, they are being invited to discover *in their own cultures* a generic lack of motivation, discipline or skill. Increasingly, in schools, as well as on training schemes, they are being asked to see in their predicament not a structural effect, but rather a personal cause or incitement to improve themselves, and prove to the world that 'anyone can make it if they try'. That is the savage presumption behind the humanistic idioms of social-and-life-skilling. Perhaps it is time to have a closer look at them.

Self-improvement – From Samuel Smiles to SLS (Social and Life-Skills)

In a recent radio interview, Sir David Young asserted that 'it is high time we went back to the philosophy of Samuel Smiles. God helps those who train themselves. Or rather, God help those who don't.' It was more than political opportunism that prompted the Chairman of the MSC to ally himself publicly with the Thatcherite project of a 'return to Victorian values'. There *is* some very old wine being poured into new bottles at the MSC. Nevertheless history does not repeat itself even if ideologies never cease to do just that. The dole schools of the 1930s do not have the same conditions of existence as the youth training schemes of the 1980s, and the contemporary forms of self-improvement exemplified in social-and-life-skilling, have quite a different *raison d'être* from that of the original Victorian version. The ideology, in fact, has a complex and contradictory provenance which takes some unravelling. In tracing a line of descent from Samuel Smiles, through the Dale Carnegie Era between the wars, to the personal growth movements of the 1960s and finally to SLS, the tensions and breaks between those successive forms are as significant as their continuities.[9]

For example, the nineteenth century version did not always relay an individualistic message about 'pulling oneself up by one's own bootstraps'. It did not necessarily involve the deferential imitation of the manners and morals of 'elders and betters'. It also informed the movement for independent working-class education, supported popular demands for better cultural amenities and living conditions and it has been an element in both the religious and secular visions of socialism. In other words it can take on co-operative forms which stand against the ethic of possessive individualism. In sharp contrast the dominant model gave an aggressive competitive edge to the notion of betterment. Here self-improvement is an exercise in contest mobility, not forelock-touching. The typical morality tale which features in this literature concerns the hero (almost always male and usually the author) setting out on life's journey, beset by the temptations of pleasure and 'vice' at every turn. The road to fame and fortune follows a very straight and narrow path dictated by conscience and ambition marching hand in hand. Along the way tempters and failures would be met, individuals whose early promise had been confounded by the evils of drink or sex, their role as much to introduce an element of suspense – would the hero fall, be led astray? – as to underline the terrible conseqences of ignoring the prescriptive code laid down as the key to success. A very ancient theme, but what is original about this code is the way it legitimises competition, makes rivalry respectable; the message often seems to be 'stand on your own feet, even if it means treading on other people's toes'.

In the last thirty years, the co-operative vision of self-improvement has virtually disintegrated, while the competitive model has undergone a series of rapid transformations. Many of the old links between material and moral betterment have snapped, but new ones have taken their place. State education promised to provide an institutionalised route to social mobility, in a way that made the lonely struggles of the autodidact or the self-made man stand out as 'heroic' exceptions to the rule. Consumer life-styles emerged in which new and improved self-images could be bought, fully-fashioned, and changed as easily as clothes. These developments are exemplified in post-war forms of rational recreation, always the mainstay of self-improvers. These forms have either become privatised and embedded in costly technologies of leisure consumption; or taken in under State provision. In the first case they constitute symbols of success, rather than a means of achieving it; in the second, they have become a means of providing 'safe activities' for 'dangerous' groups (such as the young, black, unemployed, etc.) rather than a leg up the social ladder. But perhaps the most significant shift has been the way a whole range of bodily pleasures and expressive forms which had hitherto been ruled out of bounds, have been legitimised as 'rational recreation' and incorporated within strategies of self-improvement adapted to the codes of the new middle-class. At last the old moral economy of fixed and sublimated drives gave way to a liberal therapeutics of 'personal growth' whose slogan might be 'incremental insight equals interpersonal effectiveness equals success in work and play!' Creative individualism has here become a recipe for social success, rather than a symbol of Bohemian excess. In contrast to Smiles, the subject to be improved is a private or inner self rather than a public one, yet the object is still 'promotion'. In effect, the inner-directed features of the vocation code, and the other-directed features of the career code have become inextricably fused, or rather confused!

In the diverse elements which compose Social and Life-skill training, both the Smiles model and the liberal therapeutic have their place. The former has been operationalised in so called 'assertion training' and given a radical, though no less individualistic edge; the latter can be found in various kinds of counselling of adolescents in schools, youth projects and in the Personal Guidance Bases which it is currently proposed the MSC should set up. Yet at present both approaches remain marginal to the core curriculum of SLS. The reason is not hard to find. The translation of a self-improvement programme into the formal pedagogic context of the State school or training scheme imposes its own selective constraints. What had essentially been a method of self-help, learned through the personal example of mentors who had themselves successfully mastered it, hardly provided a model for institutional provision on a large scale, nor did it fit in with the prevailing relations of educational transmission. It is nevertheless highly significant that it was at the point where the notion of *skill* was made central to self-improvement that the apprenticeship model was dropped in favour of a behaviouristic model of learning applied to the whole field of vocational preparation.[10]

Initially SLS emerged out of an apparently radical critique of State schooling, designed to expose the irrelevance of academic curricula to working-class pupils, and concerned to develop an alternative approach to learning related to their real lives outside the school gates. How did it come to be, so quickly, and easily, incorporated within youth training schemes?

Of course the notion that schools or training schemes should be preparing young people for 'life' as well as labour does help give a nice liberal gloss to an otherwise all too crude utilitarian philosophy, and it also provides a convenient safety clause when trainees reach the end of the MSC line and find there are still no jobs for them. But the promotion of SLS is not the story of the corruption of an ideal. From the beginning it was conceived as a form of compensatory education suitable for 'non-academic' children; and what had to be compensated for was not only the inadequacy of existing forms of classroom knowledge, but the deficiencies of the pupils' cultures as well. It was a *double* deficit model in which the school's failure to connect with the 'real world of work' was mirrored in a failure of the working class family to transmit the kind of communication skills and interpersonal competencies which employers were now demanding for white collar jobs. But never mind, those skills and competencies could be taught *in the same way as woodwork or metal work*.

From the outset then a new micro-technology of self improvement is proposed; the social is dissolved into the interpersonal as a condition of the expressive becoming fully instrumentalised. Behaviourist theories of learning were thus the most appropriate pedagogic model for social- and life-skilling. Amongst the pioneers in the field was the Industrial Training Research Unit with its programme entitled CRAMP (Comprehension, Reflex learning, Attitude development, Memorisation, Procedural learning).

Even more significant was the work carried out by a group of social psychologists under the direction of Michael Argyle at Oxford. Inspired by ethological studies of animal and human communication this team set out to devise a rehabilitation programme for long term inmates of prisons and mental hospitals. This started from the somewhat circular proposition that 'social deviants' had failed to learn 'normal' techniques of social interaction. In the case of mental patients and prisoners we might suspect that their long periods of incarceration might have had something to do with it but never mind, they could at least now be taught how to behave themselves in public once they were released! The programme consisted in a crash course in verbal and non-verbal communication techniques (e.g. rules for eye contact and body posture in various social settings, how to pick up and respond to social cues, how and when to smile appropriately, conversational rituals, etc.). It was assumed that once the subject had learnt to release these signals 'correctly' social relations would become unproblematic.

In many ways Michael Argyle is the Frederick Winslow Taylor of the human relations industry. Just as Taylor attempted to establish a science of production-line management based on time and motion studies, so Argyle is aiming at a science of impression management also based on breaking down social practices into standardised, quantified, and controllable units of 'interaction'. But where Taylorism was concerned to maximise the physical efficiency and output of the factory worker, Argyle's programme is somewhat more ambitious. For the norms of inter-personal efficiency he uses makes the notion of 'social skill' highly transferable between a whole range of contexts. They are not only designed to increase the productivity of the white collar worker, but also that of the housewife (tension management!). These are techniques for selling yourself to a prospective lover as well as to a personnel manager. The very transferability of these 'skills' is an index of their real disciplinary function and scope. For their effect is to anatomise the speaking body into a set of 'proper' features silently regulated by law – the law of 'free and equal exchange' (Argyle's 'interation) – which systematically conceals the structural inequalities in power governing the production of the discourse. Despite the claims that this legal body has an 'instinctual foundation', it turns out to be the bearer of a behavioural ideology combining the calculating rationality of the boardroom with the social niceties of the bourgeois drawing-room. As for the real behind the ideal it is perhaps worth noting that what it is proposed to 'reskill' the mental patient or prisoner into seems a lot closer to the fragmented routines of the deskilled labourer than to the 'whole personality of the informed citizen' that is claimed.

Given this, it might seem at first sight rather odd that social and life skills should have been so enthusiastically taken up by educationalists; but the paradigm was all to easily recast in terms of demands for a 'relevant' curriculum for early leavers. For here was a method which would teach them 'how to communicate effectively, how to make, keep and end relationships, how to make effective transitions, how to be positive about oneself, how to manage negative emotions, how to cope with unemployment, how to cope with stress, and how to be an effective member of a group'[11] and much else besides! A veritable panacea for those concerned to free working class pupils from the 'double tyranny' of mechanical solidarity and abstract thought.

At the present time a bewildering number of different practices are taken in under the umbrella of SLS. Elements from various models of self improvement (personal growth, behaviour modification and straight Sam Smiles) are being selected and combined in numerous ways. Assertion training and psychodrama may be in vogue in one programme; training in good interview manners, lectures on personal hygiene and life-style enhancement mixed together in another. The choice of approach often seems determined by the context and the personal outlook of the teacher and the fact that this very diversity allows some measure of control over what is taught should not be overlooked. Yet this also has its dangers. It has enabled SLS to invade 'soft' areas of the school curriculum, liberal studies, careers teaching and even pastoral care. In these contexts SLS tends to be narrowly confined to the rehearsal of interview techniques, filling in job application forms, signing on and the like. This is clearly no substitute for social education or even personal counselling!

In this situation it is difficult for teachers and trainers alike to distinguish what, if anything, may amount to 'really useful knowledge' in SLS and what is merely underwriting the still dominant view that unemployment is a sign of inadequacy to be compensated for. It is not easy to devise a kind of ideological litmus test, in which a particular practice shows up as red or blue! But this brief historical review has at least revealed one indicator. Whatever its surface idioms, the prevailing model of self-improvement purveys the same message – that it is possible for individuals to triumph over even the most adverse circumstances, provided they work at it hard enough, follow certain advice and act consistently in their own self-interest. Yet there has also been a more co-operative model, of the working-class improving its lot collectively rather than swarming up the social ladder *singly*, one against one. The practice of mutual aid generates its own kind of 'social and life skills' whose survival value under present circumstances is certainly no less than wearing the 'right' clothes to interviews. Yet to introduce such a notion is currently viewed as tantamount to treason by the MSC. Nevertheless, and especially in schools, we must continue to insist on the relevance of including this alternative construct under the rubric of SLS.

However, it is also important to realise some of the limitations of fighting on this terrain. Historically, self-improvement, of whatever kind, has only appealed to those sections of the lower middle- and upper working-class whose social aspirations have, for one reason or another, been structurally blocked. It has never caught on amongst the poor, the unskilled or the unemployed. But is this changing? Will the present generation of school-leavers, living, as they say, 'on the rock and roll', find more survival value in techniques of self-improvement than their predecessors did? Certainly the handbooks, teaching kits, visual aids and other SLS materials that are currently pouring off the production lines take great pains to dress up their improving message in fashionable clothes. A closer look at some of this literature may therefore be useful, both to give us a clearer idea of the kind of discursive strategies being employed by these latter day Samuel Smiles, and to help us assess what is likely to be their impact on their young readerships.

Janet and John in Thatcherland

All the texts I have looked at[12] were designed to appeal to young people whom the publicity handouts variously describe as 'non-academic', 'under-achievers', or 'poor readers with short attention spans' – in other words, the working-class. It was clear from the handouts (and the materials themselves) that a common set of assumptions was being made about 'the kids': they are ignorant of their rights and weakly motivated to defend them. They lack any kind of work experience. They have no access to useful information and advice other than that provided by official agencies and professional experts. They have difficulty in organising their lives in a rational or satisfactory way.

Now this does not remotely add up to an accurate account of the way school-leavers deal with their real situation. It is simply a deficit model of working-class culture used to provide a rationale for SLS as a form of compensatory education. As to their actual content, all the texts offered very similar information and advice about looking for a job, going for an interview, fitting in at work, claiming State benefits and getting on training or further education courses. A section on 'sex' (which usually meant contraception, abortion and VD) was usually included in the package, along with advice on 'personal relations'. Youth politics, whether to do with unemployment, housing, or cultural questions is conspicuous by its absence.

Pills of information and advice were normally sugared by a mixture of cartoons and photo-stories, in formats borrowed from commercial teenage magazines. They were obviously meant to be easily digested, to give the individual quick-acting, if not permanent, relief from a range of social ills – poverty, boredom, discrimination and so on. 'If you take this advice regularly' (before and after interviews?) 'you'll be OK' is the basic reassuring message.

Or is it? These materials gave me much food for thought, but not in quite the way their authors intended. For they contain a series of complex *meta*-messages which are far from easy to decode. The explicit prescriptions (the texts are full of lists of do's and don'ts) turn out to rest on a set of implicit ascriptions to the role of employers, social workers, teachers, doctors, lawyers, etc., which are not only contentious, but inscribe the reader as a purely passive recipient of their various discourses. Where these discourses are being most overtly informative, they are covertly at their most *per*formative, in actively constructing the situations (e.g. being arrested or sacked) which they purport merely to reflect. It is not then just a question of sugaring the pill – using popular media like cartoons or photo-stories to smuggle through an otherwise unpopular message – few of the intended readers are likely to be taken in by that. Rather, and to stretch the metaphor, we could say that these knowledge pills are both contraceptive and analgesic in their effect; they are designed to prevent school-leavers from thinking or acting realistically in any other terms than those laid down in official discourses and procedures *and* they kill the pain involved in trying to do so. In so far as anything is explained at all about the current crisis, it is not in terms of relations of conflict or contradiction between social or historical forces, but in terms of ineluctable processes stemming from inert principles of causation. Youth unemployment is caused by the recession, racism is caused by racists – a form of reasoning which is maximally calculated to put young minds to sleep!

It is in their claim to be purely factual or practical that these materials reveal themselves as ideological through and through. School-leavers are indeed being invited to enter into an imaginary relation to their predicaments; not because the ways suggested for dealing with them are in themselves impracticable, or inexact, but because they are premised on a *subject position* which turns real relations to Capital or the State upside down and inside out. For the reader who is addressed, whether directly, or indirectly, is always a *legal* subject i.e. an individual centre of contractual rights and obligations, free and equal before the law. It is from this position that we are urged to join a trade union, resist racism and sexism, start our own business, be polite to policemen and dress sensibly for interviews. It is also, as a legal subject, that the reader is supposed to recognise the situations shown, identify with the 'exemplary' figures of youth portrayed in them, and clutching a checklist of prescriptions in hand, go and do likewise.

But this is not just an exercise in conforming to external rules and regulations. These texts counsel young people to police their own behaviour, not by appealing to the wisdom or authority of 'elders and betters', but by referencing the experience of peers. The testimonies of young people who have apparently followed the advice and succeeded, is a recurring device used to lend credibility, or realism, to the text. In the process, the legal subject is subtly converted into a *judicious self*, a superego, based not on the father (whose word is no longer law) but on an imaginary peer, a double representing the reader's 'better self'.

Though this beguiling figure, the voice of self-improvement speaks, and constructs its special effects of meaning. But of course everything now depends on whether readers do indeed recognise themselves in the mirror images projected by these 'judicious selves'. I showed a sample of this literature to a group of twenty unemployed school-leavers in North London; I asked them whether they thought the situations that were portrayed in the photo-stories or cartoons were realistic, and whether the information and advice amounted to really useful knowledge. The response was almost entirely negative. They found the story-lines artificial, the language used patronising, and the information and advice completely abstracted from the real social context of their lives.

To illustrate this, let us look in more detail at one fairly typical example of the genre. The School Leavers Book (1982) sticks very closely to the core curriculum of SLS. A separate topic is dealt with on each double-page spread, and the format consists of a photo or cartoon story accompanied by a checklist of do's and don'ts. In the stories, all the young people are shown dressed sensibly, as if for interviews. They spend most of their time posed in empty space, occasionally framed by the odd corner of a table, or brick wall, saying things like 'Hi Sheila, I've been told to leave my job because I'm pregnant' or 'Magic, it's my Giro from the DHSS. I'll cash it and have some money to spend at last'. The characters are continually hailing each other, and the reader, with lines like 'Hi. Last week I went for my seventh interview and I think I've finally got it right. I thought I'd pass on a few ideas to you'. Sometimes we get what passes for a dialogue:

> *Girl A* Hi! I haven't seen you for a few months, did you get a job after all?

Girl B No, but I took your advice and applied for a place at college.

Girl C Colleges have typing, nursing, mechanics, electrical work, dressmaking, engineering, photography, art, catering, maths, hairdressing and loads of other courses and you don't always need exams to get in.

Girl A I started last week. It's OK.

As you can see these youngsters are not arresting conversationalists despite all the hailing that goes on. They would provide great material for a Monty Python sketch though! Even when relaxing down at the youth club, they are likely to have earnest discussions about the role of Industrial Tribunals, or Social Security Appeal procedures. They are surrounded by kindly officials, including the police who are presented as a more or less benevolent agency of the Welfare State. The section entitled *Arrest* begins:

> Most people only contact the police when they have some sort of a problem. They go to the police station voluntarily to register a complaint or seek information. However there are occasions when the police may seek your help. You may wish to help them, but you should also know your rights.

An even more strenuous exercise in wish fulfilment is to be found in the section dealing with trade unions. A West Indian boy and girl are shown having an argument about the pros and cons of joining one. The girl is initially hostile, but is finally won over by the lad's assertion that unions are in the vanguard of the fight against sex and race discrimination!

The script throughout is written in a bizarre mixture of Ladybird and 'bureaucratese'. There is no real dialogue or debate between the characters because whatever their role, everyone speaks either in the name of the Law or in the language of the judicious self. The Everyboys and Girls who people the stories are persons without personalities, ventriloquists' dummies manipulated by the hidden hand of an ideology not their own. The device of putting official information and advice into the mouths of a multi-ethnic cast of working-class teenagers may strike you as a rather pathetic piece of sleight-of-hand, one which tells us a lot about the authors' patronising attitudes. But the point is, it is *structurally* necessary to maintain the coherence of this particular universe of discourse. The problem the authors had to solve, whether they recognised it or not, was this: if the text is to work, in the sense of getting the message across, then readers have to identify with its 'senders' (the characters) as speaking on their behalf, or in some way representing the real world. But if the text is to work as an enunciation of official codes of practice, then everything which would enable working-class school-leavers to identify with the characters in terms of language, culture, or ideology has to be cut out. In trying to get round this problem – which the use of familiar graphic forms highlights, but does not solve – the authors are impelled to construct a story-line which is both mystifying and obtuse. Let us look at a typical case in point.

Really cool knowledge?

Two pages of the book deal with applying for a job by phone (see figure 4.1). A white boy and black girl are shown ringing up a garage in reply to an advertisement for a salesperson. The boy does it all wrong, while the girl follows all the correct procedures as laid down in the accompanying checklist. However *both* applicants are turned down. The Manager thanks them for ringing but says 'there are a lot of people we have to interview'. No other explanation is given. On the face of it then, the implication seems to be that there is no pay-off for learning 'good' interview techniques, since they make absolutely no difference to the outcome. That, indeed, is the conclusion which the young people reading this sequence, reached. Why should a book which is devoted to life and social skills put across such a self-defeating message? Why was not the black girl, shown as such an adept at 'impression management', rewarded by being offered an interview, while the lad who is made to break all the rules, has to suffer the consequences?

One reason is that if the book is to maintain any credibility with the reader, it has to maintain a semblance of economic realism. It has to take into account the fact that in a situation of structural unemployment *and* credential inflation, the links between educability and employability on which so much of the teachers' authority rests, can no longer be made with any degree of conviction. School-leavers are coming to realise that no matter how impressive their interview manners, how good their personal or academic credentials, irrespective of how many dozens of immaculately-written letters they send out or how diligently they follow the instructions in their job-hunter kits, the cards have already been dealt and theirs read 'sorry, no vacancies'.

How then to motivate them, to cool out their immediate demands for real work at a living wage, and persuade them to go on a training-scheme instead, without simultaneously practising a cruel deception? This is the problem which teachers face, and which this sequence (and the whole book) tries to solve. It does so not by suppressing the contradiction, but by displacing its terms into a magical resolution: *the salvage of individual victories out of collective defeats*.

How is this effect achieved here? Consider for a moment the position of the garage manager. Despite the marked differences between the two applicants, in terms of race, gender, and class 'attributes', he is shown addressing them identically throughout. Obviously an equal opportunities employer, he rejects them both!

In other words the manager is constructed as an exemplary legal subject. He conforms to employment legislation (the Race Relations and Sex Discrimination Acts) and this in turn legitimates his freedom to hire and fire according to the laws of the market (lots of others to interview, sorry). What in fact is being guaranteed, is his freedom *not* to hire and *not* to give any substantive reason why. The applicants are left with their 'freedom' to remain unemployed. The interview is presented as an equal exchange between free subjects, rather than what it is, an unequal power relation between capital and labour mediated by patterns of social discrimination institutionalised by the State. The symmetry of the manager's responses is necessary to maintain the legal fiction and suppress the social facts.

If he had been shown differentiating between the boy and girl, following a policy of either negative or positive discrimination, then the real relations in play would have had to be depicted simply to maintain the congruity of the story line. His silences are equally functional. Because this is an exercise in public propriety we are not told what he might really be thinking or feeling in contradistinction to what he says. No advantage can thus be taken, here, or elsewhere, of the cartoon's capacity to demystify, e.g. by using 'think-bubbles'

Whenever you are phoning for information, whether it's Social Security, an Advice Centre or for a job — be prepared Use the checklist.

to articulate a sub-text of what is truly going on but is censored, distorted or covered over in official discourse. In the process, the power of the interviewer to remain silent, to withhold information or to lie, and the interviewee's powerlessness to challenge these prerogatives without offending against the code, all this is massively endorsed – and this in a book which ostensibly upholds young people's rights!

There is however a further twist to the tale, which concerns the type of qualities associated with the occupation chosen for the exercise. Salesperson in a garage can refer equally to mens work (car salesman) or womens work (behind the counter) *without* putting in question the fundamental rule governing the sexual division of labour (the closer the job is to operating the machine, the more likely it is to be a masculine preserve).

Moreover no school leaver would be taken on as a car salesman – it is indeed regarded as a 'man's' job, not a boy's. Salesperson therefore in this context has the connotation of shop girl. The qualities which are normally demanded for shop work – selling one's self to sell the product, looking good to make the customer feel good – are of course constructed as 'essentially feminine'. Now none of this is problematised in the text. Instead the girl is shown as having effortlessly mastered the art of selling herself whereas the boy apparently sees no reason to even try. Her 'success', his 'failure', does not therefore represent some role reversal. It reinforces gender stereotypes in the crudest possible way.

At the same time a far more subtle and insidious displacement is effected in the story line. As I have said the even-handedness of the garage manager is mystifying, in that it works to conceal the real asymmetry between his class position and that of the young people, but the asymmetry that *is* shown operating between the two job applicants, is no less mystifying. For the distinction between right and wrong interview manners not only cancels the real differences between them but also conceals the fact that they are being positioned *symmetrically* within *the same system of double binds*. How does this occur?

The lad is allowed to drop his aitches, confess he doesn't really want the job, run out of money for the telephone and forget the name of the 'bloke in charge'. The nearest anyone in this book is ever permitted to come to a position with which the reader could indentify! This character can be a 'speaking subject' within a certain code of working-class masculinity, affirm something like a cultural identity, but *only as an index of social disqualification*, a transgressor of 'the law'.

The black girl, in contrast, is made to give a flawless performance of deference to white middle-class etiquette. Even when she gets the brush-off, she politely thanks the manager for his help! But she is allowed to exist only as a subject spoken for by the dominant culture, one who suppresses anything that would affirm her real identity. The line that is drawn between the two characters is not one of gender, ethnicity or class; that would destroy the whole fragile grid of legal subjectivity on which the story rests. In contrast, the distinction that *is* made reinforces the grid, for it rests on the opposition between judicious and injudicious selves.

Injudicious selves 'show themselves up', 'give themselves away', 'lose control'. Judicious selves remain *self-possessed*, on condition that they first *disown* everything that would invest them with the properties of speaking subjects. Which is better? To remain calm, cool and collected by taking the role of 'The Other' or show yourself up as being incompetent or worse, 'uncool', by 'being yourself'. That is the double bind into which *both* these characters are implicitly locked.

Self-possession has been turned into a highly convertible currency – both a selling-point for prospective employers and an insurance policy against feelings of indignation or disappointment triggered by rejection; a 'therapeutic' for dealing with anxieties of the first interview or the traumas of a first date. It is by these means that young people are supposed to conjure individual victories out of collective defeats, or, as here, black girls do better than white boys. Instead of being helped to confront their shared predicaments within a wider framework of knowledge and action, they are offered a purely personal tactic of disavowal.

What this means in classroom practice, as I found, is that even when a political issue, such as job discrimination, is implicitly posed, it cannot be clarified or made explicit within the terms of reference set out. I asked my group why they thought the garage manager had turned the applicants down. Was it because the girl was black and he was a racist? 'Well, no, because he couldn't see her, and she talked posh, so he couldn't tell by what she said.' Was it because she was a girl? 'No, because it wasn't a particularly male job anyway.' Why did the boy get rejected? 'He messed up the interview . . . no it couldn't be that 'cos the girl did everything right and she got the brush off too.' Did the manager then turn them down on different grounds? 'No.' Why? 'Because he said the same to both, treated them the same way.' But he might have been thinking different things about them? 'Well, you couldn't know, could you.' So what was the point of the story? 'We don't know. It's pointless, stupid. The people who wrote it must be mad!'

They are not mad, but they are certainly unconscious of the way their ideological grammar serves to close off any space of critical engagement by the reader, subverting their own undoubtedly progressive intentions.

I have tried to show how here the ideal of 'self-possession' plays a key-role in shifting the ideology of self-improvement onto a new terrain. In the classic Samual Smiles version, it was at least recognised that legal subjects were free to negotiate or bargain with real competitors in the market place, to find the highest price for their labour and so on. I think it is very significant that no-one in this book is shown doing so. The competition between the boy and girl is not set up in these terms at all. Rather it is invisibly structured by a purely symbolic exchange, a system of trade-offs between a public and a private self. The public self is made to adjust to undesirable realities (YTS or the Dole) by suppressing its real features (as in the case of the black girl). By the same token, the private self is made the locus of unrealisable desires (the dream job, or the job you really want, as with the boy). Subtly, the right of collective bargaining is transmuted into the obligation to conduct a purely interior negotiation between two halves of a divided self. Impression management makes its cultural capital out of just that split, even as it promises to resolve it. The full formula for its 'therapeutic' double bind should be written: 'privatise what you publicly are – publicise what you privately are not', and *enjoy* the duplicity for the sense of power it gives you over the means of self-representation.

Clearly we have come a long way from old-style bourgeois individualism. There is no place for the strong inner-directed ego, voice of conscience and morality in this scenario. Nor are young people being trained to measure themselves competitively against their peers, to run and win in the rat race. Yet elements of both the vocation and career codes are still in play; they have been transposed into the figures of a new individualism, more flexible and 'desirable' than the old, capable of adapting itself continually to the changing demands of market forces, while sustaining the illusion of its autonomy from them. It all adds up to a subject form ideally suited to a 'High Tech' version of consumer capitalism and one that is increasingly being mobilised against the residual forms of resistance which this is throwing up.[13]

The 'cooling out' of school leavers' aspirations is no longer being left to the cumulative effect of educational failure, or the sudden pressures of the labour market. A new set of pedagogic and counselling devices are being developed, of which existing forms of careers guidance and SLS are but the crude prototypes. So let us finally take a brief look at some possible trends for the future.

I think it is possible to envisage a scenario in which the whole process of dis-qualification was turned to rather different account; instead of being coerced into conformity or bribed into better ways, classroom resisters would be encouraged to follow the example of those of their peers who have learned to win against the system by pretending to play its game. In other words they could be officially counselled how to 'play it cool'.

There are probably as many styles of playing it cool as there are terms to describe the practice. It is part of the survival tactics of every subordinate group, a way of neutralising the consequences of powerlessness without challenging the prerogatives of power. Playing it cool avoids the risks of open defiance and the humiliation of abject surrender to the dominant norm. Indeed the very success of this game depends on how skilfully the ambiguous status of the practice is played upon. Its basic elements involve:

1. the construction of a position of inner detachment or mental reserve which enables people to dissociate themselves from acts of compliance imposed upon them by a superior authority;

2. the systematic inhibition of spontaneous feelings, whether positive or negative in contexts where this would be interpreted as a sign of weakness.

The central paradox of this whole manoeuvre is that it preserves the integrity of an oppositional identity only by practising a calculated duplicity: you pretend to be playing according to the official rules, whilst secretly bending them to the advantage of your own, rather different, game – that of 'loser wins'. Thus for example, a 'cool' way for young soldiers to get a free discharge from the army may be to pretend that they are gay. But if you are really gay, and happen to like army life, then the 'cool' thing to do is to pretend that you are as heterosexual as the other lads, while in secret, in the company of your gay friends, continuing to 'be yourself'.

As this example shows, 'playing it cool' is a very double-edged weapon. In some contexts it may be a rational survival tactic; in others it may be profoundly self-destructive.[14] And it is often very difficult to tell which is which – who is playing whose power game, who is losing and who winning – first because the game involves the suppression of true feelings (which is why it is a predominantly masculine technique) and second because this form of one-up-manship is simply a mirror image of real power relations, a way, precisely, of conjuring imaginary victories out of positions of real defeat.

'Playing it cool' is thus a rather more 'hip' version of the techniques of impression management already being taught to school-leavers in SLS. The cultural contexts may be different but the mechanisms (of splitting, etc.) are essentially the same, and this is what some of the new vocationalists are beginning to realise.

In our telephone interview story, if the black girl is represented as someone whose conformity to the dominant code involves the abject surrender of her identity, few readers will support her position – especially not black girls. The boy, in contrast becomes a popular hero. But what if the story-line is contextualised in a slightly different way? What if the black girl is represented as *pretending* to play 'whitey's' game, while secretly laughing up her sleeve at him? Why, then she is 'playing it cool' and it is the boy who is being stupidly 'uncool'. I offered just such a reading to a control group of school-leavers and that indeed was their response.

However it is not just a question of finding a device to persuade young people that, depite all appearance to the contrary, SLS is 'really useful knowledge' which will enable them to 'do it their way' just like Sid Vicious, if not Frank Sinatra. The MSC is now moving into the field of adolescent counselling and marriage guidance in a big way,[15] and, in the process, bringing to bear more sophisticated techniques for cooling out the unemployed. For now, within the protective frame of the therapeutic setting, they are encouraged to let out all their anger, guilt, anxiety, fears; all these feelings must be 'got out of their system' as one such counsellor put it to me 'so that they are better able to cope with the stresses of job interviews, rejection letters, and everyday family life'. In other words the State will provide an emotional safety valve, to enable the unemployed to go on 'playing it cool.'

We are living in a society in which to belong to the 'wrong' class, the 'wrong' age group or gender, to have the 'wrong' colour skin or the 'wrong' sexual orientation is to be made to pay an increasingly high price in the labour market. Under these circumstances, the appeal of impression management to those whose face would not otherwise fit, has never been greater. In the fictional 1984, Winston Smith was tortured until he really did see five fingers instead of four. In the real world of 1984, school-leavers are being invited to persuade themselves that two and two equals five, not through the medium of pain, but through the *pleasure* to be gained from successfully creating that impression. If as teachers and educational-ists we are going to resist these trends, then perhaps *we* should stop playing it quite so cool. And that must mean moving on from purely theoretical critiques to the construction of alternative practices. Wagging a finger at SLS is after all a pretty pointless academic exercise unless we are also prepared to take the risk of developing a different approach which is more, rather than less, responsive to school-leavers' needs. But there can be no really useful knowledge which does not proceed from the attempt.

II   Notes towards an alternative practice[16]

When I left school they said to me 'Why don't you sign on and get some money?' So I went to my Careers office, and they gave me a pink form and a white piece of paper. I took them to the unemployment exchange. They gave me this yellow form to fill in. When I done that, they put it in an envelope and sent me to Social Security. When you get to the Social Security you have to line up and wait your turn. When you get to your turn they give you an appointment to see someone else in a little room. Then you have to wait your turn again. When you done that interview, they tell you to go next day and sign on. When you sign on they give you a number and you got to go to that box number. My number was 16. I'll never forget it. If you've never signed on before you have to go back to your Careers Office, then back to the Unemployment, then back to the Social Security, then back to the Unemployment again. It makes you dizzy. Why do they have to make it so complicated? – *16-year-old unemployed girl*

The course gave us more confidence to ask questions. *We* could ask the questions for a change. And you could tell, a lot of the time, by the way they answered you, that they weren't expecting it, not from kids like us. – *Student on school-leavers course*

The task we set ourselves in designing and pilot-teaching a short course for early leavers was twofold: (1) to develop a form and content which would focus on precisely those issues marginalised, or mystified by the new vocationalism; (2) to address the students personal sense of priorities, while challenging the dominant, individualistic, reading of school transitions. The problem of devising an appropriate curriculum and pedagogy was never going to be an easy one to solve. For example, to offer our students a beginner's guide to the local economy and state provision might be to insult local intelligence of these matters – an instant recipe for boredom; it would also beg a series of tricky but important questions we wanted to explore with them.

These questions had everything to do with the way learning, labour and leisure are currently being redefined, not only by the discourses of the powerful, but within working-class cultures as well. Just how much of a minefield we were walking into quickly became apparent, when the first draft of the course came out with all emphasis placed on issues of learning and leisure, on the assumption that none of our school-leavers would find jobs and therefore would not be interested in labour market issues. The first premise might turn out to be true, but the second one certainly did not follow on from it! The fact is that unconsciously we had been drawn into constructing a course on the very premise we wanted to question – the idea that the transition from school to work has now inevitably to pass through the dole queue and YTS. We decided therefore to begin the course with some simple exercises working from careers literature and hobby magazines, exploring and comparing the students' own personal inventories of skill with the dominant constructs of vocation and career. We hoped this would help them differentiate more clearly between the different skill codes, and sensitise them to some of the knowledge/power relations that came into play in their transmission.

After these preparatory exercises, the main part of the course consisted in group visits to a number of work and training sites. These were chosen because they illustrated specific issues – such as sexual divisions of labour, managerial structures, attitudes and aspirations of workers and trainees, state strategies towards youth unemployment, etc. Each visit was documented, the students interviewing both managers and the 'rank and file', and taking photographs. These experiences were then explored thematically via group discussions and photo-story work, enabling students to interpret the emerging issues in the light of their own concerns. Finally the material was worked up to produce a statement in words and images on a series of presentation boards.

The other major component was the homework exercise. This ran in tandem with the day-time visits. Students were lent cameras and tape recorders to take home, to build up a personal portrait of the people, places and practices which were significant for them. The aim here was to help students contextualise the issues arising from the visits, in terms of a sharpened sense of their own social and cultural priorities, their own sense of transitions.

One pressing problem was the way students might read the deep structure of the course. Whatever we said about its aims, they might still see it as a means of railroading them through from school to YTS, thus reinforcing existing institutional closures around the transition. Most of the professionals to whom we talked certainly took it for granted that this was our 'real' function – one reason, perhaps, why we got the level of co-operation we did. Yet the course was not designed as an exercise in vocational guidance. Our purpose in getting students to look at constructs of skill was to question some of the 'taken for granted' aspects of leaving school, not to set ourselves up for cracks about kids who are fond of animals being encouraged to get jobs in butchers' shops!

That meant we somehow had to interrupt the normative sequencing rules for 'successful' transitions in planning our time-table. In fact we decided to reverse them. We would *start* the course by looking at work regimes and local labour markets, move back to inspect government training schemes and only towards the end of the fortnight deal with the mechanics of leaving school, signing on and claiming benefit.

In the event our strategy paid off. Reversing the normal order of progression seemed to give the students space to explore some of the key disjunctions between the official rules and their own – a space which both released their sense of imagination (and humour) and opened up the issues in a way that made sense to them.

As regards the curricular form itself, it seemed to straddle a number of models. In some contexts we were more concerned with states of knowledge (e.g. about government training schemes) in others, with exploring new ways of representing what was already known (e.g. the homework exercises). Above all we set out to provide a framework which would connect these two orders of knowledge, something that is easier said than done.[17]

From social studies to cultural practice

When we came to consider our general approach to teaching the course, we decided to opt initially for a version of the social studies model. This consists in turning students into 'social investigators' in the belief or hope that this generates a more critical perspective on society. We had some reservations about this model. It was already known to our students from schooldays, and familiarity seemed to have bred contempt, if our pre-course discussion with them was anything to go by; but it had the big advantage that it seemed well-suited to the documentation of our day-time visits. We remained, in any case, agnostic. We would see how our group took to this way of working. How far could they push it in the direction of their own interests and concerns?

Partly to test this, we chose strongly contrasting types of work-place or training regime for our 'investigations', for example, a workers' co-operative, a small non-unionised family firm and a large public corporation. However, this was not to be an exercise in the appreciation of diversity, or even to examine, critically, different forms of ownership and control; we rejected these more orthodox versions of the social studies approach as being too objectivist for our purposes. Instead we sought to construct an experiential framework of comparison, which corresponded to the actual range of conditions likely to be met by young workers or trainees, in the hope that out of this a number of key political issues might emerge for further discussion and project work. How similar or different were the attitudes of small co-operatives to those of small businesses? What difference did the presence or absence of trade unions make to the position of women workers, etc.? Clearly, as tutors we could have taken the lead in formulating these and similar questions. Yet even within the confines of the social studies model, we felt it might be counterproductive to give artificial priorities to issues on behalf of the group. For the danger was that the students' own concerns might then become marginalised, at best developed 'off script'. Moreover, for all that, we wanted to sensitise them to some of the 'taken for granted' aspects of their commonsensical beliefs. We therefore worked with the group to help them script the issues as they imagined they would find them, and that meant things they wanted to find out about, however instrumentally. Alas for non-directiveness, the interview scripting that emerged from the early briefing sessions was often wooden and inflexible when put into practice.

A case in point occurred on the second day, when, as a limbering-up exercise, the group went on a local walkabout, interviewing people they saw at work. They met some Telecom engineers repairing a cable in the street. The scripted questions about training opportunities failed to yield much response. In the embarrassed silence that followed, one of the girls asked diffidently enough, whether the job had any special perks. 'Talking to young girls in the street,' replied one Jack-the-lad! But our boys didn't find the ritual sexist quip at all funny for once. *This* was something they wanted to hear about. In fact Sue's question released a flow of stories from the men about moonlighting and other fiddles, the skives they used to get up to when they were apprentices, and the importance of not having the gaffer on your back. Despite the initial hiccup, a real rapport was established around the commonalities of a class experience which embraced both school and work. In the process, important, but hitherto unscripted issues, concerning discipline and resistance, control over labour processes, the hidden economy and not least, the routine sexism of working-class life, emerged in a way which allowed the students to give them proper weight; these were to be the major themes in the material which they subsequently produced.

By the third day, something like a group practice had crystallised, with the students beginning to work well together, taking turns to do interviews, operating the darkroom on a rota, transcribing tapes. The inevitable beginners' mistakes (underexposed film, tapes erased, etc.) did nothing to dampen the general enthusiasm. Their ability to master the technical rudiments, to work quickly and accurately and increasingly under their own steam, was truly impressive. The classroom began to take on the frenzied appearance of the editorial offices of some latter day 'Picture Post' with prints spreading round the walls, tapes and transcripts accumulating in an ordered clutter on the desks.

Undoubtedly much of this initial energy must be credited to the new experience of compiling evidence through the production of photo-texts. This was not quite like the social studies they had done at school. But underlying this was a more significant response. The group was beginning to take collective responsibility for generating material which reflected their, not our, concerns. A small breakthrough occurred on the fourth day, when for the first time on a visit (to some co-ops), they told us to stop chaperoning them about and leave them alone to get on with the job. They had discovered something in *this* labour process, which, like the Telecom workers, they could control and turn to their advantage. They didn't need us, as gaffers, on their backs!

Collective work seemed to exemplify the best aspects of this media version of social studies, but in other aspects we were becoming aware of some of the limitations of the model. It seemed that holding our group within this investigative frame could serve them as a strategy of *dissociation*, when it came to looking at some of the more painful realities of working-class life and labour. Actual social scientists do not have this problem, because normally the conditions they investigate do not directly touch their own real lives as middle-class professional people. But our students were not in this privileged position. What happened when they were confronted with such realities is well illustrated by their visit to a local pickle factory. This was housed in a squalid Dickensian building, with plant to match; the relaxed and informal atmosphere on the shop-floor belied its rigid division of labour – women worked the lines, bottling, labelling and packing; the men did all the heavy, skilled and supervisory jobs. The management policies of this small family firm can be judged from the fact that they refused to employ any relatives of the women workers, on the grounds that family rows would disrupt production and they had promptly sacked the only woman who tried to join a union. The declared loyalty of the women to the firm (many had been there more than twenty years the manager told us with pride) was in fact built on a profound fatalism. Conditions were not good, the wages were low, but that's the way life is, isn't it?

We had chosen this site because we thought it would force the group to address all those issues about women's work, which a screening of 'Rosie the Riveter' had earlier failed to spark off. We were wrong. As they chatted informally to the women, they made their own assessment of the place. 'It's a dump. I wouldn't work here if they paid me!' Sharon thought that even marriage might be better than this kind of 'slave labour'. The married women who were paid to do just that, agreed with her! They wouldn't want their teenage daughters to end up in the same boat. But this consensus expressed no closure of a generation gap, no solidarity of sisterhood in class. Quite the opposite. The investigative frame had simply enabled our group to protect themselves from having to take in the whole painful experience; they distanced it in terms of age and gender (as one of them put it 'it was OK for these old bags') in much the same way as, in reverse, the women insulated themselves from the situation by projecting their hopes for a better life onto a future generation (at least the youngsters might find something better to do than this). Neither view sought to challenge the appalling conditions in the factory.

When we got back to base, we asked the group to identify which aspects of the visit had affected them most. As they sifted through the source materials, it soon became clear that the only texts they felt confident in shaping were neutral descriptions of technical processes (the plant, the production stages). There was enormous resistance to representing the social relations of the workplace. This can be seen in the panels about the visit that were eventually produced – a literal reading of the labour process, followed by excerpts from the firm's publicity handout, and some uncontexted quotes from manager and employees. There are strong overtones of CSE type presentations here.

We began to see a pattern to the successes and failures of the social studies model. In situations where students felt at home, where they could empathise to some extent with the people they were interviewing, then they felt able to shape the experience within the documentary form, even treat it 'objectively'. But where they felt they were entering a hostile environment or when they could not identify in some way with the subject under investigation, then they could not treat the experience objectively or shape it into a coherent representation.

This 'law' was confirmed by a subsequent visit to a youth training scheme. Confronted by an authoritarian training manager and an environment which one of them compared unfavourably with an open Borstal, the group went into a state of silent mutiny when invited to discuss the role of YTS! Until, that is, one of them muttered that some trainees on another scheme had managed to sabotage an open day. Then someone else remembered seeing some defiant graffiti on the workshop walls. This possibility of resistance instantly galvanised the group into imaginative life. They set to to produce sheets of graffiti in similar vein. Political slogans, ritual insults, and what is politely called 'popular scatology' flowed in profusion across the page. The lesson was clear enough. It was only through these resources of meaning, these cultural forms that the students were prepared to confront the more painful possibilities of what might lie in store for them. They had pushed us beyond the social studies model in the direction of their own cultural practices and the styles of resistance with which they connected. More generally, it signified their desire to shift from the position into which we had put them, as (passive or critical) observers of society, to one where they no longer had to play it quite so cool.

Portraits in transition

What then of the group itself? We had asked the school for a dozen early leavers,[23] half girls half boys. We ended up with ten, seven boys, three girls. We were unhappy about the imbalance but we were presented with a *fait accompli* two days before the course began. We had anticipated that we would get the resisters, whom the school would be only too pleased to get rid of for a time. In this we were proved wrong. Our students formed part of that middle stratum whose school lives had been neither academically reward-ing nor spectacularly troubled. Neither 'lads' nor 'ear'oles', neither 'boffins' nor 'bother' this group has been singularly neglected by teachers and sociologists alike. As we were to discover, their positions and strategies did not fit easily into the usual pigeonholes.

For example, with one notable exception (an apprentice punk) none of our students showed any marked involvement in youth cultural styles as such. They displayed a wide range of taste in music, clothes, and leisure pursuits, without these differences provoking any conflict. Their social sense of self was furnished from autobiographical materials which did not seem to require these fashionable props. Their criticism of youth styles was precisely that they effaced individuality. But if they were not style-leaders, they were not loners either. Their friendship networks were not based on where they lived, or where they were located in school, but rather on highly specific attitudes and interests which cut across these boundaries.

Three attitudes united them as a group. The first was their low regard for CSE exams as a credential for finding work; second, their desire to leave school at the earliest possible opportunity and third their determination to 'make it' by other means. These are all inter-related, of course, but it was interesting to note that their personal aspirations had in no way been dented by their experience of failure at school, nor were they deterred *at this stage*, by the thought that their real economic prospects might be bleak.

However this was not just another case of refusing to face the future. It was simply that the school was not central to their transition strategies *whereas the family was*. Almost all of them already had some kind of work experience generated through family connections, whether through their parents, or other kin. They believed that these part-time, holiday or weekend jobs would metamorphose into full-time work on leaving school. And perhaps their confidence was not entirely misplaced, for in this part of South London, with its small firms and flourishing hidden economy, the networks of working-class kinship have proved well able to absorb the growth of single-parent families and continue to provide material and moral support. The way in which some of these families provided information and advice on employment opportunities, as well as following the time-honoured practice of 'having a word in the gaffer's ear', made the careers service seem almost an irrelevance!

The degree and type of family connectedness to the local labour market was thus a crucial variable in these early leavers' plans for the future. Another, equally important factor, and one that related to a more hidden curriculum vitae, was their mode of positioning within what Freud called the family romance. This term refers to those normative structures of projective identification through which parents and children, usually of the same sex, misrecognise in each other the social embodiment of developmental ideals constructed by the dominant culture. In the case of working-class families the pantheon of heroes and heroines used for this purpose is mainly drawn from popular culture e.g. TV, or movie stars, rock stars, sporting personalities, and the like. These furnish the models for 'supermum' or 'superdad' against which actual parents are often compared invidiously. They also provide all those 'famous' first names (e.g. Elvis, Marilyn) whose symbolic function is to inscribe the child's history in a certain genealogy of parental desire.

The family romance is thus a key ideological mechanism through which real relations of reproduction (the generational and sexual divisions of labour) are magically transformed into imaginary relations of kinship with members of another class. It is there in the fairy tales which are often told about mysteriously absent figures – the dead grandmother, the cousin in America, the uncle who won the pools – whose narrative function is to lend a halo of respectablity or romance to what otherwise might be a rather sorry story. The phantasies of adoption elaborated by some children as well as the myths of 'real origin' constructed by actual adoptees belong within the same category. There is finally the 'negative romance' as in the 'rags to riches' story. Here the conditions of working-class childhood are portrayed as more adverse than they actually were in order to maximise the achievements of the 'self-made' man (*sic*) in 'heroically' overcoming these early obstacles of birth. Thus the themes of apprenticeship are decoded in terms of career in the autobiographies of the socially mobile. Conversely working-class inheritances can be reworked in terms of the vocation code to lend an evangelical fervour to sentimental accounts of poverty and the 'good old days and ways'.

Now the point about the family romance in all its forms, and why it is so central to adolescent transitions, is that it potentially connects the child to sites of social aspiration outside both family *and* school, yet in a way that normally tempers parental envy or ambition with a sense of shared pride in origins. That very opening, instead of simply sending working-class adolescents off on a wild goose-chase in search of ideal homes, dream jobs or Mr/Ms Right drives them to construct out of materials to hand (friends, work-mates, the neighbourhood) those territories of desire (Freud's 'other scenes') which make the oppressive circumstances of working-class life and labour seem just about bearable. But other outcomes are also possible. For example, if the household is socially isolated, or its grids of cultural transmission are weak and confused, then the family romance is far less likely to be decentred and relativised. Instead it springs a narcissistic trap for the likes of Billy Liar to grow up into 'working-class heroes' whom nobody recognises except their own, secret ideal selves. The picture is complicated though by the fact that girls and boys are positioned differently both within real kinship networks, and within the field of family ideology.[18]

Some of these issues became clearer as a result of the materials generated through the homework exercise. We had asked the students to photograph the people, places and practices which were especially significant for them and then to turn them into a montage as a 'personal portrait' accompanied by an autobiographical statement. Many of the key references in these panels were imaginary – wish fulfilments revolving around high life and fast cars. Significantly it was the boys who were likely to indulge in fantasies of spectacular consumption. However the portraits also highlighted everyday experiences, interests, activities, important locations and commitments at home. The girls' portraits tended to emphasise this type of reference more than the boys, though they were not necessarily more home-centred. Elements of romance also entered in, of course, but they had a different form and function from that of the boys. We were already seeing the emergence of a double standard of representation and this, of course, reflected funda-mental differences in the girls' and boys' transitions, and the way these are organised within the grids of apprenticeship and inheri-tance.

The montages of Jane and Jamie make interesting reading from this point of view (see plates). Jane was going to be a hairdresser. She was the most definite and confident member of the group when it came to discussing plans for the future. Indeed her disinterest in school (she rarely went) stemmed from the strength of her commitment to what she already referred to as her 'career'. But then she had already made the transition to work at home. She had, as she put it, grown up with hairdressing. It was in her family. Her

JANE

I handle the cue pretty well. I'm not very photogenic.

I always used to go in the Café . . . talk to my mates, play on the machines.

The photograph of me holding the kettle . . . whenever, I go to someone's house it's always me that ends up making the tea. It's the same at home, they're always saying, 'Jane, put the kettle on.' I'm just a dogsbody. But I'm a very active person. Donna, Nicola and me, we're the only girls who play pool at Nick's Café . . . it's across the road from where Donna lives. Well, I used to go in there all the time, but now I don't so much. That's because of my boyfriend. He doesn't like me going in there. He's very possessive. If I go to the Café to get some fags he goes, 'Who was there, who did you talk to?' When I'm at home, I go out on purpose sometimes, just to annoy him. He's really boring; he just likes to stay indoors with me. But I like to go out and enjoy myself. I like pool, darts and discos. My mum sticks up for me when I have rows with my boyfriend about it. I think it's important to keep up your interests and your mates.

JAMIE

School's brilliant. I get on with everyone. I've left school already. I ain't going back no more. I'll be working, messengers, on a motor bike. My mum's buying me one – as soon as I'm 16 – I'm going to be a despatch rider. My brother used to do it, but he got the sack. He went to Buckingham Palace and nicked a pair of shoes. I might be going to work on the lorries. I've done it for about a year. Or I might work with my brother in this catering firm. Or I could just sign on. I'll probably just work on the lorries as long as I want, until it gets boring.

Mark: Every job gets boring . . . depends what you're doing, though.

Jane: If you're having a laugh and mucking about time goes quick.

mother, aunt, elder brother and cousins were all in the business. As a small girl she had watched her mother doing friends' hair at home. Quite early on she had been taught how to shampoo and set; later she had worked as a helper in the family salon. From all these sources she had picked up a wealth of knowledge about styles and techniques and how to deal with customers – skills she now fully intended to capitalise in looking for work, with the help of her family connections.

The fact that she constructed hairdressing as a career had less to do with the industry's attempt to professionalise its training structures (which in any case she had sidestepped) than the way the appalling conditions in the industry (low pay for long hours) are justified as leading step by step to the promised land of self-employment (running your own salon). Few ever make it of course, but the ambition runs deep. Jane's 'family salon' turned out to mean merely the salon where members of her family worked – part of a chain owned by a leisure combine!

Jane may have been in love with hairdressing, but she had few illusions about the actual job, especially the apprentices' lot. The photo-story she put together on this theme shows her getting the rough end of the deal from both manager and client. Equally, her description of her own, domestic, apprenticeship, may have been tinged with elements of a 'family romance', but if she was dreaming of becoming a princess of the salons, she was most certainly not waiting around for some Prince Charming to make it all come true. This comes out strongly in her comments about her boyfriend, which she included in her personal statement. It is clear from these that she was far from charmed by his attempts to lord it over her!

At the same time, Jane said, in a significant phrase, that she had grown up with hairdressing *in her fingers*. Skill for her was a natural aptitude, a cultural legacy literally embodied in her, providing a quasi-congenital link between her origins and her destiny. In fact, in this family, occupational succession was both a female and male tradition stretching back to the grandparents' generation. Thus for Jane, growing-up was most definitely an apprenticeship to an inheritance. But if she was positioned within a *strong* grid, that also meant that she experienced the tension between the two codes, between the positions of active appropriation made possible by the former and the positions of passive reproduction imposed by the latter, in a particularly acute way. This emerged clearly when she came to montage her personal portrait. She had plenty of images of herself as an active subject – 'an active person who likes playing snooker and pool' as she put it. But she also had photographs of herself passively playing out the 'little woman' role. In the first version of her panel, she positioned a large picture of herself holding a kettle in the left foreground, dominating the other, more active images. But in the final version, shown here, the emphasis is reversed. The domestic image is reduced in size, and 'bleached' so that it fades into the background against the dynamic image of her at the pool-table. Wish fulfilment or an actual process of negotiation? Jane may have wanted to follow in her mother's footsteps, but this was into hairdressing, not the kitchen sink. The purely domestic register of both codes *was* being rejected. She was struggling to challenge male preserves (as pool-player and breadwinner) while still maintaining a style of femininity (in her clothes, make-up, etc.) which was conventionally glamorous. This was possible for two reasons in her case – first because strong grids provide adolescents with a sense of continuity between where they are 'coming from' as children and where they are 'going to' as adults in terms of a class place. But this itinerary did not have to follow every signpost of the family romance, despite her boyfriend's attempt to trap her in the 'Great Indoors'. Jane's position was sufficiently decentred within a wider network of affiliation, to enable her struggle for autonomy to be endorsed as expressing kinship with other members of the family, who also had resisted the closures of 'the couple'. Her father was as proud of his daughter's skill at pool, as her mother was of the fact that Jane stood up to her boyfriend so well. She was 'taking after' her mother's brother and father's sister in these respects! A similar set of relays came into play in supporting Jane through the immediate transition from school. At first the promised job failed to materialise. It looked as if, at this critical moment, all her family connections in the business would fail to deliver the goods. Yet there were also plenty of family precedents for both this situation and for her decision to stick it out; she refused to go on a YOP scheme; she would wait until what she wanted turned up as indeed it eventually did – a position as a junior in a flourishing high-street salon.

Most working-class girls do not have so much room for manoeuvre of course. The grid of inheritance locks them into a chronic position of maturity from an early age, whence they are simultaneously exploited and idealised as 'little wives and mothers' (i.e.

domestic apprentices) both at home and in the labour market. Moreover, once they take a step outside the protective frame of their own peer group romance, girls find themselves trapped back in the double bind positions always and already assigned to them by the system of male sexual apprenticeship: baby-faced virgins or old whores.

The difference between girls' and boys' transitions is the difference between the rephrasing of a structural subordination and the resolution of a conjunctural contradiction. For girls the wage form offers a brief encounter with an autonomy which bears all the traces of 'domestication'; but for boys it signifies a licence to deny the fact of continued dependence on the family, in assuming masculine rights without adult responsibilities. This stems from the split positioning of boys within working-class culture. The rites of passage into shopfloor cultures customarily place the lad in a quasi-feminine position *vis-à-vis* male elders; he is subjected to sexual teasing, treated as a skivvy, sent on errands for 'left-handed spanners' and generally 'shown up' as soft or incompetent by the older men. At the same time, in the family culture, the boy is held in a quasi-infantile position *vis-à-vis* female elders; he is fed, cleaned up, has his clothes washed for him, and is generally babied. His assumption of masculinity and maturity involves the unconscious conservation of this infantile position in and through the disavowal of all the despised 'feminine' features associated with his 'other place'. The sexual and economic power of male elders is thus not confronted directly; rather their role at work and in the family is assumed by the boy through a series of inversions and transpositions of its symbolic terms played out in relation to mothers, sisters, girl-friends and other boys. These patterns of transference are encoded in both the family romance and in youth-cultural forms, especially in the structures of sexual apprenticeship which link both to a line of male inheritances. For example shopfloor custom has traditionally 'apprenticed' the 'virgin worker' to the 'woman who is old enough to be his mother' who sexually initiates him only to be confirmed a 'slag'. This is followed by a phase in which the young 'improver' perfects his mastery of sexual technique by seducing younger, preferably virgin girls. Out on the street meanwhile, groups of 'hard men' play at king-of-the-castle by elaborating a whole series of territorial devices to feminise and belittle other boys from the neighbourhood. Once indoors, however, the hard nut metamorphoses into the 'family man' as soon as he pays over a proportion of his wage packet to his mum for board and lodging – the payment making him feel grown up about continuing to be babied.

Unemployment, and the weakening of cultural supports, has simply had the effect of privatising these structures, restricting them to the level of phantasy, rather than elaborating them in peer-group ritual or myth. Jamie's story and personal portrait illustrate this all too clearly.

Jamie, like Jane, presented a picture of self-confidence. It was not that he had no plans for leaving school, he had too many. He could work with his step-father on the lorries, or with his brother in catering, or get a job as a despatch rider with his new motor bike, or even become a photographer (after our course!). His only problem, it seemed, was an embarrassment of riches.

It was hard to tell fact from phantasy. By his account his family connections included a famous uncle who played in a rock band and 'knew Bert Weedon', and an Aunt who had a villa in the South of France. All that we could discover about his real family was that his step-father was an unemployed bricklayer and did not get on with Jamie at all.

Throughout the course Jamie plied us with questions. Questions like 'Please, Sir, can I borrow the camera tonight?' 'Please Sir, what kind of bike did you have?' 'Please Sir, do you like Black Sabbath?' all asked in the tones of a little boy asking for sweets. Was he really thirsting for knowledge, or was it all an elaborate wind-up? The answer is 'both, and neither'. At one level he was drawing a caricature of the model son or pupil, which he might once have tried or failed to become. But as soon as we responded to his questions we found ouselves led by the nose for a bit and then slapped down by a sudden sarcasm or withdrawal, put back in our place (as teachers and male elders) *and in his*. For what Jamie was doing was leading us into a trap which had been sprung on him at school and in his family.

What is the primary experience of schooling for most working class children? It is the experience of being constantly encouraged to answer teachers' questions and then as soon as they rise to the bait (and fail to get it right) being slapped down. And what do most working class children start out wanting to do at school? Go into any 'infants' class' and you'll see. They want to 'please sir or miss' because that is the only way their desire to be recognised in the first person singular gets recognised by that strange anonymous figure of authority the State has put *in loco parentis*. Yet if Jamie's name is called in the classroom, it is usually to summon him back to a purely legal place of attendance, in which nothing that makes him, Jamie, count for much. In one sense then Jamie was simply giving us a taste of our own medicine as teachers. He was cutting us down to size and making us feel small, by playing teacher to our pupil. He was also exploiting our desire as teachers to impart knowledge, while satisfying his own for personal attention, yet subtly sending the whole process up so that he could shine in the eyes of his peers as 'piss artist', who had conned us into thinking him a teacher's pet. He won either way, or so he thought, while trapping us in his own cleft stick. That was one of the perverse pleasures he got from his game of 'please sir'.

But there was more in the game than that. It was also about turning the tables on us as male elders. Jamie was no hard man. That particular strategy of disavowal had for one reason or another been blocked off. Instead he borrowed 'feminine' techniques of seductiveness and charm and transformed them into secret props of his male self-esteem. He began by flattering us, feeding us questions, hanging on our every word, the way girls have traditionally been taught to 'hook their man'. But as soon as we picked up his words they led us in quite a different direction. They strung us along, they took us for a ride, until he got tired of it and told us, unceremoniously, where to get off – a very masculine technique, and one which all too effectively placed us in a 'one-down' feminine position.

If Jamie replayed elements of his family romance in relation to us, he deployed quite another mode of seduction towards his peers. Jamie fancied himself as a 'ladies' man', something of a Don Juan, irresistible to younger girls, attractive to older women too. He was already planning to get married, even though he was not even 'going steady'. An unproblematic inheritance of good looks supported this structure of apprenticeship. If school was so brilliant, by his account (even though he couldn't wait to leave) it seemed to be because it provided a stage on which he could romance about his sexual conquests to his more impressionable 'mates'. Yet from our observations he was very shy with girls.

So it comes about that in his personal portrait, the little-boy-lost of 'please sir' is transfigured into the suave young man about town.

The doubled image of himself in nonchalant pose, denies what it also signifies – his split positioning. Instead he has made an image of himself in a seamless web of past, present and future accomplishments. The panel seems to be saying that the world is his oyster and Jamie is one of its hidden pearls! This is a young man who is 'going places' (in the Mercedes!) and if he has an image of the council estate where he actually lives, it is only as a backdrop to show how far he has already come.

Yet behind all this, there was still a real little-boy-lost struggling to grow up. If Jamie was such a willing apprentice on the course, it was not primarily to acquire our actual skills, but to find a symbolic framework within which whatever was transmitted by elders came as a birthright, not as a legacy corrupted by a seductive power game called education or family love. For behind all the questions he asked us, was one he could not put into words, about his origins and his destiny and the real means he had to master to connect the two. For where the grids of apprenticeship and inheritance are weak and confused neither the question nor the answers are easy to articulate. Instead they sponsor the more perverse forms of individualism, in which the hidden injuries of class are patched over by ever more subtle techniques of impression management and playing it cool. Yet Jamie's position is challenged by both Mark and Jane (see panel statement). Jamie boasts that he can work on the lorries as long as he wants – 'until he gets bored with it'. Their rejoinder points the way out of this fools paradise, and back towards real, collective forms of resistance to boredom.

Jane and Jamie represent just two of the many faces of working class individualism, and the complex way this is articulated through reproduction codes. For Jane 'being her own boss' meant both standing up to boys *and* owning her own salon. Her position within the family romance made it possible for her to challenge aspects of patriarchy, but also to confuse that struggle with her petty bourgeois aspirations. What we attempted to do, through the medium of photo-story work which cross-referenced the subjective and objective aspects of school transitions, was to help her differentiate more clearly between issues of gender and class, without foreclosing their lived dialectic. For Jamie, in contrast, 'being your own boss' meant omnipotently controlling one's own image. Here, and again through the medium of photo-story construction, we attempted to unearth some of the principles of hope which were hidden behind this façade, and to ground them in a sense of shared predicament with peers. Modest aims, by no means easy to achieve or evaluate, and yet perhaps no less worthwhile for that?

I have emphasised the role of family dynamics in these school transitions for several reasons: first because, for this group, they were so central, second, because they have been largely ignored in most sociological accounts. Third, I have tried to show how a cultural studies approach can provide a more sensitive reading of transitions; instead of trying to measure conscious plans against official routes, it enables us to bring to the surface a rather different agenda, belonging to a more hidden curriculum vitae. The little differences in positioning which this reveals can make a big difference to outcomes within the limits imposed by political and economic conditions. Objectively, all our group shared a similar location in school, and all belonged to what is termed the 'respectable working-class'. Yet the variety of perspectives they adopted and the range of circumstances in which they found themselves six months after leaving school, could not be put down simply to the lottery of life chances or the 'infelicities' of individual psychology. It had more to do with their positioning within a field of family relations, both real and imaginary, which was itself socially constructed. Far from offering a counsel of despair for teachers, I believe this theoretical approach can help pinpoint alternative educational practices which can make a real difference to actual outcomes – and perhaps that is not unimportant, either personally or politically for teachers at the present time.

Taking it all back to school

One of the effects of the current crisis, is to make us feel that whatever we do as teachers makes absolutely no difference to the outcome for young people. Whatever we might like to think we are doing, we are only helping to school them for the dole. That is the message we often get, rightly or wrongly, from functionalist accounts of education and reproduction, but this view is only the flip side of that well known mental disorder, 'Teachers Hubris', the delusion that what we do in the classroom should make the whole world of difference to our pupils.

These positions are not only personal, they are political. The first leads to an underestimation of the difference that education can still make to working-class pupils, and an under-valuation of their culture too. For if codes of apprenticeship are read through the incremental grids of academic and professional career, they can *only* show up as signs of deficit. These signs can then be freely interpreted as marks of a congenital lack of intelligence and natural aptitude about which nothing can be done – a negative echo of a popular working-class fatalism concerning 'brains' and those who are born with them.

In contrast radical teachers tend to *over*value working-class culture and *over*estimate their own role as agents of social change. This is largely because they read both through the grid of vocation rather than career. Not only is teaching itself constructed as a special calling (the preserve of the charismatic elect!) but pupils' lives are meant to be educationally unfolded according to a somewhat similar plan, as the search for authentic self-expression impelled by an inner voice or 'I'. Now nothing in the ideological grammar of working class autobiographies corresponds to *this* curriculum vitae. This does not stop some people romanticising working-class culture, waxing lyrical about the authenticity of its expressive, especially youthful, forms, even investing them with an inner mission to change the world which they clearly do not possess. Only with the recession came the grim realisation that in this society, if many are called, few are chosen, and on the whole they are not, from the working-class. The collapse of the old-style progressivism has left radical teachers in a weak position to defend their practices against the demands of the new utilitarians, or to take a firm stand against those reactionary aspects of working-class culture which the Black Paperites, and then Thatcher so success-fully mobilised against us.

The antidote must lie in developing a better-proportioned sense of what specific differences alternative practices (e.g. in the field of political, social, or anti-sexist or racist education) can make to particular groups of pupils. We need other measures than the crude indices offered by the Rutter report, and they will also have to include some better rules of thumb as to where our pupils are 'coming from' in a period when cultural forms are fragmenting and changing so fast.

In fact, even in Rutter terms, the course would have to be judged a success. For example in a student group which contained a high proportion of school non-attenders (in both senses of the word) there was a 100 per cent record on the course. Some idea of the energy released can be gained from the fact that over 1000 photographs and 50 hours of tape were produced during the fortnight, from which an exhibition, comprising thirty-six panels has been made.

Perhaps more significant was the fact that their form teachers all commented on the difference the course seemed to have made to these young people. They were 'more confident', 'more grown up', more 'self-assured'. However these evaluations are judged, they were echoed in the student's own appreciation of what they had got from the course. At the very least this seems to indicate that by concentrating on expressive practices one can achieve as good 'results' as those claimed for more instrumentalist approaches.

What are the implications of the course? Are there any? Can a course like this be reproduced? If so in what form and under what conditions? We remembered the special conditions we had managed to secure for ourselves – a relatively small group, an off-school site, a block timetable, and a teacher pupil ratio of 1:5 (and even then we often felt overstretched!). Moreover, we have had the *time* to analyse and write up our practice. Readers will not need reminding that those conditions do not exist in State schools at the present time!

In retrospect it seems that this approach is most easily adaptable to the growing number of unemployed youth projects concerned to develop forms of social education and community arts. But clearly, apart from that, the methods of cultural studies turn very awkwardly on the hardening relationships between schooling and training. I am far from underestimating the inroads into general education currently being made by the MSC, and in particular by the NVTEI. The crucial question though is where and how can a fight back be best made?

Here I believe that many educationalists have been blinded by the 'success' of MSC expansionism, into locating the problem exclusively within the frame of 16–19 provision. How this has come about is easier to see than to resist. The unpleasant fact is that popular support for MSC initiatives (SLS and all) stems from the way they exploit *real* deficiencies in secondary schooling, while doing nothing to remedy them. MSC supervisors can frequently be heard boasting that they are giving their recruits a 'proper education' for the first time in their lives. The truth is that despite overall rising educational standards a minority of young people do leave school without proficiency in basic numeracy and literacy, however that is defined. Of course they always did. State schooling has never been popular amongst sizeable sections of the working-class. It does not follow that it is not a potential site for constructing a popular educational practice.

Under present conditions that is clearly a long way off. But if a start is to be made in engaging with the real terms of this crisis, then perhaps we need to rethink our line of attack. Might it not be possible, here, to take a leaf out of the MSC book, but turn the page in the opposite direction? Just as the new vocationalism has been carried from '16–19 training' into the secondary school, there could be a countermove in the opposite direction – *first to construct alternative curricular and teaching practices around the problematics of transition in the secondary school and then carry them forward into post-school education*.

Certainly, under progressive authorities like ILEA, there is still more scope for innovation in schools than in the heavily-policed YTS schemes and it is what happens to young people in secondary school that positions them *vis-à-vis* the statutory agencies of transition.

One immediate implication of this is that we need to consider ways of implementing an alternative reading of futures much earlier in school life. For example what effect might a course like ours have for third-year pupils *before* they decided on their subject options. We would guess that it would make them less easily steered, much more likely to make real choices against the grain of dominant expectations. In this context it would be important to run girls' courses to develop a feminist reading of transitions, more effectively than we were able to do.[19]

I am not, though, underestimating the obstacles to be overcome. Chief among them is the fact that the State school remains hostage to an élitist and divisive examination system. We saw what disparaging views our students had of that! They knew the CSEs they were taking represented a bankrupt currency, one that was neither cashable through the incremental banking system of 'career' nor even in terms of an ordinary unskilled job. But the examination issue underlines our point; the essential battle-lines are to be drawn in and around secondary schooling.

As to the effort reported here, I am all too aware that it has only scratched the surface of the problem. Courses for school-leavers will always be a case of 'too little too late'. The purpose in moving from a theoretical critique of the new vocationalism towards an alternative practice was in any event not just to produce a bigger and better kind of link course. It was to show that social and life-skill ideology can not only be deconstructed, but that an alternative cultural studies approach can be developed in its place.

Up until now all the subtle dialectics of educational theory have proved no match for Thatcherism's crude thoughts. But if we are to show parents and teachers, and most importantly young people themselves, that there is a realistic alternative to 'schooling for the dole' then we must begin to argue back from the strengths of our own practices. Only then can we start to claim back some of the grounds of educational advance which have been so disastrously lost.

Notes

1. The fieldwork on which this chapter draws was carried out in the London Borough of Southwark in 1982. A fuller report of these findings will appear in Cohen (1984). Some of the ideas developed here first appeared in 'Schooling for the Dole' in *New Socialist*, 3 (1982). I would like to thank Steve Butters of the Post 16 Education Centre for his many helpful suggestions, and my colleagues in the Department of Sociology at the Institute, especially Michael Young and Tony Green, for their encouragement and support. Finally Professor Basil Bernstein, Head of the Sociological Research Unit, convinced me of the need to pursue this line of enquiry, and gave much impetus to its completion.

2. Most critiques of youth training schemes tend to reduce their ideological function to one of mystification, deduced either from the political role of the MSC, or the economic policies of Thatcherism. In these terms YOPS and YTS is part of a wider strategy of crisis management which aims at restructuring capital at the expense of labour. See the contributions to Cole and Skelton (1980), Rees and Atkinson (1982), Moos (1979), Finn (1983) and LRTG (1983). The difficulty with this 'left functionalist' reading is not only that it tends to topple over into a kind of meta-conspiracy theory (see Scofield *et al.*, 1983) but that in doing so it ignores the specific effectivity of ideological *forms* of training, and their relation to issues of educa-

tional practice. In emphasising this dimension the present chapter is close to the perspective developed by contributors to Wolpe (1983).

3. These initiatives can be found emerging from various parts of the political spectrum. For example, Ed Berman, of Interaction, one of Mrs Thatcher's policy advisers on community development in the inner city, has pioneered a programme to teach unemployed youth a range of entrepreneurial skills to help them market their own cultural products more profitably. Meanwhile Professor Newman is developing a programme of 'life-style enhancement' for the Labour administration at the GLC. This approach is especially popular amongst black self-help and community projects. Its origins, however, are to be found in the rather different circumstances of the 'idle rich' in the West Coast of the USA. These unfortunate people, with more time and money on their hands than they knew what to do with turned to specially trained 'leisure counsellors' to advise them on forms of rational recreation and 'life course planning'.

4. Wiener (1982) traces the prevalence of an 'anti-industrial spirit' at a time when Britain was supposedly the 'workshop of the world' to the fact that the cultural codes of aristocracy remained the referential model to which both the bourgeoisie and lower middle class aspired. Bailey's study of the rational recreation movement (1978) provides the missing link for understanding how popular revulsion against factory conditions came to be channelled into the safer pursuits of the Great Outdoors. For examples of how this whole problematic has been recast in contemporary debates see Ball (1979); Watts (1983) Veal *et al*. (1983). For a neo-Marxist version of the post-industrial society thesis see Gorz (1983); also the more pragmatic arguments of Sherman and Jenkins (1979).

5. Many accounts of youth unemployment are so anxious to avoid making young people responsible for their predicament that they go to the opposite extreme and portray them as passive victims of conditions they neither understand or control (White and Brocklington, 1983). Psychological accounts tend to pathologise the experience, focusing on stress factors and the individual's inner resources for coping (Stokes, 1983). A more adequate acount would have to relate the structural position of youth labour within the capitalist economy to the changing forms of cultural reproduction within which the lived meanings of unemployment are constructed. Casson (1979) still offers the best overview of the political economy of youth unemployment.

6. In most studies the relations between discipline and skill have either been taken for granted, or treated in a rather one-sided way. Marxist approaches (Thompson, 1967; More, 1980; Braverman, 1974) tend

to treat discipline as a purely repressive instrument of capitalist coercion pitted against skill as a purely expressive agency of proletarian knowledge. Foucault (1978) challenges this reading, arguing that discipline *empowers* the subject through its regulation of bodies; conversely skill regulates the subject through the *mastery* of techniques. Apart from a study of monitorial schools (Jones and Williamson, 1979) this perspective has yet to be brought to bear on understanding contemporary changes in skill/discipline regimes. The view taken here is that the new vocationalism not only corresponds externally to changes in the mental/manual division of labour, but that it involves reconstructing mind/body relations within the social-isation process. Historically the shift is from regimes where the ordering of the young body is modelled on the operation of the machine engine, while the mind is drilled to programme it with instructions, to regimes where the body is enclosed within its own autonomic processes, while the training of young minds is modelled on the operations of the digital computer. From a perspective totally hostile to Foucault's 'archaeology of knowledge' the studies of Marcuse (1964) and Elias (1978) nevertheless powerfully confirm his key insights. See also Sohn-Rethel (1978).

7. See, for example, Brailsford (1983), Cambell and Jones (1983) and Smith (1983).

8. Much of what follows draws on a theory of reproduction codes developed in Cohen (1984). In specifying the distinctive features of four such codes and tracing the history of their articulations to the youth question it became apparent that skill was an important though often hidden, referent. It entered into the construction of both the grid of subject positions, and the gender markers of im/maturity which act as 'diachronic shifters' between these positions. For an account of the role which inheritance, vocation and career codes play in the formation of educational ideology and class discourse see Bisseret (1978). An application of this theory to understanding changing patterns of political socialisation within the working class can be found in Cohen (1983).

9. Historical accounts of youth policy and provision have tended to overemphasise these continuities. See, for example, the otherwise interesting study by Horne (1984). Samuel Smiles' classic texts (1859 and 1894) are a fascinating source for discourse analysis, as is the juvenile literature of the period which articulates many of the same themes. Historical studies of rational recreation and self-improve-ment (Bailey, 1978; Morris, 1970), though useful, tend to give a purely positivist reading of these texts. A similar difficulty is present in the account of self-help movements between the wars by Susman

(1979). Lasch (1980) develops a trenchant critique of the post-war personal growth movement from the vantage-point of both psychoanalytic theory and the American tradition of cultural studies.

10. In tracing the provenance of the disparate elements that make up social and life skills ideology I have followed Griffith (1983) in concentrating on its core problematics and forms of implantation. This is not about assessing the relative influence of this or that text. Thus I have taken the work of Argyle (1978, 1980) as paradigmatic because in my view it exemplifies a problematic which is elsewhere present in more submerged or disguised forms (e.g. Priestley and Maguire, 1978; Hopson and Scally, 1981a, b). This is not to deny the specificity of these more explicitly educational variants, or the role which particular institutional relay systems may play in modifying elements of the ideology (e.g. the work of the Further Education Unit, 1980, 1981, 1982).

11. Quotation from Hopson and Scally in *Liberal Education*, 44 (1981).

12. The materials I reviewed were published between 1979 and 1982. Many of them were produced in association with the National Extension College, and were linked to a new wave of 'teen TV' programmes. They included *Roadshow*, *Jobmate*, *16Up*, *Help*, *Just the Job* and *The Job Hunter Kit*. I also looked at materials produced by the Careers Research and Advisory Centre.

13. The classic historical study of possessive individualism (Macpherson, 1962) treats it as a political ideology corresponding to capitalist property relations. Its specific conditions of reproduction as *behavioural* ideology have rarely been studied with the same historical depth, but see Busfield (1974) on its family forms. The approach adopted here is based on the pioneering work of Edelman (1979), who, in outlining the constitution of legal subject forms and their relation to the development of new consciousness industries, paved the way for a more sophisticated theory of individualism in its changing modalities. The shift analysed here is from the competitive form of status and property acquisition to a non-competitive but self-possessive form. In psychoanalytic terms this corresponds to a regression from secondary to primary narcissism as the basis of cultural identifications (see Chassaguet-Smirgel, 1976, and Lasch, 1980). Williams (1983) makes some interesting comments on what he defines as the 'mobile privatisation' of the new working class which seems to be an intermediate form between the competitive and the self-possessive.

14. Winnicott (1965), from a Kleinian perspective, argues that the splitting mechanisms described here are attributable to developmental difficulties which prevent a 'normal' process of integration in the

subject. However, this defence mechanism appears to be a normative feature of cultural forms which facilitate the survival of 'underdog' groups. It is significant, however, that most strategies of consciousness-raising involving these groups (e.g. sexual or ethnic minorities) challenge 'splitting', and aim to set in motion a collective process of self-affirmation. Whether these techniques amount to a genuine form of integration, or whether they merely lead to a separatist closure around a peer group romance seems open to debate. But they are certainly an improvement on playing it cool.

15. The counselling ideology deployed by the MSC is set out in Miller (1983a, b). Procktor (1978) provides an overview of the current state of the counselling industry – essentially a mishmash of conflicting and diluted models of psychotherapy. The study of adolescents' responses to counselling by Porteus and Fisher (1980) hardly inspires confidence. For a withering critique of the function of 'pseudo-psy' therapies in the field of state intervention see Donzelot (1979).

16. The course described here was planned and taught in collaboration with Adrian Chappell of the Cockpit Cultural Studies Department. A more detailed discussion of this project can be found in Cohen and Chappell (1983). *Leavers Believers*, an exhibition of work produced by students on the course, is available on hire from the Cockpit Gallery, Princeton Street, London, WC1. The course would not have been possible without the active support of John Stevens, then Head of Social Studies at Walworth School, Southwark, and now ILEA Advisor on Political Education. Our thanks to him and to the students for their enthusiastic commitment.

17. Our curriculum model combined elements of collect and integrated codes in the terms developed by Bernstein (1974). Our teaching methods involved weak classification and strong framing. See Cohen and Chappell (1983).

18. This approach, which involves a shift from a notion of transitions to one of transpositions, is developed further in Cohen (1984).

19. Further courses are currently being developed as part of a wider project of collaboration between the Cockpit Cultural Studies and the Post-16 Education Centre. This project has been funded by the Greater London Council, and involves the production of a school leavers' guide to the crisis – a photo-text for use in social education – and two further exhibitions.

References

Argyle, M., *Social Skills and Mental Health* (London: Methuen, 1978).
Argyle, M., *Social Skills and Work* (London: Methuen, 1980).
Bailey, P., *Leisure and Class in Victorian Britain* (London: Routledge & Kegan Paul, 1978).
Ball, C. and M., *Fit for Work* (London: Chameleon, 1979).
Barker, D., *Sex and Generation* (London: Tavistock, 1980).
Berg, I., *Education and Jobs* (Harmondsworth: Penguin, 1973).
Bernstein, B., *Class, Codes Control*, vol. 3 (London: Routledge & Kegan Paul, 1977).
Bisseret, N., *Education, Class Language and Ideology* (London: Routledge & Kegan Paul, 1978).
Brailsford, P., *Give us a Break* (London: MSC, 1983).
Braverman, H., *Labour and Monopoly Capital* (New York: Monthly Review Press, 1974).
Busfield, J., 'Ideologies and Reproduction' in Richards, M., (ed.), *The Integration of a Child into a Social World* (Cambridge University Press, 1974).
Campbell, M. and Jones, D., *Asian Youths in the Labour Market* (EEC/DES, 1983).
Casson, M., *Youth Unemployment* (London: Macmillan, 1979).
Chassaguet-Smirgel, J., 'Some Thoughts on the Ego Ideal', *Psychoanalytic Quarterly*, vol. 45, 1976.
Cohen, P., 'Losing the Generation Game', *New Socialist*, 14, 1983.
Cohen, P., *Stopping the Wheels* (London: Macmillan, 1984).
Cohen, P. and Chappell, A., 'Leavers and the Three 'L's', *Schooling and Culture*, 13, 1983.
Cole, M. and Skelton, B. (eds) *Blind Alley* (Hesketh, 1980).
Donzelot, J., *The Policing of Families* (London: Hutchinson, 1979).
Edelman, B., *Ownership of the Image* (London: Routledge & Kegan Paul, 1979).
Elias, N., *The Civilising Process* (London: Methuen, 1975).
Finn, D., 'The Youth Training Scheme', *Youth and Policy*, vol. I, 4.
Foucault, M., *Discipline and Punish* (London: Allen Lane, 1978).
Further Education Unit, *Vocational Preparation* (1981), *Developing Social and Life Skills* (1980), *Basic Skills* (1982).
Gorz, A., *Farewell to the Working Class* (London: Pluto, 1983).
Griffith, A., *Skilling for Life/Living for Skill* (Toronto: OISE, 1983).
Hopson, B. and Scally, M., *Lifeskills Training* (London: McGraw-Hill, 1981).

Hopson, B. and Scally, M., 'Life-skills Teaching in Schools and Colleges', *Liberal Education*, no. 44, 1981.

Horne, J., 'Youth Unemployment Programmes – A Historical Account', in Gleeson, D., (ed.), *Youth Training and the Search for Work* (London: Routledge & Kegan Paul, 1984).

Jones, K. and Williamson, K., 'The Birth of the Schoolroom', *Ideology and Consciousness*, 6, 1979.

Labour Party, *16–19 Learning for Life* (London, 1983).

Labour Research Training Group, *Training and the State* (1983).

Lasch, C., *The Culture of Narcissism* (London: Abacus, 1980).

Macpherson, C.B., *The Political Theory of Possessive Individualism* (Oxford: Blackwell, 1962).

Marcuse, H., *One Dimensional Man* (London: Routledge & Kegan Paul, 1964).

Miller, J. *et al.*, *Tutoring* (FEU/NICEC, 1983).

Miller, J. *et al.*, *Towards a Personal Guidance Base* (FEU, 1983).

Moos, M., *Government Youth Training Policy and its Impact on Further Education* (Birmingham: CCCS, 1979).

More, C., *Skill and the Working Class* (London: Croom-Helm, 1980).

Morris, R.J., 'The History of Self Help', *New Society*, 3 December 1970.

Porteus, M. and Fisher, C., 'Counselling Support and Advice – The Adolescent Viewpoint', *British Journal of Guidance and Counselling*, vol. 8, no. 1, 1980.

Priestley, P. and MacGuire, J., *Social Skills and Personal Problem Solving* (London: Tavistock, 1978).

Procktor, B., *Counselling Shop* (London: Deutsch, 1978).

Rees, T. and Atkinson, P., *Youth Unemployment and State Intervention* (London: Routledge & Kegan Paul, 1982).

School Leavers Book (1982) (London: Longmans Resources Unit).

Scofield, P., Preston, E. and Jacques, E., *The Tories' Poisoned Apple* (ILP, 1983).

Sennett, R. and Cobb, J., *The Hidden Injuries of Class* (Cambridge University Press, 1977).

Sherman, B. and Jenkins, C., *The Collapse of Work* (London: Methuen, 1979).

Smiles, S., *Self Help* (London: Murray, 1859).

Smiles, S., *Character* (London: Murray, 1894).

Smith, G., *Young People's Responses to YOP* (Oxford Dept of Social and Administrative Studies, 1981).

Sohn-Rethel, A., *Intellectual and Manual Labour* (London: Macmillan, 1978).

Stokes, G., 'Out of School, Out of Work', *Youth and Policy*, 2, 2, 1983.

Susman, W., *Culture and Commitment 1929–45* (London: Academic Press, 1979).

Thompson, E.P., 'Time, Work Discipline and Industrial Capitalism', *Past and Present*, 38, 1967.

Veal, G., Parker, H. and Coalton, W., *Work and Leisure: Unemployment, Technology and Life Style*, Leisure Studies Association, 15, 1983.

Watts, A.G., *Unemployment, Education and the Future of Work* (London: Macmillan, 1983).

White, R. and Brockinton, L., *Tales out of School* (London: Routledge & Kegan Paul, 1983).

Wiener, M., *The Decline of the Industrial Spirit* (London: Croom-Helm, 1982).

Williams, R., 'End of an Era', *New Left Review*, 181, 1983.

Winnicott, D.W., 'Ego Distortion in Terms of True and False Self', in *The Maturational Process and the Facilitating Environment* (London: Tavistock, 1965).

Wolpe, A.M. (ed.), *Is There Anyone Here from Education?* (London: Pluto, 1983).

5

From Vocational Guidance to life Skills: Historical Perspectives on Careers Education

Inge Bates

In recent years the teaching profession has taken an increasing interest in careers education and its currently popular variant, social and life skills. Several thousand teachers have now participated in the numerous in-service courses which provide an introduction to the subject paradigm and pedagogy. Such courses are not generally places for reflective critical scrutiny of the curriculum package which is being presented; there is a tendency to dwell on what might be termed the superstructure rather than the substructure of the subject or, in other words, the topics, teaching materials and methods rather than on underlying premises and assumptions.

This chapter[1] outlines some of the key stages in the development of the professional conceptualisation of careers education, beginning with the 'talent-matching' model which provided a formula for vocational guidance in the early part of the century, following the birth and progress of the 'developmental' model which became dominant in the 1960s and finally suggesting the impact on careers education of the economic climate of the late 1970s and 1980s and massive rises in youth unemployment. The focus is on the substructure of the subject, or the subject paradigm, in which a central theme has been commitment to the goal of encouraging individual self-development and self-actualisation. It is argued that, consequently, there is an inevitable tension between careers education and society, which must logically vary inversely with the opportunities conducive to the achievement of self-development which society offers. This dimension of careers education makes it particularly prone to shifts in emphasis as its proponents attempt to reconcile their general aims with changes in the economic and social climate.

Overall, the account reveals that careers education, in common with other school subjects, is not a stable monolithic entity, but rather a contested territory which has attracted a number of interest groups, and where the determination of boundaries has perhaps been influenced as much by historical and political factors and their repercussions for careers educators, as by unpressured, disinterested judgements about the educational needs of young people. Moreover, in the case of careers education, compared with other school subjects, the territory is a particularly significant resource since it covers the sensitive political area of young peoples' attitudes towards employment and unemployment.

Recently, particularly since the 'Great Debate' and the massive rises in youth unemployment, the careers education movement has been joined by other interests with a common focus on an alleged need for a more vocational emphasis in the school curriculum. The general growth of interest in this area, and pressures towards change, make it more urgent that careers educators and others involved in 'preparation for working life' disentangle and assess the various meanings of 'preparation' and clarify their aims regarding their own role in this process.

The beginnings of vocational guidance

In the past the word vocation had a religious significance, referring to the experience of being *called* by God to a particular way of life and thus associated with spiritual satisfaction, commitment and individual responsibility.

> Heaven is his vocation and therefore he counts earthly employments avocations. (OED example of usage)

This meaning is a far cry from contemporary usage in the context of expressions such as vocational guidance, unified vocational preparation, or vocational skills, which refer to activities perhaps better understood as avocational. The contrast serves to highlight what appears to have been a perennial problem for teachers and counsellors employed in the management of the transition from school to work, namely, a fundamental ambivalence regarding their role, particularly those aspects sometimes referred to distastefully in teacher parlance as 'providing fodder for industry'. 'Vocational guidance', 'careers education', and 'social and life skills' all help to dignify the activities they describe, underlining their morally worthwhile aspects and diverting attention from other more controversial functions such as occupational selection, socialisation and, in recent years, occupational simulation,[2] all of which fit less easily within the traditionally liberal and humanist concerns of the profession.

Signs of tension between ideology and practice are apparent in the earliest version of vocational guidance, commonly termed the 'talent-matching' model. British accounts of the growth of careers education and guidance (for example, Daws, 1968; Hopson and Hayes, 1968; Watts, 1973) have usually begun by distinguishing this earlier 'traditional' or 'talent-matching' approach to careers work from a more recent model, which is often described as involving a 'developmental' or 'educational' approach. As the name suggests, the 'talent-matching' model rested on a concept of matching clients' interests, abilities and values with opportunities in the labour market. It was generally distinguished from vocational selection, in that it was client rather than employer-oriented.

> vocational selection chiefly interests proprietors, management and employers. Their desire is to find the best possible workers. The whole problem of selection is contained in the choice of these most efficient workers, and the discovery of means of making this choice . . . The problem of vocational guidance on the other hand, is to discover the most suitable occupation for a given individual with given abilities. (Claparède, 1922)

However, while the image of the model was client-centred, giving prominence to human talent and suggesting the identification of jobs which would match this talent, there would seem to have been a close affinity with vocational selection, particularly since practitioners depended heavily on the use of employers' vocational selection tests (see for example, Allen and Smith, 1932). These tests derived from the field of vocational psychology, a branch of industrial psychology which had, by the early part of the century, begun analysis of occupational skills and sought to identify related human characteristics. The analysis, in precise detail, of numerous occupations in terms of skill components (visual discrimination,

quick reaction time, steady attention) and other critical requirements formed the basis of constructing selection tests which were
widely adopted by employers. Writers such as Munsterberg in
Germany advertised the benefits from these improved selection
procedures.

> The employers can hope that in all departments better work will
> be done as soon as better adapted individuals can be obtained;
> and on the other hand, those who are hoping to make their
> working energies more effective may expect . . . greater joy in
> work, deeper satisfaction and more harmonious unfolding of the
> personality. (Munsterberg, 1913)

Munsterberg here adopts the stance, which has become usual in
vocational guidance literature, of stressing the mutual interests of
employers and clients.

The batteries of tests developed for the purpose of vocational
selection were becoming available during the formative years of
vocational guidance and thus came to be assimilated by an emergent
profession otherwise lacking conceptual models and technical aids.
'Talent-matching' principles came into the hands of vocational
guidance via this route and, through their use of employers'
selection tests, counsellors must to some extent have focused on job
requirements rather than human talent. Despite the ideology of the
profession, their receptivity to such aids is not altogether surprising
given the constraints of the labour market. Unless scope for
self-realisation had been a specific principle underlying job design,
it is difficult to imagine how vocational counsellors could have
implemented genuinely 'talent-matching' principles, a fact which
did not pass altogether unnoticed. For example Angus Macrae
wrote:

> The vocational psychologist dreams of a day when having
> constructed a silhouette representing the characteristics of the
> person examined, he will proceed to superimpose this human
> profile on a number of occupational profiles until he finds one
> with which it exactly coincides. But in his waking moments he
> knows that that day will never arrive. Boys and girls are not
> fashioned after stereotyped patterns designed in relation to the
> needs of human occupations. (Macrae, 1932)

Thus Macrae implicitly acknowledged that vocational psychologists were forced to view human talent through the lens of job requirements rather than vice-versa. What perhaps is interesting, and requires explanation, is not so much that counsellors found themselves allocating young people to occupations many of which cannot have appeared to provide much opportunity for personal fulfilment, but that they remained committed to an ideology which was more client-centred and idealistic. These were fertile conditions for producing the kind of personal frustration and disillusionment which appears to be common among careers officers today.

How was the vocational guidance profession in the pre-war period reconciled to the potential contradiction between their general aims and the constraints of 'opportunity structure' which Roberts has emphasised in more recent years, and to what extent did this constitute a dilemma? From a brief examination of the literature of this period it appears that an important factor, which affected the construction of the problem, was the assumption that human attributes were largely psychologically determined and could be taken as given.

The work of Earle, for example, reflects this belief and his recommendations concerning both educational and vocational guidance proceed from the premise that human ability can be regarded as innate.

> Persons whose abilities are not of a high order cannot, in the first place, complete satisfactorily a general course of education, . . . and so cannot, in the second place, become sufficiently equipped for a successful career in the more complex occupations of life . . . And inasmuch as the general education of the more capable child is a *direct* preparation for his *occupational life*, so the less capable child is entitled to receive a suitable preparation for *his* occupational life. (Earle, 1933)

Earle employs the terms 'more' and 'less capable' unencumbered by the insights into these categories which research and theory in the sociology of education has provided in recent years. Children's abilities, it is assumed, suit them for more or less 'complex' occupations. Ken Roberts' (1975; 1977; 1981) argument that human abilities and aspirations may be significantly determined by an interlocking relationship between the occupational structure, family and education was not yet under consideration in the field of vocational guidance. Thus practitioners could operate the 'matching' principle relatively untroubled by the implications this debate would eventually have for their own role.

Vocational guidance in the first half of this century had only a peripheral place within schools. It was regarded as a social service comparable, for example, with a medical service, and no claims were made for any educational potential and, hence, for a place on the school curriculum. Its institutional base was the Juvenile Employment Service (later to become the Youth Employment Service and more recently the Careers Service), created in 1909 as a result of the Labour Exchanges Act, which had provided a national system of labour exchanges intended to facilitate the distribution of labour. Typically, the service provided 'vocational guidance' through a single talk to pupils in schools followed by an individual guidance interview, during which a decision would probably be reached about the best kind of employment for the young person concerned. Compared with more modern approaches the role of the client was relatively passive. It was up to the vocational adviser to do the work, acquiring specialist information on jobs, diagnosing the young person's abilities and making an appropriate job recommendation. Given the assumptions of the model there was no reason to regard a single interview along these lines as an inappropriate or inadequate context for guidance. Moreover, in the inter-war years the social context in which the Juvenile Employment Service operated made it unlikely that young people would be offered a more in-depth or extended variety of counselling. The widespread adolescent unemployment of this period meant that youth employment officers were faced with the more urgent problem of simply finding school-leavers jobs. Again Macrae acknowledged this point:

> In these unprosperous days, many young people are less concerned with the difficulty of choosing suitable work than with the difficulty of finding any sort of work at all. (Macrae, 1934)

Thus in so far as the 'talent-matching' model actually operated it seems likely that in these circumstances it would have been fairly distorted; the problem was more likely to have been the currently familiar one of 'placing' rather than 'matching' young people to jobs.

Daws (1971) dates the appearance of the careers teacher in schools somewhere between 1926 and 1932. His (or her) role was similar to that of the youth employment officer, concentrating on making contacts with employers and thus helping young people to find employment. It gradually became common practice in schools for one teacher to have responsibility for careers advice, although advising sixth formers tended to be dealt with as a separate process by heads or senior members of staff. The careers teacher would be responsible for keeping careers brochures in the school library, and arranging occasional careers talks and pupils' interviews with the youth employment officer. Until the 1960s, there was little published discussion of the careers teacher's role.

From vocational guidance to careers education

Major changes and expansion in the vocational guidance scene in Britain are generally regarded as beginning around 1960. By the end of the 1960s the 'talent-matching' model had undergone fairly extensive overhaul, with the elaboration of a theoretically grounded and much more individually oriented 'developmental' model which remains dominant. The new model stressed the then fashionable educational values of human potentiality, self-actualisation and autonomy and, on this platform, its proponents were able to argue not only for school time but for curriculum time for the new 'careers education' (Schools Council, 1972). Given the favourable economic climate and educational trends of the 1960s, the model was launched at an auspicious moment. Official approbation came with Schools Council (1972) and DES (1973) reports recommending widespread adoption of careers education by schools along the lines of the 'developmental' model. With the gradual allocation of curriculum time for careers education and guidance, teaching for and about the world of work began to acquire an independent and larger presence in schools than hitherto, and the legitimacy of vocational preparation as an educational enterprise was implicitly conceded by the teaching profession. The details of these developments are discussed more fully below and it is suggested that, while in many respects 'careers education' was a great advance on the 'talent-matching' model of vocational guidance, there were problems within the 'developmental' model which echoed the tension between vocational guidance and vocational selection of the earlier period. The account concentrates on changes which affected the school context and does not include parallel changes which affected the Youth Employment Service.[3]

The developmental model

The changed conceptual basis for careers education was largely the result of American research and theorising in the field of vocational guidance, particularly the work of Ginzberg (1951) and Super (1953 and 1957). The rapid growth of interest in vocational guidance in the US during this period has been associated with the national trauma triggered by the launching of Sputnik in 1957, one of the consequences of which was a heightened interest in the maximum utilisation of manpower resources; Ginzberg's own work was undertaken within the framework of a project called the 'Conservation of Human Resources Project'. Within this general context Ginzberg came to focus on the question of how people make occupational choices. In 1951 Ginzberg and his colleagues published *Occupational Choice: An Approach to General Theory*. Super (1953) provided a modified version of this theoretical framework. These theories have come to be commonly termed the 'developmental' theories of occupational choice.

The 'developmental' theories present a concept of occupational choice as the outcome of a long-term process of vocational development and adjustment, not as the isolated and relatively sudden event which seemed to be the implicit assumption of the talent-matching model. In the process of vocational development as described by Super, primacy is attached to the role of the 'self-concept':

> ... the process of vocational adjustment is the process of implementing a self-concept, and the degree of satisfaction attained is proportionate to the degree to which the self concept has been implemented. (Super, 1953)

Super argued that one of the priorities for vocational guidance was to assist the development of the self-concept. The reasoning seems to be that the better a person's appreciation of their abilities, interests and values, the more likely they are to make a satisfactory occupational choice.

Contrary to the suggestion of some writers (Roberts, 1977; Speakman, 1976) who have criticised these theories as psychologically based and neglectful of economic and social determinants of occupational choice, both Ginzberg and Super do take account of these factors. Super's analysis, for example, implicitly acknowledges the limitations of the labour market, which may require job choices not particularly congruent with the self-concept and thus not likely to be associated with job satisfaction:

> Surely this is the crux of the problem ... the nature of the compromise between self and reality, the degree to which and conditions under which one yields to the other, and the way in which this compromise is effected. (Super, 1953)

Presumably, 'the conditions under which one yields to the other' might include high levels of unemployment and 'a yielding of the self-concept to reality' can accommodate the lowering of job expectations which people typically experience in the current climate. Nor, as Law (1976) has noted, is the self-concept viewed as an exclusively psychological phenomenon:

> The process of vocational development is essentially that of developing and implementing a self-concept: it is a compromise process in which the self-concept is a product of the interaction of inherited aptitudes, neural and endocrine make-up, *opportunity to play various roles, and evaluations of the extent to which the results of role playing meet with the approval of superiors and fellows.* (Super, 1953, emphasis added)

While the definition is not couched in a sociological vocabulary, the reference to the significance of 'role-playing' and the 'approval of fellows' touches gingerly, if it does not embrace, theories of occupational socialisation subsequently developed by writers such as Roberts (1977) and Willis (1977).

The problem in the 'developmental' theories would seem to lie not in their neglect of labour market constraints or social and cultural influences on occupational choice, but in the significance which they attach to these factors and, in particular, the extent to which they view them as superable. Ginzberg and Super appear to approach the problem of occupational choice from a broadly functionalist perspective in which the handicaps of some young people are viewed as dysfunctional and detrimental to their own interests and the interests of the wider society. The view is problematic in so far as it does not address the possibility that the social and cultural factors identified may be functional from the point of view of reproducing a stratified labour market. Examined in this light, such career disadvantages appear highly resilient and unlikely to dissolve through the influence of vocational guidance.

In Britain the 'developmental' theories of occupational choice were taken up notably by Daws (1968) and Hopson and Hayes (1968, 1971), both based at what was then the Vocational Guidance Research Unit at Leeds. These writers argued that in order to be effective vocational guidance should run parallel to the process of vocational development and be sensitive to the various life-stages identified by Ginzberg and Super. From this perspective, existing guidance provision, based mainly on a single interview at the point of employment entry, seemed inadequate; it was too brief and occurred at too late a stage for successful intervention. Thus guidance came to be viewed as a long-term process involving student learning in a basic triad of areas, 'self-awareness', 'occupational awareness' and 'decision-making', these being related to aspects of vocational development. A fourth area, variously defined, is generally annexed to the model. This is broadly concerned with preparation for transition into the post-school environment (see, for example, Watts and Herr, 1976).

One further step was necessary in order to effect the shift from vocational guidance to careers education. As it stood, the model invited incorporation within social service type provision rather than within education. Claims for school curriculum time have been characteristically expressed in terms of definitions of knowledge and skills deemed worthy of transmission from one generation to the next. Writers on careers education suggested that careers work in schools should not so much guide pupils' choices directly, but teach skills and knowledge in the areas of self-awareness, occupational awareness and decision-making, so that young people were better equipped to make these choices for themselves (Watts,

1973); in this way careers education would provide a kind of learning which would be useful to students throughout life, particularly given the possibility of repeated job changes. The disassociation of vocational guidance from the functions of providing information and advice and the alternative stress on helping pupils to make decisions for themselves appears also to have been influenced by developments in theories of counselling, particularly the ideas of Carl Rogers (see *Client-Centred Therapy*, Rogers, 1951). Similarly, outside the classroom in the individual interview context, a complementary counselling model was generally advocated on the grounds that it allowed the client to play a more active, self-determining role in the decision-making process.

Continuity and change

It is usual in vocational guidance literature to stress the distinction between the new 'developmental' model and the former 'talent-matching' approach (Daws, 1968; Hayes and Hopson, 1971). The following account contrasts the two approaches, but in doing so draws attention to continuing as well as changed assumptions and to the implications of the modifications to the paradigm for the relationship between vocational guidance and manpower requirements.

A basic similarity between both formulae for vocational guidance relates to their underlying image of the opportunity structure. Both models have tended to present the world of work and the opportunity structure as a set of given conditions within which vocational guidance (or careers education) operates. Writers may lament the nature of the world of work but their assumptions about the dynamics of change do not generally ascribe a significant role to careers education. Hopson and Hough, for example, suggest that:

> those of our young people who have not already been socialised to expect little from their jobs, often become rapidly disillusioned with the cynicism and mindlessness encountered at the workplace. However much we might deplore the cause and the effect this is a well documented fact, and consequently, we should not encourage our young people to expect from their jobs that which they are certainly not to receive (Hopson and Hough, 1973)

This view leads these authors to an emphasis on leisure pursuits as an alternative form of self-expression and fulfilment.

Proponents of both approaches have also stressed the economic importance of improved vocational guidance:

> If British economic prosperity is to flourish and grow as it must, we have to ensure that the threat of limited manpower resources is removed by improving the quality of the manpower we have . . . We must also ensure that the needs of the industries upon which our national wealth most crucially depends are at all times adequately met. (Daws, 1968)

The argument implicitly acknowledges a subordinate function for careers education in relation to economic developments.

Despite a taken-for-granted model of the opportunity structure and an emphasis on the economic merits of vocational guidance or careers education, pioneers in both approaches have viewed their activity as primarily relating to individual needs and interests. This, however, introduces the major difference between them.

This distinction consists of the different assumptions of the two models concerning the fixity of human potential. In the 'talent-matching' period abilities tended to be regarded as pre-determined by innate psychological factors. In contrast, the 'developmental' model takes account of the influence of socialisation processes. Vocational guidance is seen as having the potential to intervene between the individual and the social factors shaping his or her development and aspirations, and thus able to create conditions in which young people can become aware of and transcend influences such as social class background. The assumptions of the 'developmental' model are thus more ambitious than those of the 'talent-matching' version; the counsellor becomes responsible for acting as a catalyst in individual development, not merely a reflector of fixed individual qualities.

A second, related difference exists in the emphasis in the 'develomental' model on the active participation of the client. The client is no longer regarded as a passive recipient of information about him/herself, but is expected to explore their own abilities and interests together with information about possible occupations. Thus the new model does not dispense altogether with 'talent-matching' but converts it to an *extended* and *client-controlled* process. The new model is tantamount to do-it-yourself 'talent-matching.

As a consequence of these two modifications the 'developmental' model is much more individually-oriented than its predecessor. The focus is on the recognition and development of possibly dormant human abilities and interests, thus aiming at a form of consciousness-raising. The increased emphasis on self-development creates the theoretical possibility that careers education could produce large numbers of young people who would not readily be reconciled to the opportunities available to them. Consequently, the model could become dysfunctional from the point of view of manpower requirements. How did careers education pioneers seek to resolve the tension between the aims of their activity and the opportunity structure? As has already been noted, in the 'talent-matching' era this issue was generally safely submerged by the assumption that people are fitted for some occupations rather than others by virtue of natural ability. From the mid-1970s this question began to recieve serious attention in the literature on careers education. However, initially, it was not regarded as an important issue or a flaw in the model.

For example, Hayes and Hopson expressed the view that counsellors should not be overly concerned with jobs available but should concentrate on helping clients to develop and formulate their aspirations:

> the counsellor should not use such information [manpower data] to direct young people into particular lines of study or towards those occupations where serious skill shortages have been predicted. Ensuring that the community's future manpower requirements are satisfied is not the counsellor's job. His responsibility is to his students (Hayes and Hopson, 1971)

However, these writers did not give any indication that they considered this separation of responsibilities might be deleterious for the economy or for individual adjustment.

Daws (1968) also gave attention to this issue and recognised the possibility that the occupational structure might not readily accommodate the ambitions of young people who had benefited from vocational guidance:

It is worth experimenting with the assignment of guidance to a school-based officer while shifting the onus of placement . . . on to an employent-based officer. It would not matter if the result of such an arrangement was that half our school leavers crystallised a preference for, say, industrial design, provided they all recognised the improbability of their realising such an ambition. The most talented and determined would still achieve their objective. The remainder would settle for second preferences. (Daws, 1968)

Thus Daws acknowledged that occupational entry may eventually be determined by a *compromise* between individual wishes and the opportunities available. His argument hinges, however, on assumptions about the degree of compromise involved in the settlement and the numbers likely to be affected. He expects sufficient overlap between opportunities available and individual choices to allow 'the remainder to settle for second preferences'. In the absence of such overlap his predictions would not be fulfilled; a scenario could be hypothetically constructed, for example, in which the 'remainder' would find their initial choices completely irrelevant and only a minority would enjoy the possibility of taking up 'second preferences'.

In so far as careers educators viewed the non-utilisation of human talent in the employment context as a significant problem, it was resolved by bringing *non-occupational roles* into the equation. Hopson and Hough, for example, having noted the lack of intrinsic satisfaction in many kinds of employment, argued the importance of activities outside of paid employment, as channels for self-expression:

For one person fulfilment might be through his family life, for another through his craftsmanship in his job, a third may live for his mountaineering at weekends, a fourth for his marrows and broad beans, and another through his community life.
If we are really concerned with helping people to develop a sense of purpose then we must truly accept that we are concerned with his *life* and not just his *living*. (Hopson and Hough, 1973)

It is this dimension of careers education which explains the terminology used in some statements of aims where instead of

occupational awareness, which might be expected, we find 'opportunity awareness'.[1]

Summarising the similarities and differences between vocational
guidance of the earlier period and the new careers education, it can
be concluded that the two approaches are in many respects similar.
In particular their proponents have faced an important common
dilemma arising from a combination of commitment to individual
self-realisation together with a recognition that not all forms of
employment offer such possibilities. It would appear that – perhaps
for psychological, political or ethical reasons or a mixture of all
three – pioneers in this field have not allowed their ideology to rest
in an obvious state of contradiction. Consequently in the earlier
period 'natural ability' was stressed and 'less able' clients were
considered potentially satisfied by limited occupational roles which
might be considered frustrating and a wastage of talent for the more
able. In the 1960s this view was less acceptable, research and theory
having offered glimpses of the complex relationship between
manifest ability and socialisation. This change in intellectual climate
led to an emphasis on rolling back the effects of socialisation through
long-term careers education along the lines of the 'developmental'
model. It was hoped that the human abilities and aspirations
potentially unfurled as a result would be more or less accommodated by the occupational structure, or if not, would find expression
in leisure-time pursuits.

The take-up in education

Despite its apparent potential to produce misfits, careers education
was taken up by the educational establishment. From the 1960s
onwards a flurry of reports and papers began to appear directly
or indirectly concerned with the role of the careers teacher (e.g.
Ministry of Education: Forward From School, 1962; Newsom
Report, 1963; DES: Careers Guidance in Schools, 1965; Joint
Four: The Careers Teacher, 1967). Two documents were particularly significant and are useful in illustrating how careers education
was promoted.

Official approval of the concept of careers education was first
indicated in 1972 when the term was used in a Schools Council
Working Party report on the transition from school to work. The

report *Careers Education in the Seventies* develops a definition of careers education in the context of a wider discussion of secondary education in general and the relationship between education and the economy. The argument for careers education is couched largely in terms of changing economic needs and predictions of skill shortages:

> All the indications are that, despite the contrary appearance of occasional periods of recession . . . manpower need at skilled levels is likely to out-run supply throughout the foreseeable future. To compensate for this quantitative deficiency, it will be necessary to develop every scrap of talent that emerges from our schools and to encourage its development in a way that is relevant to the economic and social needs of the country.
> It is no longer possible to contemplate a relatively stable employment world within which a pupil can find a place that will provide him with a living for half a century . . . It follows from this that the most needed qualities of today's school-leavers are adaptability and flexibility.

Having elaborated upon this theme, in the next breath as it were, the report rescues careers education from the role of mere servant to the economy:

> This is not to argue that in considering how it might best serve all its purposes the school should uncritically accept the larger society into which its pupils will go. Certainly, however, it must help the pupils to take their place in that larger society and in doing so must be concerned to help them adjust to things as they find them. But its purposes must go beyond merely adjustive ends. It must consider, too, how it might best prepare young people to make constructive criticisms of the society they inherit so as to change and improve it. Those who would define the objectives of the school in the manner of a market research organisation by cataloguing the competencies needed to adjust to and maintain the status quo have failed to understand this stimulative and creative function of our educational system . . .

The report throughout makes regular reference to liberal and progessive traditions, apparently seeking to reassure readers of the educational legitimacy of what is being advocated and offering parent and pupil attitudes as further support for the thesis:

> the great majority of parents and pupils see preparation for work as a central function of the school . . . and this demand may seem to conflict with the liberal tradition of the teaching profession, which emphasizes personal development, self-expression, habits of critical thinking and so on, as the most important values of education . . . Many of the difficulties seen by teachers are more apparent than real, however, as a liberal education is above all an education for choice and the ability to chose wisely is the most important skill that any guidance programme must seek to foster.

In general the remarks on the relationship between education and society reflect a view of education as possessing an 'independent stance towards society and the economy' and a commitment to education as a means of social change. The emphasis on the latter might be seen to place the Working Party's views towards the progressive end of a spectrum of possible liberal positions, a stance which was perhaps more acceptable in the climate of the late 1960s than a decade later. Against the backdrop of this general discussion the report begins to outline and shade in a definition of careers education in which basically liberal values are embedded. The definition which emerges includes the basic components of the 'developmental' approach – the teaching of self-awareness, occupational (or opportunity) awareness, decision-making and preparation for transition.

Similar aims provided the criteria for a survey of careers education provision undertaken by the DES and published in the report, *Careers Education in Secondary Schools* (1973). The survey reveals that 25 per cent of schools included in the study provided careers education in the third year, 72 per cent in the fourth year and 45 per cent in the fifth year. 38 per cent of schools surveyed offered pupils a work experience programme. One conclusion of the report, apparently presaging the 'Great Debate', was that 'it seems clear that many schools in this country are not effectively in touch with the working world' and leads to a recommendation that for 'all boys and girls careers education should be a continuous process and an important element in the curriculum'. To this end a general strengthening of careers work in school is proposed, together with improved and expanded in-service training.

Despite the general emphasis of the DES survey on a paucity of careers education provision, all the signs were that curriculum innovation in this area was already gaining momentum. Indeed, given the difficulties which have usually been associated with attempts to launch new school subjects outside the traditional subject compartments (see, for example, Crick, 1981; Goodson, 1983), careers education was experiencing an exceptionally rapid take-off. In 1969 the National Association of Careers Teachers had been formed. In 1971 the Schools Council had set up the Careers Education and Guidance Project. There were university and college training courses in counselling and careers education and guidance and various organisations were providing short in-service courses for careers teachers. The DES survey itself was able to establish 73 per cent of comprehensive schools claimed one or more teachers who had experienced at least a brief period of in-service training and 11 per cent of all schools claimed to have a teacher who had attended a course of one term or longer.

The curriculum credentials of careers education were a necessary but insufficient condition for official recognition and the extension of provision in schools. The case has been made for other new school subjects but the history of their early development has been more chequered. Thus careers education is something of an anomaly and its relatively easy entry requires explanation. Part of the explanation would appear to be associated with the educational and economic climate of the 1960s.

In education the 1960s were a period of expansion, optimism and egalitarianism. Floud and Halsey's general interest in the economic benefits of releasing 'reserves of ability' and related critique of the tripartite system of education also extended to vocational guidance provision:

> It is also desirable that the policy of vocational guidance should be re-oriented in a deliberate attempt to increase the fluidity of the supply of labour. To be effective for this purpose guidance cannot afford to begin its work only at the end of the children's school days, concentrating on the end-products of the educational process . . . The question is whether a national guidance policy, aimed at stimulating the ambitions of the unselected

school population and tackling the problem of social assimilation which underlies the wastage of able working class children from the grammar schools, does not demand the appointment of counsellors or guidance officers to the staffs of all secondary schools . . . (Floud and Halsey, 1956)

Comprehensivisation, the widening of curricular options, the creation in 1963 of the Schools Council from the Department of Education's Curriculum Study Group, the curriculum innovation movement, the Plowden report, the emphasis on pupil rather than subject-centred teaching – were all associated with the ideals of extending equality of opportunity, developing individual autonomy and removing constraints upon educational and occupational choice. Careers education, with its emphasis on self-selection for occupations, could be considered a logical outcome, a replacement for institutional mechanisms for channelling children into different careers. The fashionable themes of equality of opportunity and education as an economic investment were woven into the text of the new careers education and guidance ideology.

At the same time the prospect of the raising of the school leaving age drew attention to the problem of producing a curriculum which would engage the attention of the former school-leaver, and subjects such as social studies and careers education were viewed as possible solutions possessing the magic motivational ingredient of relevance. In these conditions careers education was able to set sail with the wind, briefly, in its favour.

The mood in education in the 1960s and early 1970s was also related to economic and associated occupational factors. Economic arguments characterised both American and British arguments for expansion in careers education. In Britain, writers on vocational guidance (Daws, 1968; Roberts, 1971; Craft, 1973; Watts, 1973) were able to point to changes taking place in the economy and the increasing demand for skilled workers, particularly in the tertiary sector. The expansion of the supply of professional, administrative and clerical jobs meant that more young people than previously could contemplate the possibility of a 'career', with its connotations of progress through a hierarchy of jobs, than simply a job. At the same time conditions, compared with the pre-war era, were of relatively full employment and in these circumstances most young people could contemplate some degree of job choice, between fields, if not levels, of employment. Moreover, predictions were that the demand for labour would exceed the supply for the foreseeable future (Ministry of Labour, 1964). In the climate of concern for maximum utilisation of manpower more attention was paid to training, resulting in the 1964 Industrial Training Act. Young people were thus increasingly likely to be faced with choices, not simply between jobs but between training programmes and, as more jobs required a training investment, the problem of choice became more complicated. In addition, Schools Council Working Paper 40 (1972) pointed out that as a result of technological change, occupations were changing at an ever-increasing rate. Jobs were appearing and disappearing and, consequently, people could not assume they would be engaged in the same occupation for many years. This meant the possibility of repeated job changes, which it was hoped could be facilitated by teaching skills in the area of career self-management.

In summary, the 1960s provided highly fertile conditions for the production of a new concept of careers education and its adoption by schools. Changed economic and educational circumstances focused attention on the role of vocational guidance and created a disposition towards acceptance of the 'developmental model', with its assumptions about the possibility for people to make occupational choices congruent, or at least compatible, with their self concepts. However, the model seems to have been inherently unstable. This instability derives largely from the fact that it implies a rather rosy image of the world of work and the opportunities it presents for the exercise of human potential (or, alternatively, takes a very dim view of human potential). There is abundant evidence within other fields, such as industrial sociology that occupational roles are determined by other factors than their scope for human development, and, further, that opportunities for job satisfaction are differentially distributed.[4] Given the inequalities which characterise the occupational structure, it is difficult to imagine how choice, or in other words self-selection, could become an important determinant of occupational entry without producing a problem of over-supply of candidates for some occupations. Even if the assumption is made that human abilities in relation to jobs vary widely, and allowance is made for a mediating influence of this variable on personal ambition, then it still seems likely that the maximisation of the influence of personal choice on occupational entry would create a considerable problem of supply and demand for jobs. Unless a large proportion of the population can be assumed to be masochistically inclined, or extraordinarily lacking in self interest, only the removal of inequalities of satisfaction, status and reward would seem to permit genuine self-selection to operate as an efficient mechanism for the distribution of labour. What seems to be required from the point of view of economic needs are mechanisms for constraining rather than enhancing occupational choice. In the 1960s, with expanding opportunies and a general mood of optimism, the image of occupational choice underlying the 'developmental' model could be sustained without appearing absurdly to distort the everyday experience of young people and the common sense of their teachers and counsellors. Its maintenance depended, however, on the continuation of these conditions which were, by the time careers education was becoming a curricular reality in the early 1970s, already disappearing.

The 1970s: internal debate and external pressure

In general, the position in which careers education seems to have been most comfortable is one where it can 'serve both masters'. Through the 1970s economic recession, a shrinking labour market and rising levels of unemployment heightened the tension between human interests and manpower requirements which had been lying slack in the 1960s. During this period it became more difficult for careers education to face both ways, with related repercussions for the progress of the 'developmental' model. The political issues which are never far below the surface in careers education were becoming more explicit. In 1976 Watts and Herr raised the question of the 'socio-political' aims of careers education, arguing that this is one of the most important and least discussed issues for the careers education movement:

> all educational theories are in the end political theories. But careers education is directly concerned with the relationship between education and the allocation of life-chances, and is therefore political in a particularly direct sense, especially in a society which is characterised by considerable variations of remuneration and status between different occupations. (Watts and Herr, 1976)

Similarly Law's (1976) reference to the need for a path between 'ovine compliance and bloody revolution' reflects the growing awareness of the political implications of teaching in this area.

In this climate the 'developmental' approach developed twists in emphasis. In particular, three themes became more striking in the work of different writers on careers education and guidance. These are categorised here as: a *social change* emphasis; an *individual adjustment* emphasis; and an *alternative roles* emphasis. The term 'emphasis' is used to denote that these themes were not generally advocated as replacements for the 'developmental' model which, in any case, was sufficiently broad in its typical formulation to accommodate a variety of interpretations. Nor were they necessarily viewed as mutually exclusive. Rather they represent themes which were highlighted in the careers education literature of the 1970s, sometimes by proponents of the 'developmental' approach and sometimes by other researchers who argued the implications of their own work for careers education.

At the same time, the 1970s witnessed the emergence of a new educational ideology, concerned with teaching about and in preparation for industry, emanating from sources outside the field of careers education (Government and Industry) and transmitted to relevant audiences through the documents, conferences and media coverage of the Great Debate, 1976–77. This will be termed the *industrial needs* emphasis. While this did not usurp, and in some ways boosted, the spread of careers education in schools, it implicitly defined the political perspective from which the study of industry and the world of work in schools should be approached.

For analytical purposes the four strands which have now been identified are treated separately below, but this is not to suggest they need all be, or have been regarded as, incompatible dimensions of careers education.

The social change emphasis

Watts and Herr (1976), in their discussion of the socio-political aims of careers education, raise the question of a 'social change' approach as a theoretical possibility. They suggest that individually-oriented approaches 'may implicitly include social change as a by-product or subsidiary aim, but an approach which focuses *primarily* on social change might for instance see its function as being to make students aware of how exploitative the employment system is'. In fact, social change had already made an appearance as a declared aim for careers education, both as a subsidiary aim and as a more central theme. For Hopson and Hough it appears to have been at least a subsidiary aim:

> Another motive for preparing this book lay in the belief that so much of current educational practice is static, aimed at adjusting the student to the status quo. Instead it could be dynamic, providing him with the means to change his environment. (Hopson and Hough, 1973)

The Schools Council Careers Education and Guidance Project, at one stage of its development, made social change a central and integrating theme in its philosophy:

> But what about the large group of children for whom choosing between different jobs and their accompanying lifestyles can, in reality, make only a marginal difference to the quality of life and who, moreover, must struggle harder to develop any genuine self-awareness given the concepts of themselves imposed by their environment. For these children the relevance of choosing is less accessible. It is not choosing which will answer the problems they experience at work . . . but changing, changing the conditions of work, changing the society in which they live. (Schools Council Careers Education and Guidance Project, 1975)

Coming from outside the field of careers education, Willis's work (1977) provided suggestions for strategies through which education, particularly careers teachers, might contribute to fundamental structural change. At practitioner level the theme of change, and young people as 'agents of change', was fashionable in the early 1970s, and was a frequent topic of discussion at careers education conferences in those years.

Proponents of a 'change' model, or at least a 'change' ingredient in careers education, are essentially resisting the tendency to reify the world of work and the opportunity structure which has been identified as a general characteristic of the 'developmental' approach. Perceiving a probability of mismatch between the human potential which it is their job to develop, and job opportunities (to which they attach different degrees of significance), they take a route out of the dilemma this poses by representing employment opportunities as susceptible to change and improvement and their own clients as potential agents in this process.

The individual adjustment emphasis

This is in a sense an opposite to the 'change' variant outlined above. 'Adjustment' is being used here to refer to the view that an element within careers education, or its overall purpose, should be fitting pupils into the world of work. Essentially, this approach addresses the same dilemma as the 'social change emphasis' – the perceived tension between individual requirements and employment opportunities – but resolves it by focusing on the human side of the equation; it is the young person who is to be adjusted, not the world of work. Teaching 'adjustment' has been a recurring theme within a number of versions of the 'developmental' model and its significance has been drawn out and emphasised by Ken Roberts in the 1970s. Using Watts and Herr's (1976) classification of 'sociopolitical' aims of careers education the adjustment emphasis falls within the 'social control' category. It is perhaps a sign of the equivocal attitude of the profession towards the function of social control that this dimension of vocational guidance is sometimes treated with a certain amount of ambiguity and embarrassment.

Daws, Hopson and Hough, and Watts and Herr are among the writers who have paid attention to the concept of 'adjustment' within the framework of the 'developmental' model. Daws' (1971) concern is with those young people who lack 'social skills and insights and simple habits such as punctuality' and 'may too readily show hostility to those who would teach or supervise them'. He argues that they need 'help to enable them to anticipate the various demands of working life and to survive there'. He is careful to point out that such help need not be regarded as a form of 'anticipatory socialisation', involving the school in imitating a work environment, but rather as the provision of 'anticipatory insights'. The distinction is similar to the traditional one between 'training' and 'education'. It seems likely, however, that this distinction, while apparently theoretically tenable, will become confused when translated into practice in the school context. It is difficult to imagine, for example, how education on the subject of employer requirements such as punctuality can remain dissociated from the school discipline system.

Hopson and Hough (1973) also introduced an adjustment dimension into careers education. In support of their argument the authors quote Daws (1970) who had identified skills possessed by the 'employables'. They included:

> A willingness to pace one's work rate according to the require-
> ments of fellow workers and supervisors . . .
> a readiness to respond to peer group conformity pressures on the
> job, in such matters as dress, speech, attitudes and values, and
> habits of informal interaction of various kinds . . .
> a general disposition to accept and attempt to *adjust* to a variety
> of unfamiliar practices and features in the work context that are
> initially a potent source of anxiety and stress. (Hopson and
> Hough, 1973, emphasis added)

Hopson and Hough, like Daws, expressed a particular concern with young people who appear to lack such skills and argued that careers education could equip them in these areas. Conscious of the potential critique that this amounted to 'conditioning young people to fit into "bourgeois society" ' they argued that without such skills young people were prevented from choosing between alternative kinds of employment. The use of the concept of skills further shields their recommendations from criticism on the grounds of illiberality. In a move which has now become alarmingly commonplace, the teaching of attitudes and habits is subsumed within the teaching of skills. Thus in a manner not dissimilar to Daws, the 'adjustment' aspect of careers education is disassociated from direct training or socialisation and deposited within the boundaries of a liberal definition of education.

In each of the above examples 'adjustment' is one element within a broader concept of careers education and guidance. Moreover, it can be seen from earlier references to the work of the same authors that helping pupils to adjust is not necessarily viewed as incompatible with a wider, or subsidiary aim of helping pupils to change, or cause adjustment within the world of work, thereby creating opportunities more congruent with their own needs and abilities and perhaps reducing the extent to which adjustment is required of *them*. These two dimensions of careers education are both incorporated within some models (Hopson and Hough, 1973; Watts and Herr, 1976; Schools Council Careers Education and Guidance Project, 1976), although the models differ with respect to the significance they attach to each aim.

A stronger case for the 'adjustment emphasis' has been stated by Ken Roberts, who has argued that adjustment must inevitably occupy a central position in the purpose of careers education. Roberts' critique of the 'developmental' theories of occupational choice led to an alternative formulation of aims for careers education and guidance, reflecting the 'opportunity structure' theory of employment entry. Arguing that industrial societies face the problem of adjusting individuals to jobs which allow little scope for self-expression, he suggests that careers education and guidance should concentrate on easing adjustment and on placement, rather than on promoting self-knowledge. Roberts acknowledges that the position he outlines is likely to be less attractive to the profession but suggests that, in the long run, it is more likely to produce a service which is in the interests of clients:

> Talk of adjusting individuals to often limited opportunities may not be very inspiring. Refusing to recognize this as the effective role that guidance can play, however, will not change society for the better. The net result will merely be to leave individuals less adjusted to the world as it is. (Roberts, 1975)

Thus Roberts offers the vocational guidance profession a rationale for a definition of aims which, unlike the formulae emanating from within the field, takes its cue from characteristics of the occupational structure rather than from human attributes.

The two themes of 'social change' and 'individual adjustment' are sometimes flanks of the 'developmental' approach and at other times have been proposed as central principles in careers education philosophy, as in the case of the writings of Willis and Ken Roberts.

The alternative roles emphasis

This theme was introduced in connection with the discussion of careers education in the 1960s and early 1970s. It refers to the strand of thinking in careers education which stresses the opportunities which people have in life to play a number of roles outside the employment context.

Starting from a common commitment to enabling individuals to achieve maximum self-fulfilment, writers on careers education (e.g. Hopson and Hough, 1973; Schools Council Careers Education and Guidance Project, 1975; Super, 1975; Watts, 1978) have considered in a variety of ways the significance of roles and activities outside of paid employment. Daws (1971) takes account of sociological evidence that lifestyles are heavily determined by occupations and recommends that careers education should proceed on the assumption that helping an individual choose a job is tantamount to helping him or her choose a way of life. Other writers have attached different kinds of significance to activities outside of paid employment. At the risk of ignoring differences between their positions they (e.g. Hopson and Hough, 1973; Super, 1975; Watts and Herr, 1976; Watts, 1978) suggest that these activities can provide alternative sources of self-fulfilment and respect when such satisfactions cannot be derived from paid employment. Concepts of 'work' (Hopson and Hough, 1973) and of 'career' (Watts and Herr, 1976; Watts, 1978) are proposed which include leisure activities involving the expenditure of effort and roles such as family roles and community roles:

> . . . attention has to paid to the fact that many even of those who do work for major portions of their lives, draw their main satisfactions outside their occupations . . . The implication of this is that if careers education is concerned with helping individuals to find identity and self-fulfilment in terms of their own values, an exclusive focus on work roles will be of limited value to those for whom work is not likely to be 'a central life interest'. (Watts and Herr, 1976).

An extension of the concept of career along these lines enabled Super (1975) to argue, in an address to the Institute of Careers Officers, that 'careers counselling will be life-counselling'.

The 'alternative roles emphasis' represents a further solution to the problems posed for the careers education movement by their observation of a lack of fit between human needs and talents on the one hand and labour market opportunities on the other. It reflects the recognition by careers educators of the existence of jobs which allow little scope for personal development and suggests that surrogate satisfactions are available. The 'alternative roles emphasis' thus has the appearance of rescuing the 'developmental' model from the accusation of irrelevance to the needs of the underemployed or unemployed, while avoiding the overt political overtones of Watts and Herr's 'social change' or 'social control' categories.

The theme was present in the earliest British versions of the 'developmental' approach. As a feature of the original model it appears to have been introduced mainly to cater for the problem of underemployment or non-utilisation of the human resources which careers educators saw it as their goal to develop. In the later 1970s the 'alternative roles emphasis' has become more prominent in careers education literature, particularly in the work of Watts (1978) and Hopson and Scally (1981), apparently on account of its ideological potential to cater for the related problem of unemployment. Watts (1978), for example, in an article significantly titled 'The Implications of School-Leaver Unemployment for Careers Education in Schools', has argued for teaching in the areas of 'leisure skills' and 'alternative opportunity awareness' in the context of broader programmes concerned with education for and about unemployment.

This approach to careers education, while apparently politically innocuous, raises more questions than it settles. Firstly, there is the problem that the patterns of inequality which characterise the occupational structure also affect patterns of recreation. Consequently, the opportunity structure is not magically levelled by taking account of leisure opportunities for self-development, as sometimes seems to have been implied (see, for example, Hopson and Hough, 1973). Secondly, by defining unpaid activities such as housework and childcare as work, careers educators again take a step which leads potentially in a politically radical direction for, unless these roles are paid for, they do not represent genuine career options. Watts (1978) has acknowledged this point. The article already quoted concludes with a discussion of the future of work in society and the suggestion that guaranteed incomes will need to be made available for those wishing to pursue alternative roles if these forms of employment are to become meaningful career choices. In a more recent paper Watts has stressed the political issues this move would entail:

> There is no shortage of work in our society, only at present a shortage of paid employment. The issues that have to be faced are what forms of work society is prepared to pay for, how these forms of work are to be distributed within society and how such distribution is to be related to the generation and distribution of wealth. (Watts, 1981)

The three themes of 'social change', 'individual adjustment' and 'alternative roles' can all be regarded as attempts to resolve the common dilemma experienced by those whose own occupations are located at the interface of human potential and the opportunity structure. These themes are not peculiar to careers education but occur widely in educational discourse. However, they surface particularly readily in philosophising about careers education on account of its position at the 'sharp end' of the relationship between education and the economy.

The industrial needs emphasis

Careers education in the 1970s was inevitably affected by the 'Great Debate' on education initiated by Callaghan's Ruskin College Speech in October 1976. Detailed analysis of the 'Great Debate', its causes and implications, is beyond the scope of this research. The focus here is on the specific implications for careers education. In general the 'Great Debate' was experienced by the careers education and guidance movement as undermining its established values. For example Watts (1979), in an unpublished conference paper, commented on gradual adjustments in the DES position on careers education and guidance and observed that the understanding of industry and development of skills for employability emphasised in the official documents of the 'Great Debate' were distinctly different from the aims of careers education.

In what sense could messages of the 'Great Debate' be considered in conflict with careers education? It is possible to argue the opposite case – for example, that their constant stress on teaching in preparation for work was supportive rather than corrosive of careers education ideology, in that they lent a considerable weight of official support to the further development of this general area of the curriculum. 'Educating Our Children' (DES, 1977a), the background paper for the regional conferences, specifies 'School and Working Life' as one of the four themes of the debate. The same paper advocated the inclusion of careers education and guidance in the core curriculum, and later identified four objectives for careers education which include 'self-awareness' and 'decision-making' and appear to be derived from the dominant 'developmental' model. The Green Paper, 'Education in Schools' (DES, 1977b), recommends that schools should give greater priority to careers education and that careers teachers should have more status; readers are referred to the document 'Careers Education in Secondary Schools' [Schools Council, 1972] for guidelines on careers education, which had outlined a broadly 'developmental' model.

The threat to careers education was indirect and occurred on two levels. First, the 'Great Debate' reflected a trend towards defining and limiting the boundaries of teacher autonomy. The very initiation of a public debate on education, involving the unprecedented consultation of industrial organisations and parents as well as educational organisations, served as an explicit reminder to the teaching profession, and thus indirectly to the careers education movement, that the curriculum was not solely their responsibility to determine. Statements made in the course of the debate underline this assumption. For example, the document 'Education in Schools', having reviewed briefly public criticism of education asserts that:

> Education, like any other public service, is answerable to the society which it serves and which pays for it, so these criticisms must be given a fair hearing. (DES, 1977b)

Thus the 'Great Debate', irrespective of its content, simply as a *means* of intervening in education helped to change the political context in which educational issues were discussed. For careers educators the implications of this change were particularly pertinent. The debate had extended an invitation to those outside the field of careers education to contribute, at least indirectly, to the definition of an educational ideology related to the world of work. The careers education movement had, implicitly, claimed responsibility in a similar area. The Government's consultation of other interest groups, representing 'society' and 'industry', rather than first and foremost young people, strengthened the position of other contenders for influence on this part of the school curriculum, thus effecting a *relative* reduction in the influence of the careers education movement.

Second, the content of contributions to the 'Great Debate' helped to confer legitimacy upon a new 'industrial needs emphasis' which it was suggested should properly inform teaching in this area of the school curriculum. In the course of the 'Great Debate' the Government did not seek to dispense with careers education as an approach to teaching about industry and the world of work in general. What seemed to be suggested was that industry, and preparation for industry, deserve a place in the school curriculum for reasons *over and above* those of helping pupils to choose future careers and of smoothing their transition into work. Industry, it was argued, should be examined in terms of its general contribution to society. Thus extra-individual reasons are introduced as a justification for the study in schools of some of the traditional subject matter of vocational guidance and careers education.

The education and industry theme is introduced in the document 'Educating Our Children' (DES, 1977a) by way of reference to public criticism of education on the grounds that it is out of touch with industry. The criticisms most directly relevant to careers education are related to young people's attitudes towards industry. The document reports public concern about 'negative attitudes to work and the discipline it entails' and also the view that 'pupils, especially the more able, are prejudiced against work in productive trade and industry'. The construction of the problem, or at least part of the problem (young people's negative attitudes towards industry) lends plausibility to the solution which is proposed: schools need to develop 'knowledge and understanding of the world of work'. The reasoning appears to be that 'negative' attitudes towards industry must reflect lack of knowledge and understanding; schools can remedy this situation by developing more contacts with industry and giving it more consideration within the curriculum. The definition of the problem and the proposed solution are openly derived from consideration of the needs of the economy:

not enough people are equipped with the skills, knowledge and understanding of our economy which are necessary to the country's well-being. (DES, 1977a)

It is industry and the 'country' which are alleged to find young people's 'negative' attitudes a problem, not young people themselves. In this manner an additional ideology for teaching about industry is sketched out. The curriculum product appears on first sight to be open to a range of political interpretations; the function, however, which must inevitably affect the content is to *repair* attitudes towards and conceptions of industry.

The 'industrial needs emphasis' is not concerned with 'self-awareness' and 'decision-making skills' and so in these areas there is no overlap with careers education. The potential conflict between the two approaches arises because the 'industrial needs' slant openly ignores the traditional educational emphasis (rhetorical or otherwise) on 'critical awareness' and asserts that industry must be presented in a positive light. The various documents of the 'Great Debate' repeatedly elevate the role of manufacturing industry in society by stipulating a rather simplistic definition of its function as a producer of Britain's national wealth:

Young people need to reach maturity with a basic understanding of the economy and its activities, especially manufacturing industry, which are necessary for the creation of Britain's wealth. It is an important task for secondary schools to develop this understanding, and opportunities for its development should be offered to pupils of all abilities. These opportunities are needed not only by young people who may have careers in industry later but perhaps even more by those who may work elsewhere, so that the role of industry becomes *soundly appreciated* by society in general. (DES, 1977b, emphasis added)

It is this aspect of the 'industrial needs emphasis' which is antithetic to the spirit in which the 'developmental' model was launched. The contrast can usefully be highlighted by a further extract from the Schools Council working paper quoted previously:

they [schools] must avoid the danger of becoming little more than advance agents of the economy. If this happens three things go wrong: firstly, in effect children are on the labour market from their earliest years, judged constantly in terms of their future usefulness or earning power. Second, schools lose their independent stance towards social problems, which should enable young people to study constructively and *critically all aspects of our society, including its economic arrangements*. (Schools Council, 1972, emphasis added)

The TUC (1977) voiced similar comment on the limitations of the definition of the relationship between education and industry which appeared to inform the official papers of the 'Great Debate'.

The 'Great Debate' was not without practical consequences. Partly as a result of its regional conferences, a host of developments were initiated or encouraged at the local level, including teacher secondment to industry, school–industry twinning schemes involving teachers and employers in discussing the curriculum and the expansion of work experience. Examples of such developments are discussed in a DES (1981) booklet 'Schools and Working Life' which reports school activities designed to help pupils 'appreciate the importance of industry and commerce to the community'. Watts (1983) and Eggleston (1982) provide further examples of developments at the school level. Unconnected with any established academic discipline, and with the official boost of the 'Great Debate', curriculum development in this area has been able to bypass the traditional gatekeepers of school knowledge (the examining boards), and to infuse teaching not only in the careers education and guidance area but 'across the curriculum'. The ideological impact of the 'Great Debate' was experienced by the Schools Council Careers Education and Guidance Project in the course of a Schools Council enquiry (1977) into the project's materials. One of the main points at issue between the Schools Council and the project was the latter's presentation of industry within its teaching materials. In their discussions and correspondence with the project team, Schools Council representatives stressed the view that work and industry should be represented in a more 'positive' light. As a result of the enquiry and the resulting negotiations, the Council's views, which appeared sensitive to the Government's 'industrial needs emphasis (not surprisingly perhaps given the vulnerability of the Council at this time), led to some modifications to the project's published materials.[5]

Summarising developments in the 1970s, economic and political conditions affected thinking on careers education as a result of endogenous and exogenous influences. The shrinking labour market and growing levels of youth unemployment were the background to internal debate among those with academic and professional interests in careers education. The debate focused particularly on the adequacy of the 'developmental' model, its dimensions now being set in relief against a labour market characterised by more limited job choice and increasing unemployment. Consensus about aims and priorities began to splinter. It was their observation of constraints upon job choice which encouraged the Schools Council Careers Education and Guidance Project to sail against the wind towards a 'social change emphasis' in careers education; the same observation appeared to trigger Roberts' critique of the 'developmental' model and the alternative 'adjustment' approach which he saw as necessary. The emergence of these themes in the academic discourse on careers education can be seen in part as attempts to provide more pertinent guidelines in the face of changing economic circumstances. Likewise, the 'alternative roles emphasis' highlights an aspect of careers education which could cast an almost optimistic light on the implications of unemployment for careers education and guidance.

At the same time the careers education movement could not remain insulated from the wider debate about education and industry, which pointed towards a greater emphasis on adjustment and the presentation of industry in a favourable light. First, by involving non-educational interests in the subjects being debated, it caused a relative reduction in the influence of the careers education movement over the area of the school curriculum directly concerned with the relationship between education and industry. Second, it helped to confer legitimacy on an 'industrial needs emphasis' which to some extent competes with the 'developmental' model of careers education in determining the treatment of the world of work within the curriculum.

While the themes within careers education ideology outlined here are separable within the literature they are not necessarily treated as incompatible, but rather have been combined in a variety of ways. For example, proponents of a 'developmental' model may include an 'alternative roles emphasis', may also include teaching 'adjustment' and may have 'social change' as a subsidiary aim; this is possibly the most popular version. At practitioner level, it is likely that the various strands, which might be seen as conflicting, will not be viewed as alternatives but rather as part of one general ideology typically summed up, on the rhetorical and promotional plane, by the definition of careers education as 'preparation for life'.

The 1980s

Since the 'Great Debate' and the massive rises in youth unemployment the school–work interface has become an extremely active scene, as evidenced for example by weekly news coverage in the *Times Educational Supplement* 'School to Work' page. The proliferation of developments and their recency means that their coverage in this paper is inevitably more sketchy and more speculative than the preceding analysis.

What emerges clearly is that the treatment of the 'world of work' and 'preparation for working life' have become a focus of a variety of both international and national pressures for change in the whole school curriculum, and 'work' and 'skills' have become keywords in a multi-faceted movement for curricular change. Some practical consequences of this trend have been: the development of certificates and examinations in vocational education with an 'A' level in Industrial Studies being offered by the Oxford GCE Board from 1984 and a new Certificate of Pre-Vocational Education for 17-year-olds; the increased popularity of teaching in the social and lifeskills area as one educational solution to the problems posed by youth unemployment; and the (new) 'Technical and Vocational Educational Initiative' involving provision for technical and vocational courses for 14- to 18-year-olds to be set up by the Manpower Services Commission. But 'vocationalising' the curriculum has gone beyond areas such as technical education and careers education with obvious 'vocational' links. Curriculum innovation in other areas such as English, history, mathematics and the sciences has sought to highlight the industrial and career implications of these subjects. The examples commended in the DES (1981) booklet 'Schools and Working Life' are illustrative of this general trend.

How is the intense interest in the development of a curriculum which allocates more space to 'skills for adult and working life' to be understood? A variety of factors, operating at different levels, can be suggested as candidates for a place in the overall explanation of these complex events. The general importance of the current economic and political climate, the rise of youth unemployment and the role of the MSC have been discussed elsewhere in this book. As Willis and Clarke have argued, industry, government and the MSC have viewed change in this direction as a means of encouraging relevant qualities in the labour force and, additionally, as a means of occupying unemployed youth. However, the phenomenon cannot simply be viewed as a version of top-down curriculum development, reflecting industrial and governmental interests. The education system in Britain is less malleable than this (if becoming more so) and teachers are capable of resisting and filtering innovations which do not coincide with their own interests, or their perception of the interests of children. Teacher concerns, although inevitably tempered by the need to further their own careers or, failing that, at least ensure personal survival, tend to be informed by liberal educational values which are not easily compatible with a functional model of education. Thus teacher co-operation with what at first sight appears to be a fundamental erosion of their territory and ideology needs to be accounted for. The following explanation suggests aspects of teacher interests in the movement for 'vocationalising' the curriculum.

In the background are the repercussions for schools of the educational changes which took place in the 1960s, particularly comprehensivisation, ROSLA and the accompanying curriculum innovation movement. Hovering above the educational landscape, academics in curriculum studies and the new sociology of education have focused attention on internal aspects of school life such as the contents of the curriculum and classroom interaction and control. Curriculum questions, particularly that of motivating the 'non-academic' child, are not therefore surprises on education's agenda but have been incubating in staffrooms, colleges and conferences for a number of years. Various solutions have been attempted and struggled with, including the Schools Council and Nuffield projects, many of which have been seen to flounder in the classroom. More recently with the 'Great Debate', the rise of the MSC and the moves towards defining the core curriculum, teachers have found that the 'secret garden of the curriculum' is merely an allotment, on loan, open to the public gaze, where cultivation is expected to be undertaken with regard for utility and economy. In the absence of alternative solutions to the problem of motivation and in the presence of official blessing for the 'vocational' solution, the popularity of 'world of work' and 'skills' teaching is more readily explicable.

In the foreground more specific aspects of teacher interest can be discerned. First, the long-simmering pupil motivation problem has, if anything, intensified in recent years. Given a situation in which no amount of qualifications can secure jobs for many young people, it is more difficult to persuade pupils of the value of lessons and, consequently, classroom control and teacher survival through lessons are more often at stake. Furthermore, falling rolls, teacher absenteeism, the disappearance of promotion prospects, the threat of redundancy or redeployment and the effects of education cuts on the fabric of school buildings (with the consequence, for example, that buckets can sometimes be found in classrooms to catch water from leaking roofs; splendid material for larking about!) all add to the sense of strain currently experienced by teachers. Something has to be done with the pupils. Something also has to be done to make teachers' lives easier. The development of a more vocational flavour in the school curriculum in part represents a concession to pupil definitions of what is relevant and in their interests.

Pupil pressures can be seen chiefly in terms of their own highly instrumental attitudes towards school subjects, the existence of which has been well documented (see Schools Council, 1968). For 'academic' pupils most school subjects are vocational in the sense that they provide the necessary qualifications for entry into further and higher education. These pupils easily become disruptive and scornful in lessons such as careers education or religious education, which they do not view as in their career interests. Likewise, 'non-academic' pupils, particularly those entered for few, if any, CSEs, apply pressure for job-related subject matter in lessons. Whether or not pupil perspectives reflect a form of 'false consciousness' of their interests is a separate and complex issue, which does not affect their capacity to demand from teachers more vocational input. Pupil complaints that lessons are boring and moans of 'What's this got to do with getting me a job?' are commonplace and, as unemployment rises, so does interest in job information, preparation and training. It is this situation which leads to the apparent paradox of increased vocational preparation in the school curriculum at a time of disappearing jobs; the solution assuages the anxieties which the job market produces and satisfies customers that everything possible is being done for them. Teachers are then caught in a double bind. By providing job preparation and information they risk raising expectations which cannot be fulfilled. By not doing so, they risk the accusation from pupils and parents that they are assuming and imposing on pupils a future of unemployment. Many respond by providing a judicious mixture of job information and preparation for unemployment, the latter under the guise of 'education for leisure' or 'coping skills'.

More speculatively, there is a further dimension to pupil interests in careers education and social and lifeskills, linked with the style of pedagogy which has become associated with these subjects. As currently constituted lessons of this type are generally not cognitively demanding. For pupils, compared with other lessons, they are 'easy', which means that there is no pressure to write, think hard or work alone. Generally they are discussion lessons and this means teachers avoid pupil resentment at being made to 'work'. Often the lesson involves small group discussion, which has further potential attraction for pupils. Small group work provides splendid cover for unofficial and semi-official activity (see Bates, 1983) and, when teachers need a few moments' respite, a form of collusion may operate with teachers turning a blind eye to unofficial activity providing it remains below a certain level.

In recent years the widely observed teacher predisposition to choose lessons which 'go down well' with pupils (e.g. Parsons, 1981) has tended to be interpreted as a 'coping strategy' (Hargreaves, 1978), reflecting the tendency to off-load educational objectives when under pressure to ensure personal survival. The above arguments concerning the pupil appeal of careers education and social and lifeskills suggest that curriculum development in these areas can be seen partly in this light. Once teachers are providing a curriculum which is about the world of work or skills in getting jobs and surviving unemployment, they expect to have some armour against pupil complaints of irrelevance. The informal pedagogy has further advantages. From a teacher perspective, once pupils are in small groups, unless matters get out of hand, a burden slips off the shoulders of the teacher; she or he can no longer act as a centre of communications and surveillance. Noise and movement of a kind which teachers are often desperately trying to suppress become legitimate and need not be seen as a sign of incompetence. Analysed in these terms 'work' and 'social and lifeskills' begin to resemble a 'coping strategy' officially sanctioned as a school subject.

However, while the appeal to teachers of lessons of this type may partly be explained in this way, it is not simply a matter of indulgency as a mechanism of control. The 'coping' advantages are intertwined with what are perceived as the educational merits of teaching in this area. Barnes, in a brief discussion of 'Lifeskills Teaching', identifies a tradition of teacher interest in education of this type:

> At the 'academic' end of the scale, teachers would give priority to learning in subject-areas, while at the other end there would be greater emphasis on the skills, attitudes and know-how that are likely to be useful in everyday life . . . A secondary schoolteacher concerned mainly with the teaching of less able older pupils may over the years move away from emphasising the imposition of knowledge that he himself learnt in college towards an insistence that the curriculum should be 'relevant' to pupils' concerns. This change can come quite naturally as he comes to see the issue through his pupils' eyes and finds out what curriculum content helps him to manage classes of unenthusiastic young people. (Barnes, 1982)

While the reference to 'managing classes of unenthusiastic young people' suggests the coping strategy potential, it is also implied that teachers can come to view lifeskills as more useful knowledge than academic subject teaching.

When contrasted with academic subject teaching, which is the comparison teachers tend to make, a further dimension of the school image of lifeskills teaching begins to emerge. These developments are generally associated with 'progressive' rather than 'reactionary' tendencies in classroom politics. Radical and 'progressive' currents in educational thinking have long criticised the academic emphasis in the school curriculum, and the degree of control exercised by examining boards, as associated with hierarchical classroom relations, a conservative selection and organisation of knowledge and encouraging a form of competition in which working-class children are relatively disadvantaged. Schools have their conservative and 'progressive' factions, 'talk and chalk' teachers and 'trendies', and in staffroom politics curriculum innovation in the direction of 'relevance' tends to be regarded as the territory of the 'progressives'. The informal pedagogy which characterises careers education is disapproved of by many traditional teachers, who will view noise coming from the classroom as the first obvious indicator of teacher incompetence and a cause, rather than a means of coping with, the school's growing discipline problems. Consequently, teacher investment in curriculum development in this area, particularly in the more traditional and formal schools, is not without risks and is bound up with a 'progressive', even 'radical', self-image.

Finally, teacher interests can be related to their own career concerns and more generally to the self-interest of the teaching profession. With opportunities for promotion now extremely limited, teachers are particularly alert to the potential benefits of careers education, or social and lifeskills as another 'string to the bow', likely to enhance their mobility in the current climate. These individual interests are reinforced by the wider school interest in vocational courses, encouraged by explicit statements from the MSC approving such developments (see NTI White Paper, Department of Employment, 1981) and, more recently, the advent of Technical and Vocational Educational Initiative providing an alternative vocational route through the school curriculum for pupils from the age of 14. At the same time, at the upper end of the school, particularly given the situation of falling rolls, teachers are keen to attract at least a proportion of 16-year-old school-leavers who might otherwise go on to further education or YTS.

The above analysis almost certainly leaves out many pieces in the jigsaw which would fully explain the changing profile of the school curriculum and the omnipresence of 'work' and 'skills'. However, given the considerations outlined here, teacher receptiveness to these changes begins to be more readily explained. Yet it should not be concluded that the apparent collaboration of the teaching profession with industrial and governmental interests necessarily means that the latter have achieved a significant victory in the curriculum debate. Rather the debate has, moved to a more specific and important terrain. Having conceded vocational preparation in principle, the question has become one of what kind of preparation to provide or, more specifically, what kind of vocational preparation is compatible with broader educational goals. The capaciousness of the concepts of 'vocational preparation' and 'lifeskills' means that they are open to a wide range of interpretations at the 'macro' official level and further reinterpretation at the 'micro' classroom level.

Returning to the specific field of careers education and guidance, clearly it could not remain insulated from the intense activity on its borders. The account of careers education up to the 'Great Debate' revealed that the world of work, preparation for transition (to work or unemployment) and decision-making skills were already central themes in the subject paradigm. Jamieson and Lightfoot (1982) provide evidence that school provision for teaching about industry has been mainly through careers lessons. Careers educators have thus been in a position to benefit from the wider interest in vocational preparation, having already developed the requisite teacher training resources. The report (1981–2) of the National Institute for Careers Education and Counselling, perhaps the most significant provider of teacher training in this area, notes that:

When the Institute was launched in 1975, its main work was concerned with the development of careers work in schools. In recent years, it has substantially increased its work with the 16–19 age group, particularly that focussed around developments in colleges of further education and in YOP.

An indication of the scale of NICEC activity can also be gleaned from the report. An appendix lists 100 events organised by NICEC at venues throughout the UK and attended by approximately 2000 participants ('field staff seminars', 'materials workshops', consultations, courses, conferences and seminars). In addition, 57 lectures and 32 publications by NICEC staff are listed for the same year. The themes include topics such as 'Social and Lifeskills in YOP.', 'Guidance and Counselling in Vocational Preparation' and 'Unemployment and the Implications for the Curriculum' in addition to the more usual careers education and counselling topics. A second key institution, the Counselling and Career Development Unit (formerly the Vocational Guidance Research Unit), has specialised in recent years in providing in-service teacher training in 'Life Skills Teaching'; staff estimate that their 'cascade' model of training now reaches several thousand teachers and other interested persons annually. In general, by drawing out the 'social and life skills' aspects, and taking on board the problem of youth unemployment, the careers education movement appears to have ensured its survival and further development in the 1980s. The changes in name and focus of the second institution mentioned, the Counselling and Career Development Unit at Leeds University, provides a neat symbolic reflection of key stages of development in this field: from vocational guidance, to careers education, to social and life skills.

Summary and conclusions

Writing in 1914 of the major growth of interest in vocational guidance and vocational education in the States, a Dr Leonard Ayres described this as the 'beginning of the most fundamental revolution in education since the Renaissance'. This revolution seems to have been imported into Britain in the 1960s and now to be in full swing.

Focusing on careers education, which has been a significant strand in the wider movement, this chapter has distinguished four main phases of historical development, although the last of these, being currently in progress, has only been touched upon. Beginning with the 'talent-matching' period this account has suggested that the vocational guidance scene was dramatically transformed in the 1960s, and that the changes were linked with the relatively favourable economic climate, the expansion of employment and training opportunities, the dismantling, through comprehensivisation, of one major mechanism for channelling pupils towards occupational destinations and the rise of progressive educational ideologies. This was an extremely conducive climate for launching careers education in schools, since it could be projected as in the interests of all young people and thus dissolve any resistance emanating from traditional teacher suspicion of vocational preparation. In the 1970s the potential contradiction between encouraging self-development and awareness of opportunities became more apparent. It is not therefore surprising that in this period writers on careers education moved in a variety of directions in attempts to overcome (the 'social change emphasis'), reconcile (the 'alternative roles emphasis'), or iron out (the 'individual adjustment emphasis'), the contradiction. In the late 1970s and the 1980s, with massive rises in youth unemployment, and significant occupational choice becoming a luxury enjoyed by a few, the careers education label would seem to have become rather a liability. At the same time, however, there has been a rush of activity at the school–work interface and, through its expertise in this area the careers education movement has flourished and has found social and lifeskills a marriageable partner.

The chapter demonstrates that, throughout these various phases, the path towards defining careers education priorities has been dogged by the question of what kind of stance careers educators should adopt towards economic requirements. The 'developmental' model of careers education, with its commitment to facilitating personal growth, revolves around essentially humanist ideals. This leads to tension when promoted in any society where opportunities for self-development are very limited or unequally distributed. Implemented in a society in which work was organised to reflect human needs and interests, the model might synchronise more easily with its social context and the concept of vocation might regain its original meaning. In the absence of such a society the careers education movement almost inevitably comes under pressure to mollify its message, if not at the level of rhetoric then in the translation of rhetoric into reality. In the present climate there is, on account of the surrounding curricular developments outlined, considerable pressure towards an emphasis on adjustment and industrial requirements. In fact, there is now an unprecedented situation in which industrial representatives now have a direct hand in education through the production of teaching materials, and through their involvement with educational conferences, school–industry courses and teacher secondment schemes. While careers education may remain distinct from these developments at the level of its formulated ideology, on a practical level there is inevitably considerable intermingling. Does this matter?

The question can be approached from numerous angles. One obvious angle already suggested is the personal growth perspective of the 'developmental' model itself. A related critique is from the standpoint of traditional educational values. In terms of these values there is an important distinction between education and vocational preparation. Philosophers and writers on education of various persuasions have generally defined its aims in terms which include the development of 'critical awareness', which assumes that education has at least a degree of independence in relation to its economic and social context. Dewey (1916) clearly spelled out the dangers potentially involved in an erosion of the division between education and vocational preparation:

> Any scheme for vocational education which takes its point of departure from the industrial regime that now exists is likely to assume and to perpetuate its divisions and weaknesses, and thus to become an instrument in accomplishing the feudal dogma of social predestination . . . To split the system, and give to others, less fortunately situated, an education conceived mainly as specific trade preparation, is to treat the schools as an agency for transferring the older division of labour and leisure, culture and service, mind and body, directed and directive class, into a society nominally democratic. (Dewey, 1916)

The issue at stake is the nature of the relationship between education and the economy and, in particular, education's capacity to contribute to the development of critical consciousness and social change.

Of course, the degree to which education fulfils this aim for all children or is capable of doing so given other constraints – in other words the question of education's autonomy – has been much debated. However, the debate has concerned the difference between intention and practice, rather than the validity of the aim. While teachers remain committed in principle to 'critical awareness', whatever compromises occur in the classroom, these remain compromises, measured more or less frequently by teachers against their more idealistic goals. The dissonance between intentions and practice may cause discomfort and heartache which can result in a variety of moves, such as flight from the classroom (see Gracey, 1972), working for improved conditions in schools, or abnegation of aims ('becoming realistic'). At present the first two routes must appear to be effectively blocked. One can appreciate, therefore, the attraction of a reformulation of priorities which offloads the necessity to pursue what are perhaps the more difficult educational aims in relation to 'less able' children in favour of a 'skills' emphasis with its utilitarian flavour. It should be recognised, however, that this solution may involve an inegalitarian adjustment of aims and a slackening of the concept of 'education'.

The purpose here is not to discredit teaching about the 'world of work' and 'social and lifeskills'. Critics of 'social and lifeskills' (Davies, 1979; Atkinson, Rees, Shone and Williamson, 1982) seem to miss some of the possibilities which this type of teaching offers. The subject matter in these areas seems to contain many useful elements which are not obviously accommodated within the traditional, academic curriculum. If schools are to provide minimum skills for survival in society, in addition to their other goals, there *is* a case that these now extend well beyond literacy and numeracy and that without a battery of skills in, for example, managing relationships, assertiveness, self-organisation of time during periods of unemployment, many young people will be relatively disadvantaged. The question of what kind of society it is which requires large-scale, formal provision for training in social skills in order to avoid failure, demoralisation or mental and physical illness, does not need to be begged in order to accept the utility of such preparation. The issues here are not dissimilar from those which have exercised feminists, some of whom have doubted the desirability of developing aggressive 'masculine' models of working in order to make their presence felt. Such developments have been viewed as representing the assimilation of patriarchal values, when many women would prefer to see the world become a gentler and more human place where one doesn't need to attend assertiveness training courses in order to avoid being trampled underfoot. Yet feminists run such courses, have learned not to be interrupted in argument and teach classes in self-defence.

This leads to a second point, which is that 'preparation for work' and 'social and lifeskills' are essentially very elastic concepts, their meaning depending on what it is assumed young people are being 'prepared' or becoming 'skilled' for. It is partly the capacious, catch-all character of the terminology which has ensured its popularity. The only essential qualification for skills teaching appears to be that there is an emphasis on *how to* and perhaps also on *immediacy*; it is about teaching someone something which they may be able to use *soon* rather than 'learning for its own sake' or for the purpose of more distant application. It is partly through the utilitarian and pragmatic slant of social and lifeskills that the appeal to working class values is made. Beyond this, the vagueness of definition allows teachers and youth workers to determine for themselves the subject content of courses. To this end the assumptions and approaches found in the social and lifeskills curriculum packages need to be critically appraised by practitioners in the light of their own assessment of the knowledge, experience and likely future lives of young people. If programmes are based on inadequate assumptions about the experience and views of young people, they will not in any case go down well for long in the classroom. The important question for teachers and youth workers is not whether they are for or against social and lifeskills or work preparation, but the definition of the content of the activity. Moreover, compared with other areas of the curriculum, where the syllabus is determined by examination constraints, in these areas teachers have considerable scope for influence.

Returning to the theme of critical awareness, the suggestion is here that where the world of work (or unemployment) is touched upon within the school curriculum, whether in television programmes, school–industry courses, craft courses or careers education, it should not simply be regarded as a cause for preparation – thus implicitly conveying a conception of reified relations between people and work. The incorporation of the 'world of work' within *education* means it should become *subject* not object; the subject of critical enquiry regarding, for example, its historical development, organisational structure, products and requirements. Clearly, teaching about work then becomes a profoundly political subject but no more to be avoided than, as Crick (1981) and others have argued, political education. There are no easy steps from here to drawing up a school curriculum in this area. But without progress in this direction, the introduction of a more vocational emphasis in the curriculum is in danger of becoming a built-in mechanism in schools for accommodating children to the 'career' implications of present economic, social and political conditions and to whatever future developments take place.

Notes

1. In addition to comments from the other contributors to this book, I am grateful to Tony Watts, Ken Roberts, Ivor Goodson and Ralph Williams for reading and commenting on an earlier draft of this paper.
2. This appears to be the main function of YTS and its predecessors.

3.   These developments have been examined by Roberts (1971).
4.   See review and discussion of this literature in Fox (1974).
5.   This is documented in a PhD thesis by the author.

References

Allen, E. P. and Smith, P., *The Value of Vocational Tests as Aids to Choice of Employment* (City of Birmingham Education Committee, 1932).

Atkinson, P., Rees, T. L., Shone, D. and Williamson, H., 'Social and Life Skills: The Latest Case of Compensatory Education' in Rees, T. L. and Atkinson, P., *Youth Unemployment and State Intervention* (London: Routledge & Kegan Paul, 1982).

Ayres, L. P., *Report of the Committee on High Schools and Training Schools* (New York: Board of Education, 1914).

Barnes, D., *Practical Curriculum Study* (London: Routledge & Kegan Paul, 1982).

Bates, I., 'Participatory Teaching Methods in Theory and in Practice: The Schools Council "Careers" Project in School', *British Journal of Guidance and Counselling*, July, 1983.

Claparède, E., *Problems and Methods of Vocational Guidance* (Geneva, ILO, 1922).

Craft, M., 'The Social Context of Careers Guidance' in Jackson, R. (ed.) *Careers Guidance: Practice and Problems* (London: Edward Arnold, 1973).

Crick, B., 'The Dog That Didn't Bark', in White *et al.*, *No Minister: a critique of the DES paper 'The School Curriculum'* (University of London, Institute of Education, Bedford Way Papers, 4, 1981).

Davies, B., 'In Whose Interests? – from social education to social and lifeskills training' (Leicester: National Youth Bureau, Occasional Paper, 1979).

Daws, P., *A Good Start in Life* (Cambridge: CRAC, 1968).

Daws, P., *The Unemployed* (Institute of Youth Employment Yearbook, 1969–70).

Daws, P., 'The Role of the Careers Teacher,' pp. 1–19 in Hayes, J. and Hopson, B., *Careers Guidance* (London: Heinemann, 1971).

DES., *Careers Guidance in Schools* (London: HMSO, 1965).

DES, *Careers Education in Secondary Schools*, Education Survey 18 (London: HMSO, 1973).

DES, *Educating our Children* (London: HMSO, 1977a).

DES, *Education in Schools* (London: HMSO, 1977b).

DES, *Schools and Working Life: Some Initiatives* (London: HMSO, 1981).

Department of Employment, *A New Training Initiative: A Programme for Action* (London: HMSO, 1981).

Dewey, J., *Democracy and Education* (New York: Macmillan, 1916).

Earle, F. M., *Psychology and The Choice of Career* (London: Methuen, 1933).

Eggleston, J., *Work Experience in Secondary School* (London: Routledge & Kegan Paul, 1982).

Floud, J. and Halsey, A. H., 'English Secondary Schools and the Supply of Labour', in *The Year Book of Education, 1956*, reprinted in Halsey, A. H., Floud, J. and Anderson, C. *Education, Economy and Society* (New York: Free Press of Glencoe, 1961).

Fox, A., *Beyond Contract: Work, Power and Trust Relations* (London: Faber & Faber, 1974).

Ginzberg, E., *et al.*, *Occupational Choice: An Approach to a General Theory* (New York: Columbia University Press, 1951).

Goodson, I., *School Subjects and Curriculum Change* (London: Croom Helm, 1983).

Gracey, H., *Curriculum or Craftsmanship: Elementary School Teachers in a Bureaucratic System* (University of Chicago Press, 1972).

Hargreaves, A., 'The Significance of Classroom Coping Strategies', in Barton, L. and Meighan, R., *Sociological Interpretations of Schooling and Classrooms: A Reappraisal* (England: Nafferton Books, 1978).

Hayes, J. and Hopson, B., *Careers Guidance* (London: Heinemann, 1971).

Hopson, B. and Hayes, J., *The Theory and Practice of Vocational Guidance* (London: Pergamon Press, 1968).

Hopson, B. and Hough, P., *Exercises in Personal and Career Development* (Cambridge: CRAC, 1973).

Hopson, B. and Scally, M., *Lifeskills Teaching* (London: McGraw-Hill, 1981).

Jamieson, I. and Lightfoot, M., *Schools and Industry* (London: Schools Council, 1982).

Joint Four, *The Careers Teacher*, 1967.

Law, B., 'Tinker, Tailor, Psychologist or Sociologist,' in *Careers Advisor*, vol. 3, no. 4, 1976.

Law, B., 'Community Interaction: a 'Mid-Range' Focus for Theories of Career Development in Young Adults', *British Journal of Guidance and Counselling*, vol. 9, no. 2, 1981.

Macrae, A., *Talents and Temperaments: The Psychology of Vocational Guidance* (London: Nisbet, 1932).

Macrae, A., *The Case for Vocational Guidance* (London: Pitman, 1934).

Ministry of Education, *Forward from School* (London: HMSO, 1962).

Ministry of Education, *The Newsom Report* (London: HMSO, 1963).

Ministry of Labour, Manpower Studies 1, *The Pattern of the Future* (London: HMSO, 1964).

Munsterberg, H., *Psychology and Industrial Efficiency* (Boston: Houghton Mifflin, 1913).

National Institute for Careers Education and Counselling, Report for 1981–2.

Parsons, C., *The Schools Council Geography for the Young School Leaver Project: A Case Study in Curriculum Change* (Ph.D. thesis, University of Leeds, 1981).

Lady Plowden, *Children and their Primary Schools*, A Report of the Central Advisory Council for Education, 1967.

Roberts, K., *From School to Work* (Newton Abbot: David & Charles, 1971).

Roberts, K., 'The Developmental Theory of Occupational Choice: A Critique and an Alternative', in Esland, G., Salaman, G. and Speakman, A., *People and Work* (Edinburgh: Holmes McDougall, 1975).

Roberts, K., 'The Social Conditions, Consequences and Limitations of Careers Guidance', *The British Journal of Guidance and Counselling*, vol. 5, no. 1, 1977.

Roberts, K., 'The Sociology of Work Entry and Occupational Choice' in Watts, A. G., Super, P. E. and Kidd, J. M., *Career Development in Britain* (Cambridge: Hobsons Press, 1981).

Rogers, C. R., *Client-Centred Therapy* (Cambridge, Massachusetts: Riverside Press, 1951).

Schools Council, Enquiry 1, *Young School-Leavers* (London: HMSO, 1968).

Schools Council, *Careers Education in the 1970s* (London: Evans/Methuen Educational, 1972).

Schools Council Careers Education and Guidance Project, '*Towards Policy on 16–19*', (mimeo) 1975.

Schools Council Careers Education and Guidance Project, *Work: Part 1* (Milton Keynes: Longman, 1976).

Speakman, M., 'A Sociological Perspective on the Developmental Theories of Occupational Choice', in *Careers Advisor*, vol. 3, no. 3, 1976.

Super, D. E., 'A Theory of Vocational Development', *American Psychologist*, vol. 8, no. 4, 1953.

Super, D. E., *The Psychology of Careers* (New York: Harper and Row, 1957).

Super, D. E., 'Career Counselling in an Industrial Society', address at Institute of Careers Officers, North West Branch meeting, March 1975. (mimeo).

Super, D. E., 'Approaches to Occupational Choice and Career Development', in Watts, A. G., Super, D. E. and Kidd, J. M., *Careers Development in Britain* (Cambridge: Hobsons Press, 1981).

Watts, A. G., 'A Structure for Careers Education,' in Jackson, R. (ed.)

Careers Guidance: Practice and Problems (London: Edward Arnold, 1973).

Watts, A. G. and Herr, E. L., 'Careers Education in Britain and the USA: Contrasts and Common Problems', *British Journal of Guidance and Counselling*, vol. 4, no. 2, 1976.

Watts, A. G., 'The Implications of School-leaver Unemployment for Careers Education in Schools', *Journal of Curriculum Studies*, vol. 10, no. 3, 1978.

Watts, A. G., 'The Potential Contribution of the School Curriculum to Careers Guidance', paper presented at NICEC/IAEVG/UNESCO conference on 'Guidance and the School Curriculum', July 1979.

Watts, A. G., An introduction to 'Schools, Youth and Work', *Educational Analysis*, 1981, vol. 3, no. 2, Falmer Press.

Watts, A. G. *Work Experience and Schools* (London: Heinemann, 1983).

Willis, P., *Learning to Labour* (Farnborough: Saxon House, 1977).

6

Conclusion: Theory and Practice

Paul Willis

It is easier to provide educational critiques than to provide educational alternatives and practical applications. It is especially hard to provide advice on 'practice' which actually stands a chance of being adopted in complex school situations which are actually determined by a whole variety of pressures and forces that the classroom teacher knows only too well but cannot influence.

The six of us involved in talking through the issues and writing the chapters of this book certainly share a concern with the way in which education is changing: the rise of 'work in the curriculum'; the spread of techniques around social and life skills training; the fundamental reorientation – be it through a bewildering variety of change and experimentation – nevertheless a fundamental reorientation of the school curriculum, especially as it affects the working class, from a liberal humanist and relatively autonomous perspective to a much more technicist, applied and industry-linked perspective. We are seeing a tendency towards the vocationalisation of the whole timetable. However, we do not share a detailed view of what a progressive attitude towards these changes should be, nor can we offer a tight alternative curriculum. This is hardly surprising, given the overall flux of the situation and the multi-faceted forms of change and development in actual schools. The outside 'structural' situation is still developing, and for many of the reasons discussed, teachers, and particularly careers teachers, cannot freely 'choose' a particular approach and subject matter even if they were entirely certain as to its most desirable form. Nor do we feel that it is necessarily helpful to supply yet another outside and potentially 'idealist' programme for action, when particular opportunities and possibilities must be a matter for judgement by particular teachers and groups of teachers in their own schools. Individual contributors to the book have drawn out their own specific conclusions and recommendations in the particular fields they have surveyed in their respective chapters. We have not attempted to hide differences of emphasis, or our different evaluations of the real scope for salvaging anything useful and progressive from the current form of educational changes.

Recognising the openness of the situation, however, and accepting a variety of emphases between ourselves, does not mean that we accept the inevitability of the current total disarray on the left, liberal and progressive wings of education.

We believe that certain general principles and issues can be agreed as a framework within which both to criticise current developments and to think through a coherent approach to actual teaching situations within schools as they are currently, and predominantly, constituted. This conclusion attempts to set out briefly the principles and framework which have informed, to some degree, all of the chapters of this book, and which give some guidance towards classroom practice. We believe that they are now often part of 'best practice' classroom activity.

We have argued that certain educational 'solutions' flow from the way in which larger questions about the main society are defined in the first place. The dominant view of the current economic and youth employment crisis has led – through a whole range of mechanisms and influences – to an educational view that schools should be further subordinated to industry, and that their main job is to produce better, more skilled, disciplined and flexible workers. The MSC and Youth Training Scheme type of definitions of skill explored by Philip Cohen in Chapter 4 have become dominant in official discourses, and appear to be carrying all before them – reorganising many aspects of the curriculum across the board.

However, we have also argued that official aims, intentions and rhetorics have never been much of a guide to what actually happens in schools, nor to the type and character of the pupils and future citizens produced. Certainly there are effects flowing from these official views – but not always those which are desired or planned. Meanwhile it is the actual experiences, and what we have called the material cultures of the young, which provide the foundation and 'common sense' for student responses to schooling. It is these cultural resources which make it possible to plan for the future according to a highly complex map of gender, race, class and age meanings in relation to real economic structures and possibilities. Chapter 2 by Dan Finn shows, for instance, that most working-class young people, far from being ignorant about the world of work, have massive experience of it, and of the disciplines and freedoms of the wage, through juvenile labour.

Inge Bates suggests in Chapter 5 that the developmental careers model of the 1960s and early 1970s was made possible by the expansion of real opportunities in the economy and by pupils' interests in reaching them.

Standing, so to speak, 'between' the official approaches in education and the material experiences and cultures of the pupils come, of course, the school and its teachers. The school in a more formal way, and the classroom teacher in a direct way, are always negotiating two versions of reality. And this negotiation is not usually on neutral ground. The overriding imperative in many schools – sometimes the more powerful for being unspoken – is control and classroom survival. Rob Moore (Chapter 3) suggests that social and life skills training has been adopted in classrooms not primarily for its internal or official logic, but for its effectiveness in controlling pupils who quite simply don't want to be in schools.

We think it helpful if these three 'levels', or areas of concern, are recognised and used to analyse the actual educational opportunities in particular schools. For convenience let us call them the 'official', the 'cultural' and the 'practical'.

Now in terms of thinking through the possibilities in a particular conjuncture in a particular town or neighbourhood in a particular school, the crucial consideration may well be *the areas of overlap between these things*: the identification of topics and approaches it is feasible to operate in schools at the moment from the 'practical' and 'official' point of view, but which may also have relevance and bite from the point of view of 'the cultural'. In Phil Cohen's example of an alternative practice, the situation allowed a good deal of 'overlap' with the 'official', enforcing relatively little disjunction between 'the cultural' and 'the practical'. Most situations are not so open. But there are always 'overlaps'.

Although we have emphasised the 'separate' experiences and responses of pupils, and the ways in which their own cultures and experiences can be denied or insulted, and although we have argued that actual transitions and coming to terms with a future happen on this terrain, it would be quite wrong to assume that pupils do not have a major stake in that world of work which is currently massively dominated by MSC-type definitions. But they have a stake in it from *their own* point of view.

It is this point of view which must be borne in mind, and it is a set of attitudes and interests which were missing from much of the old traditionalism and/or progressivism in their liberal humanist guises. The 'new vocationalism' has drawn much of its credibility from its apparent bridging of this previous gap. On the other hand, just because we might find ourselves agreeing with an analysis which suggests that the conventional curriculum offers very little to working-class youngsters, we should not assume that a near compulsory period of post-school training, or a vocationalising of the whole curriculum, will offer much that is better – or indeed that pupils will not reject such 'relevant' offerings with the same power that they use sometimes to undermine conventional schooling. Nor can we simply assume that the popular support of parents, who see their children at least getting something that looks like training and holds the possibility of jobs, will be unequivocal, or will not evaporate in the face of cheap labour schemes with a gloss of 'skills training' followed by prolonged unemployment.

Indeed, a massive training scheme which purports to be a 'permanent bridge to work', but which will result in a vast number of trainees being returned to the dole queue, would seem like a recipe for disaster in these terms. Certainly, in many Mode 'A' YTS schemes where there is a possibility for jobs, trainees will 'behave themselves'. But in the placements where there is little or no hope for work, the potential for resistance and refusal is enormous and, depending on the type of local control, likely to be realised. Just as we will be unable to understand the response of the new trainees of Thatcher's Britain without reference to their likely destiny after training, so should we expect and understand the likelihood of some negative trainee responses to feed back into the schools and affect the cultural and social processes there. In that backwash the 'new vocationalism' is likely to be as brittle and fragile as the progressivism which it is allegedly replacing.

So what is the working-class interest in the 'world of work'? Young working-class people are not directly interested in the 'success of industry', nor in discipline, nor in transferrable skills, nor in flexible working – 'work' from the employer's point of view. They want the power of 'skill' in the market-place of jobs, local information about, and local access to jobs and to the wage.

This may lead to some common meeting grounds with official policy. Joining the Youth Training Scheme may now be the *only* way into work; it may be that going through the motions of politeness and subserviance may now by the only way to get a job interview under the new regime of SLS job etiquette; it may be that getting all possible information about local jobs may be the only chance of a job; it may be that getting some kind of paper certification is necessary to demonstrate real or potential skills or even apparent capacity for work itself. In this light it is hardly surprising that teachers find that problems of classroom control and of motivation can be dealt with in role-playing, mock interviewing and varieties of showing the 'going price' in SLS. These topics can have an impact at the cultural level because they speak to student material cultures as they relate to the future work situation and to the new institutional bridges into it. That is why they can work as control devices. Also there is 'official' sanction and space for dealing with 'work'. But, we argue, this overlap should be developed from the working-class perspective. The focus should not be the general abstract one – always a danger sign – of the 'good worker' (that is, industry's view). Nor should training oneself for this abstract role become some kind of answer to unemployment. This is to define the whole area from the point of view of habituation to work and job discipline. Instead the emphasis might be on the concrete, practical, specific and local – really useful – knowledge and information relative to the pupils and their actual futures.

Of course there are severe difficulties in any approach when the youth labour market may simply have disappeared in the local economy. But why hide the difficulties? This is a severe problem, most of all for working class interests. The idealist abstract, the image of the 'good worker' with all the elaborations about the skill and motivation necessary to get work (from the employer's point of view), is simply dishonest. It is likely to lead to public and private forms of 'blaming the victim' – young people are unemployed because they don't measure up to the exacting standards of today's labour requirements. It will not provide more jobs, nor meet the needs of the young. It will meet instead the needs of society for a form of social control and pre-emption of opposition and revolt

oddly through an imposition of discipline, flexibility, work socialisation and some future promise of work. Safely warehoused workers
for when Capital decides to invoice them out! Safely stacked only
for future release against a promissory note which may never be
redeemed.

Of course there should be teaching *about* – i.e. not 'for' – work in
such situations. Certainly unemployment should not be presented,
for instance, as a golden 'leisure' opportunity. Furthermore,
competition for scarce jobs may well mean individualistic demands
for job-getting and presentational skills. But the general chances of
finding work can be presented objectively, and welfare and citizens'
rights can be presented as honourable alternatives. The crisis for the
whole local economy and society can be discussed, and the causes
and local dimensions of the problem can be exposed and criticised –
just as the local political, self-help and community responses to the
problems can be discussed and developed. A working class perspective on unemployment must recognise the problem and work for a
solution, not spirit it away in the implied inadequacy of workers
and in self-preparation for some future promised land – when no
land is like that anyway.

In generally thinking through how best to utilise the area of the
overlap between the 'official', the 'cultural' and the 'practical', we
have found it useful continuously to bear in mind a number of
principles:

1. The need, generally, to reduce the gap between the 'official'
    and 'the informal' within the exigencies of the 'practical'.
    Certainly it is crazy that the group who, in fact, know most
    about the real cultural, social and economic dimensions of work
    and who are most ready to accept its most boring and exploited
    forms, are the ones to get most preparation for basic work as if
    they were entirely ignorant of such things.
2. The value of seeking to identify within the 'official' what is most
    progressive and realistic in relation to the 'cultural' and
    'practical' levels. For instance, although we are critical of some
    of its content, the 'new realism' in the curriculum and the
    techniques around SLS at least recognise some of the limita-
    tions of the liberal humanist educational perspective and the
    fact that traditional subjects and techniques have anyway been
    rejected by up to a half of all young people. The MSC-inspired

devotion to skills and the practical is, in its own way, a critique of the self-delusions of the post-war social democratic hope in education. So much might be shared and built upon by progressives in education. Furthermore, a lot of the rhetoric surrounding the MSC and new developments in education concerns race and gender equality. These things can be taken at face value and pushed to their limits. Also there are promising starting points in safety and health education.

3. The fact that the current crisis is not one of working-class children and their abilities – it will be solved (or not) at another level: that of production and the economy.

4. The importance of trying to deal with the 'world of work' from a working-class perspective – its struggles and conflicts as well as apparently consensual views of necessary skills: the role of trade unions; the widespread and informal practices of work control and sharing which actually make working life bearable and compatible with some basic qualities of human dignity. Realist and ethnographic pictures of work could be used to counter, and show the underlying complex reality of the stereotypes of the 'lazy worker' and the 'British disease' which underly so many views of what should be done to train the next generation of workers.

5. The importance of avoiding a view of young people as having no culture and living in some kind of experiential vacuum which requires, basically, forms of remedial and compensatory education. Not 'the youngster *is* the problem', but 'the youngster *has* problems'.

6. The importance of maintaining maximally open tracks, and opening up new ones stretching into adulthood, for return to the academic, traditional and elite streams which will still exist. Though they may serve class and cultural reproduction and the transmission of privilege, they will still offer the best chance of upward mobility to individuals in the working-class.

7. The importance of other related educational demands and reforms. We should not lose sight of the base-line organisational and material reforms – mandatory grants, redistribution of capitation and resources, reform of the examination system, tertiary reorganisation – which are desperately necessary if we are to achieve even a formally comprehensive system. What we should be calling for in general here is a simultaneously cultural

and material re-interpretation and development of the comprehensive principle and its applications to those new trends, changes and structures of the 1970s and 1980s, many of which are being used to reintroduce a vulgar and crass tripartism.

Of course, the attempt to operate these principles in the area of overlap between the 'official', the 'cultural' and the 'practical' might require a degree of 'appearance management' amongst teachers themselves. Some more general parts of the curriculum, such as social education and social studies, might offer greater possibilities than the narrower, vocational forms of social and life skills training. The approach we are suggesting requires some sophistication and flexibility in dealing with the 'official', as well as a sympathetic and sensitive eye for the 'cultural'. Practical problems of survival and control in the classroom can always threaten any logic. But there is no reason to adopt industrial and managerial definitions and interests in thinking through a position and a practice in the changing seas of education. The sense of alien takeover in the current right wing 'realist' restructuring of education may blind us to the opportunities we should certainly recognise were that restructuring 'our own'. A certain kind of interest in work and production must in any case be a central plank in progressive views of education. Certainly there is neither mileage nor justification in a simple call for a return to previous methods and subject boundaries.

Our shared position, then, is simply this: a clearer view of the overlaps in the different realms influencing and constituting the field of education, and a flexible, locally informed attempt to work on and through this for working-class and subordinate interests, can help to set a course through the current chaos and disillusion. There are opportunities as well as problems in a sea of troubles.

Author and Name Index

Subject Index

Page numbers in *italic* refer to tabular matter.